MARLBOROUGH'S SELF-TAUGHT SERIES

TURKISH SELF-TAUGHT

BY NATURAL METHOD
WITH ENGLISH
PHONETIC PRONUNCIATION

MARLBOROUGH'S SELF-TAUGHT SERIES

TURKISH SELF-TAUGHT

**BY NATURAL METHOD
WITH ENGLISH
PHONETIC PRONUNCIATION**

**REVISED AND ENLARGED
VOCABULARIES AND PHRASES**

F. A. ATTAOULLAH

GYAN

Published by

GYAN

Gyan Publishing House
5, Ansari Road
Daryaganj, New Delhi-110002
Phone: 011-47034999, 9811692060
E-mail: books@gyanbooks.com

Distribution Network
gyanbooks.com
India, USA, Canada, UK, Australia, France

ISBN : 978-81-212-3085-8 (PB)
First Published, London, 1942

2nd Impression 2020

Printed at: Gyan Press, Delhi.

Turkish Self-Taught
Author: F. A. Attaoullah

Marlborough's Self-Taught Series

TURKISH SELF-TAUGHT

IN LATIN CHARACTERS

By the Natural Method

WITH THE

English Phonetic Pronunciation

Revised and Enlarged

VOCABULARIES and PHRASES

Specially prepared and written

by

FUAD A. ATTAOULLAH, B.A., B.Sc.

FIFTH EDITION

MADE AND PRINTED IN GREAT BRITAIN

LONDON

E. MARLBOROUGH & CO., LTD.,

1942

FOREWORD

by His Excellency Dr. Tevfik Rüştü Aras

ÖN SÖZ

DOKTOR TEVFİK RÜŞTÜ ARAS TARAFINDAN LÜTFEN VERİLMİŞTİR.

Müsveddesini bana gönderdiğiniz İngilizce konuşanlara Türkçe öğretmek için yazılan Gramer ve Musahabe'yi gördüm.

Dünyada diğer dilleri konuşanlara nisbetle adedi en çok olan İngilizce bilenlerin Eski Dünyanın üç Kıt'asında ötedenberi yayılmış olan Türkçeyi öğrenmeleri her iki dili söyleyenlerin faydasınadır.

Bu itibarla bu vadide emek sarfetmeği takdire lâyık görürüm. Ve çalışanları iyi bir iş görecekleri için teşci etmek isterim.

Gramer ve Musahabe'niz bu itibarla beğenilmeğe değeri olan ve yerinde edilen bir himmettir.

DR. T. R. ARAS.

(Gramer ayrıca tab edilmiştir. F.A.)

AN APPRECIATION

BY

SIR WYNDHAM DEEDES

(*who served the Ottoman Empire in the Imperial Gendarmerie and in the Civil Inspectorate*).

It gives me great pleasure to welcome a book of this class, and its publication comes at a most propitious time. Turkey is, to-day, standing side by side with the Allies, and it is essential that a means should be available whereby her language may be thoroughly and easily learnt, in order to appreciate better her ideals. The English language is being taught throughout Turkey, and the Turkish President himself, a very great friend of Britain, took up its study a few years ago, and now speaks it fluently.

I wholeheartedly recommend the book to the English public, particularly at a time when it is so important for England and Turkey to know more of each other's life and culture.

Wyndham Deedes

TO THE MEMORY OF

ATATÜRK

THIS BOOK IS AFFECTIONATELY AND GRATEFULLY DEDICATED.

THE name of the GHAZİ MUSTAPHA KEMAL PASHA, renamed by a grateful nation, KEMAL ATATÜRK or KEMAL FATHER OF THE TURKS, will always be intimately associated by all peoples with the constitution and progress of Modern Turkey. The measure of the reform ntroduced under his administration has wrought a marvellous change, which will be increasingly appreciated as Turkey takes her rightful place in the Commonwealth of Nations.

Among the foremost of these reforms was the nationalization of the language on a purely Turkish basis, with its efficacy in stamping out illiteracy from among the nation.

The fate of his country had made a deep impression on his soul, for he was ever conscious of the gradual breaking up of the Turkish Empire. He could see the last flickering flame of the National Independence in danger of being totally extinguished.

Turkey must be saved. She must live to play the part for which Providence had cast her. He realized and appreciated the call to guide and lead her, and with prophetic vision, and conscious of the errors committed in the past, set himself to the gigantic task.

The extent and breadth of his outlook, and his experience of the horrors of war, together with his conviction of its utter futility, filled his heart with an unbounded, burning desire to see Turkey at peace with the rest of the world.

He laid the foundation for the re-rapprochement of the Democracies of the East with the Democracies of the West, and this happy position must now be maintained, for much good will emerge from this friendship which lies in the hearts of the Turkish people, ready to be bestowed on the offer of fellowship extended to them.

Animated with the desire to see the crystallization of this Anglo-Turkish understanding, and appreciating that peoples can more truly understand each other when they can speak together in each other's language, I have prepared this book in a humble endeavour to help achieve this end.

FUAD A. ATTAOULLAH.

CONTENTS

Conversational Phrases and Sentences

T.G. Where quoted refers to "Turkish Grammar"
PH. ,, ,, ,, ,, "Phonetics"

PREFACE

For many years European and Ottoman Turkish linguists, as well as many Ottoman Turkish grammarians, who had applied themselves to the close study of the Turkish language, were firmly under the impression that its harmony and fluidity was in a large measure due to the presence of Persian and Arabic words, and to the introduction of grammatical forms identified with these languages, and it was generally feared that if these were eliminated a purely Turkish language would severely suffer by the loss of these peculiar characteristics.

The controversy arising out of this belief resulted in a general lethargy and the postponement of serious attempts to reconstitute the language on a purely Turkish basis, the language meanwhile becoming more and more assailed by foreign elements. During this period a most eminent and learned scholar produced the first Turkish grammar, which has contributed largely to the creation of the present melodious and expressive language with its extensive vocabulary and rich variety of inflections so euphonically constituted as to produce the rhythm and cadence which has been the admiration of all linguists.

Unfortunately, however, from the Turkish Nationalist point of view, this was moulded on the Arabic grammar and this fact resulted in considerable linguistic confusion.

The language of the learned now became a more or less composite one, being made up of Turkish, Arabic, and Persian vocabularies, the influence of the latter two predominating, and at one time there were almost two distinct languages; that of the learned, and that of the ordinary man in the street, who for lack of State controlled and compulsory education could not learn the former, and was therefore unable to understand the cultivated tongue. At a later period another attempt was made to regulate and improve the grammar, again by a very well known authority, whose mastery of the Turkish language is indisputable. It was a very good lay-out of the Turkish language on a modern style, where a clearer explanation than hitherto was given, together with many illustrative examples, but it did not make any attempt at radical reform, although the author mentioned in his book that such a move was necessary. There were two other factors also which added to the confusion. One was the gradual introduction into the language of French and English words by pedantic scholars who had been educated in Europe, and perhaps did not possess full mastery of their mother tongue. The other was the influence the European literature had on the principles of phrase formation, this bringing about what might be termed a Turko-European style which was unintelligible and out of tune with the rules of the real Ottoman-Arabic-Persian style. The introduction of these outside elements naturally caused the language to deviate more and more from its true original and gradually the nucleus itself became effaced.

It is with distress that we note how superficially the reforms were approached. It was very obvious that the outstanding deficiency in the language, as then constructed, was the inability by means of its alphabet, which was severely lacking in vowel forms, to orthographically reproduce in a correct and easy manner the true sounds of the Turkish tongue, the existing four vowels being sadly insufficient for this purpose.

Two of these vowels, *i* and *o*, were used to represent several different sounds, which were determined by the quality and type of the consonant accompanying them. At one time a move was made to remedy this defect by creating the necessary letters to vowelize the Turkish word, but here again difficulty was encountered, for the movement was frustrated by the orthodox and reactionary feelings of the calligraphists, the orthographers, and the printers, the former priding themselves on the beauty of the style of which they were the authors and which was the result of years of painstaking toil, and the latter not wishing to have to undertake extra work in type-setting. Another important contributory factor was the prevailing method of teaching which at that time was very inefficient. Thus it can be seen that there were many obstacles to be surmounted and conflicting opinions to be conciliated before any satisfactory reform could be effected.

It was at this crisis that the language found in Atatürk, as did the nation in its larger and comprehensive sense, its saviour. In spite of the deep-rooted superstition and belief that it would be impossible ever to resuscitate the original mother tongue of the Turks, he, with his vast knowledge, most cleverly dug out of the depths of literary chaos the unsoiled original structure of the language. He also was able to explain in full detail all the intricacies of the working of the essential factors, and proved this structure to be in the nature of a mother tongue such as Sanskrit.

His decision, therefore, to drop entirely all the various existing methods, to eliminate all foreign words without distinction, and to bring back into use all Turkish vocabularies, to adopt the Latin characters generally, and to adapt them to the requirements of the language (where necessary creating new ones for the special sounds) was another proof of the genius of Atatürk. We can now understand why this reform was welcomed by the nation with such sincere feelings of appreciation and gratitude. When telling a large gathering of people present at a garden party, the benefit the language and the nation alike would reap from the change over from the Kufic script to Latin characters, the reassuring words of Atatürk, "I am sure of it and I want you also to be sure of it," were drowned in deafening applause.

Without the slightest hesitation, everyone, from the high official down to the man in the street, set himself to the task of learning the new alphabet. Atatürk at Ankara at his own experimental and training school, and İsmet İnönü at Malatya, both in front of the blackboard, conducted classes personally, thus taking the lead in this stupendous task which they had undertaken and which they had set their energies to bring to fruition. It was a great achievement, and it is entirely wrong to think that the change in the language was just a matter of discarding the old characters and substituting the Latin ones, with the idea of making it conform to Western standards. On the contrary, it was a radical reform, brought about by the desire to make the language once more Turkish by bringing back into use all Turkish grammatical rules and vocabularies, replacing the old mêlée of adjunct and disjunct Arabic characters by a new Turkish alphabet composed of single consonants, and a complete set of vowels, all of adjunct character, and discarding all foreign words which had crept in (Turkicizing any for which there was no true Turkish equivalent), thereby making one national language, common to all classes. It brought to a happy conclusion the chaotic struggle which had been going on for the past century. In the words of Ismet Inönü : " With these new characters the great Turkish nation will enter a new world of enlightenment . . . we believe therein with a true assurance and honest conviction " ; we can read his approval and appreciation of the action of Atatürk, and his feelings of confidence were shared by the whole nation.

The Turkish language is particularly comprehensive for it provides all the necessary words including the most minute nuances, to express the deepest subtleties of the mind, the full vigour of the human feelings, and all the elements found in nature, by means of its word-building capacity.

A very careful study of the alphabet, the explanation of the division and working of the vowels and consonants, together with the graduation of sounds is of the utmost importance in obtaining the correct pronunciation.

To obtain a *correct Turkish pronunciation* it is essential and imperative for the student to *study and grasp the information given in the classification of vowels and consonants*.

The language is very much in accordance with the modern science of phonetics. It is formed of sounds which are the natural result of the laws of position and inflection of the tongue, and the movements of the lips and jaws, and no strain is put on any organ. There is only one way of pronouncing each letter. The letter "*o*", for instance, gives only one sound, not several as in the English " n*o*, n*o*t, n*o*ne ", etc. There are no diphthongs as in the English " ph*oe*nix, m*ai*n, m*oo*n, br*ea*d, v*oi*d, n*ei*ther ", etc. When two vowels come together they each retain their own individual sound. There are no digraphs, that is two letters put together to represent one sound as in " *ph*ysic, bri*dg*e, *ch*ur*ch*, nor*th*, rou*gh*," etc. There are no mute letters as in " spit*e*, yello*w*, wou*l*d, tong*ue*, t*w*o, *w*rit*e*, *k*nit ", etc. Every letter in every word is sounded individually, and every word is pronounced exactly as it is written. Consequently the reading of the language is very easy once the student has acquainted himself thoroughly with the correct pronunciation, particularly of the vowels.

A very interesting and particular characteristic feature of the language is the predominance of soft and melodious tones As will be seen this is entirely due to the balanced grouping together of the "hard" and "soft" sounds, the vowels *A*, *I*, *O*, *U*, being the "hard" ones, and *E*, *İ*, *Ö*, *Ü*, the "soft". The formation of words, of adjectives, of verbs, and of phrases, are all subject to this fundamental rule, and suffixes in formation of adjectives, of verbal nouns and others, post-positions, and inflection affixes, will all in their turn ***be in pairs,*** one being ***soft*** for the ***soft words,*** and the other ***hard*** for the ***hard words.*** The verb conjugation follows the same rule except in the present tense. I have given a very full explanation of this in the Grammar which I have prepared separately.

Consonants also are divided into groups, ***sharp, flat,*** and ***neutral.*** The neutral ones are often found together with the other two, where they serve to reduce to a certain extent any harshness in a word which might be found to be out of harmony with the euphony of the language as a whole, and which is so common with other languages.

I trust that the vocabularies and phrases contained herein will be of great help to the student, and I look forward to the day when the study of the Turkish language will be in far larger measure taken up by the younger generation of the Commonwealth of the English-speaking peoples, and shall be happy to know that this work has helped the furtherance of that aim.

F. A. ATTAOULLAH.

THE TURKISH LECTURE AND READING ROOM,
62 CHANCERY LANE,
W.C. 2.
also at:
57 EDGWAREBURY LANE,
EDGWARE, MIDDX.

TURKISH SELF-TAUGHT

PHONETICS

THE TURKISH ALPHABET

THE characters of the new Turkish alphabet have been adopted from the Latin alphabet, but only those letters suitable to the language have been taken, with the addition of a few special characters. It is composed of twenty-nine letters, twenty-one of which are consonants and eight vowels.

A, B, C, Ç, D, E, F, G, G, H, I, İ, J, K, L, M, N, O, Ö, P, R, S, Ş, T, Ü, U, V, Y, Z. There are also three special characters Â, Î, Û, which are nothing but the same three letters in the alphabet but pronounced with a longer sound, this being denoted by the circumflex sign.

To acquire the exact and correct sounds of the letters in the Turkish alphabet I will ask the student to detach himself entirely from that of the English, French, or German, and read with great attention the following :—

Character		Name	Pronunciation	Phonetics Use
A	a	A	as the sound of *u* in the English words *sun, up*	u
Â	â	AA	(1) as the sound of *a* in the English words *car, father*	a͡a
			(2) except when following a *k* or *g*, when the sound of an *i* is inserted before the *a*, making it sound as if written *kia* or *gia* (see also Ph. 3)	i͡a
B	b	BE(h)	as the sound of *b* in the English word *bat*	b
C	c	JE(h)	as the sound of *j* in the English word *jump*	j
Ç	ç	CHE(h)	as the sound of *ch* in the English word *church*	ch
D	d	DE(h)	as the sound of *d* in the English word *dog*	d

Character		Name	Pronunciation	Phonetics Used
E	e	E(h)	as the sound of *e* in the English word *net*	e
F	f	FE(h)	as the sound of *f* in the English word *fat*	f
G	g	GE(h)	as the sound of *g* in the English word *gown*	g
Ğ	ğ	GHE(h)	as the sound of *gh* in the English word *leghorn*	gh

(Alph. 1) This letter is always in the middle or at the end of a word, never at the beginning.

(Alph. 2) It is a very soft semi-mute consonant as in the Turkish word *dağ* (dugh).

In the middle of a word it is almost lost in the throat, causing in the meantime a pause on the preceding vowel of the syllable, when followed by a cons. or vowel as in the words *sağlam* (sughlum), *ağıl* (ughi(r)l).

(Alph. 3) If following the consonant "*n*" (as in "sanğat") the pronunciation is stronger, almost as if written "sunghut".

(Alph. 4) Getting lost in the throat, causing the same pause on the preceding vowel, but merging into the succeeding vowel sound by way of changing into that vowel, or a *y*, when followed by a soft vowel, as in the Turkish words *yiğirmi, göğüs*, which are pronounced: yiyirmi; göyüs.

Character		Name	Pronunciation	Phonetics Used
H	h	HE(h)	as the sound of *h* in the English word *hat*	h
I	ı	İ(r)	as the sound of *er* and *ir* in the words *father, fir*. ***Never takes acc.*** ^.	i(r)
İ	i	İ	as the sound of *i* in the English words *mid, mince*	i
Î(Î)	î(î)	EE	as the sound of *ee* in the English word *weed*. ***Actually printed*** î .	ee
J	j	JE(h)	as the soft sound of the *s* in the middle of the words *leisure, measure* or as the letter *j* in the French words *jour, jardin*	j
K	k	KE(h)	as the sound of *k* in the English word *king*	k
L	l	LE(h)	as the sound of *l* in the English word *lamb*	l
M	m	ME(h)	as the sound of *m* in the English word *mug*	m
N	n	NE(h)	as the sound of *n* in the English word *net*	n

Character		Name	Pronunciation	Phonetics Used
O	o	AU	as the sound of *au* in the English words *fault, vault*	âû
Ö	ö	EU	as the sound of *ur* in the English words *demur, further*; or as the sound of *eu* in the French word *peu* .	êû
P	p	PE(h)	as the sound of *p* in the English word *pin*	p
R	r	RE(h)	as the sound of *r* in the English word *rock*. **It must always be sounded when it comes at the end of the word**	r
S	s	SE(h)	as the sound of *s* in the English word *soap*	s
Ş	ş	SHE(h)	as the sound of *sh* in the English word *shop*	sh
T	t	TE(h)	as the sound of *t* in the English word *time*	t
U	u	OO	as the sound of *u* in the English word *pull*, with the same length of stress; or as the sound of *oo* in the English word *stood* . . .	o͡o
Û	û	Û	as the long sound of *u* in the English word *rule*; or as the sound of *oo* in the English word *cool* with the same length of sound (see Ph. 3) . .	û
Ü	ü	EW	as the sound of *eu* in the English words *lieu*; or as the sound of *u* in the French words *tu, fût*; or as the sound of *ü* in the German word *über*	e͡w
V	v	VE(h)	as the sound of *v* in the English word *violet*	v
Y	y	YE(h)	as the sound of *y* in the English word *yellow*	y
Z	z	ZE(h)	as the sound of *z* in the English word *zebra*	z

(1) It is of great importance to make the distinction between *i* (i) and *ı* (i(*r*)); *ı* (i(*r*)) and *ö* (e͡u); *o* (a͡u) and *u* (o͡o); *u* (o͡o) and *ü* (e͡w).

(1*a*) Great care must be taken to sound the letter "***r***" when it comes at the end of a word, as otherwise confusion will arise, especially when the "***r***" is the final letter of a suffix, as —*güzel***dir** = it ***is*** good *biçak***lar** = knives
*güzel***di** = it ***was*** good *biçak***la** = with a knife

(2) The three special characters ***â***, ***î***, and ***û***, which appear, generally speaking, only in words of Arabic or Persian origin, are not harder than usual, but longer in the continuity of the sound, and great care must be taken in putting in this sign, as there are also other words which are spelt the same, but without the sign, and their meaning is entirely different.
Examples:—*âdet* = custom and *adet* = number.
sâdet = happiness and *sadet* = boundary.
hâlâ = as yet and *hala* = auntie.
dînî = religious and *dîni* = the religion (obj. case).

(3) We shall learn as we go along of the importance of forming words in a euphonious manner, or, in other words, of the juxtaposition of **hard** or **soft syllables** in the formation of words. There are, however, still words of Persian and Arabic extraction beginning with or including the letters ***k***, ***g***, ***l*** and ***s***, which appear not to be governed by this rule, yet these words are not altogether out of place as far as the general euphony of the language is concerned. In these cases the vowels are directly affected. They are lengthened, and the sound of the consonant is softened. For example:—***kâ***, ***gâ***, ***kû***, ***gû***, instead of being hard are pronounced softly as if an "i" were in front of the vowel. **To denote where this takes place a circumflex** sign is placed over the vowel. Examples:—***kâr*** is pronounced "kiar"; *rüz**gâr*** is pronounced "rüzgiar"; ***kû**fi* is pronounced "kiufi"; *ef**kâr*** is pronounced "efkiar"; *zade**gân*** is pronounced "zadegian".

The letter "***l***" has a strong influence over the vowels, particularly the HARD ones, which it SOFTENS. This effect is marked by placing the same circumflex sign over the vowel which precedes or follows the "***l***". Examples:—

lû**zum*, *i**lâ**veten*, ***lâ**zım*, *mü**lâ**kat*, *su**âl

NOTE.—Usually such words are of foreign origin.

RULE.—When ***â*** or ***û*** follows immediately after ***k*** and ***l***, and when ***â*** follows ***g*** they are pronounced as explained above, but any of these vowels with the circumflex sign, following any other letter except **s,** are pronounced only as long or broad vowels. When following **s** they are a little softer.

(4) In the pronunciation of Turkish words the syllables are, generally speaking, all of more or less the same length, slight emphasis being placed on the **last syllable,** or, in words of only one *syllable,* on the **last consonant.** Examples :—

*ba**l*** (honey)	emphasis on the	" ***l*** "
*kire**mit*** (tile)	,, ,,	" ***mit*** "
*sala**ta*** (salad)	,, ,,	" ***ta*** "

(4*a*) When suffixes are added (in word formation, etc.), the accent is still on the *last syllable,* it being transferred from the *last syllable* of the *original word* to the **last syllable** of the **newly** formed *word.* Examples :—

*bal**dan*** (from honey).
*kiremi**tin*** (of the tile).
*salata**lık*** (greens for salad purpose).

(5) This rule is broken with certain Arabic and Persian words taken into the language. In this case, the second syllable is separated from the first, the two syllables being pronounced separately with a very slight pause between, both parts being equally stressed. This separation is marked by an apostrophe between the syllables. As :—***kal'****e,* ***mes'ul,*** ***mes'****ele,* ***kat'****iyet.*

(5*a*) Turkish words are uttered in an almost calculated breath, and as will be seen, when any suffix is to be added, the appropriate one will be one which is in harmony with the last syllable, this being one of the factors creating the " fluidity " of the word.

(5*b*) This fluidity, however, is broken by some foreign words similar to (5), except that the *emphasis* is on the *part preceding* the apostrophe, this latter coming after a *vowel.* Examples :—***te'****diye* = payment ***müste'****cir* = tenant
ru'*yet* = sight ***me'****mur* = official

(5*c*) Note.—This kind of word is gradually being changed, the apostrophe being dropped.

SYLLABLES

(6) Turkish syllables are composed of **one vowel** with **one** or **two consonants** following it or **one consonant preceding it,** as :—

al, ard, sa, nal, halt, etc.
el, ırk, da, kın, denk, etc.
ön, ört, ne, göz, dört, etc.

Two consonants **preceding** a vowel are only found in foreign words taken into the language.

(6*a*) In words of two syllables or more only the last one can be of more than three letters, as :—

*dördün**cü**, köp**rü**, öl**dürt***

(6*b*) A vowel can form a syllable by itself only at the beginning of a Turkish word but can form a syllable by itself in the middle and at the end of foreign words taken into the language :— ***evet, emek, daire, mânia***

VOWELS

(7) The vowels are divided into two sections :—

LIP vowels and **TEETH** vowels.

When the lip vowels are uttered, the teeth do not show and the lips protrude.

o, u, ö, ü (pronounced au͡, o͡o, eu͡, e͡w), are lip vowels as will be seen in the following examples :—

kol (kau͡l) = " arm ". **gök** (geu͡k) = " sky ".
pul (po͡ol) = " stamp ". **süt** (se͡wt) = " milk ".

(7*a*) The teeth vowels are obtained through drawing the lips back a very little and showing the teeth.

a, e, ı, i (u, e, i(*r*), i) are teeth vowels. Examples :—

dal (dul) = ***branch.*** **yıl** (yi(*r*)l) = ***year.***
tel (tel) = ***wire.*** **fil** (fil) = ***elephant.***

(7*b*) These are again divided into sounds which we will call " wide " and " narrow ".

(7*c*) When the mouth has to be opened widely to correctly pronounce the vowel it is called " wide ".

a, e, o, ö (u, e, au͡, eu͡) are wide, as in :—

bal (bul) = ***honey.*** **yol** (yau͡l) = ***road.***
bel (bel) = ***waist.*** **köy** (keuy) = ***village.***

(7*d*) If the mouth has only to be opened a little way the vowel will be narrow.

ı, i, u, ü, (*i*(*r*), *i*, o͡o, e͡w) are narrow, as in :—

kıl (ki(*r*)l) = ***hair.*** **çul** (cho͡ol) = ***haircloth.***
dil (dil) = ***tongue.*** **gül** (ge͡wl) = ***rose.***

(8) Vowels are again divided, into " hard ", ***a, ı, o, u,*** as in :—

m*a*l (mul) = *possession.* **k*o*y** (kaûy) = *bay.*

k*ı*l (ki(*r*)l) = *bristle.* **k*u*l** (kôol) = *servant.*

(9) and into " soft ", ***e, i, ö, ü,*** as in :—

k*e*l (kel) = *ringwormy.* **g*ö*l** (geûl) = *lake.*

ç*i*l (chil) = *bright.* **g*ü*l** (gewl) = *rose.*

The latter two, the "***hard***" and "***soft***" vowels, are among the fundamentals of the language and must be memorized.

CONSONANTS

(10) In the utterance of the consonants the lips either meet and remain closed, remain apart, or meet and open again, and in the meantime the position and movement of the tongue creates sounds of various tones. These sounds can be divided into four categories :—

(11) LIP consonants . . . *b, p, m, f, v.*

(12) TEETH-GUMS consonants . *l, d, n, t.*

(13) FRONT PALATE consonants . *c, ç, j, r, s, ş, z.*

(14) REAR PALATE consonants . *g, h, k, y, ğ.*

(15) The consonants are again divided into three classes :—

The SHARP, the FLAT, and the NEUTRAL.

(15*a*) A *flat* consonant is easily uttered, and when stress is put upon it, it becomes a " sharp " one, its equivalent.

(15*b*) A *sharp* consonant is produced under effort, is strong, and has an assimilatory power over a " flat " consonant.

(15*c*) A *neutral* consonant, irrespective of its condition at the time of utterance, has no power to effect, and is not subject to alteration.

Flat.	*Sharp.*	*Neutral.*
C	Ç	L
V	F	M
B	P	N
G	K	R
Z	S	Y
J	Ş	Ğ
D	T	
	H	

(16) The student will notice by studying Turkish words that consonants of the **same class group** *themselves* **together,** as :— ***Baca, Paça, Koç, Peçe, Kesik, Sepet, Kepek, Kıskaç,*** etc.

(16*a*) This division is of vast importance and wide application. Many rules in the formation of words, adjectives, etc., are directly controlled by it. Where the rule seems to fail, in that, between two consonants of one class, a consonant of the opposite class or a neutral one had been placed, it will be found that the sound position of the medial consonant had been influenced by the vowels in the word, as in ***kabak, görücü, mercimek***, *taslak, kanat, yumurta*, etc.

WORDS and VERB ROOTS

(17) Turkish words and verb roots will either be hard (***a, ı, o, u***) or soft (***e, i, ö, ü***), according to the vowels they contain. In both cases of course, they will either end with a vowel or consonant, but when they do the latter it could either be a ***sharp*** consonant (***ç, p, t, k***, etc.), a *flat* one (***g, v, z, j***, etc.), (these are very few, see 31*c* and 31*cc*) or a ***neutral*** one (***l, m, n, r, y, ğ***), and it is most essential to take notice of the structure of the word or verb root so that the correct " endings " can be applied when forming the various " cases ", etc., as will be seen later on.

Verb Root (with Infin. end)	Words (nouns, etc.)	
kana-mak	*baba*	= hard (vowel ending).
dene-mek	*dede*	= soft (vowel ending).
sok-mak	*kabak*	= hard (sharp cons. end.).
küs-mek	*kümes*	= soft (sharp cons. end.).
sav-mak	*saylav*	= hard (flat cons. end.).
gör-mek	*şeker*	= soft (neutral cons. end.).

(18) Words, as we know, are composed of single sounds, or of several sounds in formation. In the Turkish euphony the sounds are divided into two groups, the " soft subdued " ones, and the " hard strong " ones, the hard and soft vowels being the controlling factors. There is one prevailing rule and that is that a word is either all hard or hardish, or all soft or softish (34*a*). A hard syllable is never put in direct contact with a soft syllable in any word which is of Turkish origin.

ROOT WORDS and SUFFIXES (or ENDINGS)

(18*a*) There is always graduation of sound, no sudden fall nor rise from hard to soft or vice versa as explained a little further on. This rule is the natural result of the mouth work, according to the latest scientific research in the sphere of phonetics, that is, that some particular vowels force the utterance of some particular consonants, and vice versa. In the Grammar the student will learn that for all the various cases, for adjective formation, etc., there are hard and soft endings, both, of course, meaning exactly the same, so that, to a word composed of soft syllables he will add a soft ending, and to a hard word, a hard ending, ***the vowel in the LAST syllable determining the one to be used.***

Hard word with hard ending.		Soft word with soft ending.	
*ara-**lık***	= space	*iyi-**lik***	= kindness
*balık-**çı***	= fisherman	*ekmek-**çi***	= baker
*kur-**untu***	= delusion	*süpür-**üntü***	= rubbish
*tabak-**lar***	= plates	*teneke-**ler***	= tins

(This rule, however, does not apply in the terminations of the present tense in the verb conjugations, but of this we shall speak later on.)

GRADUATION OF SOUNDS

(19) The Turkish vowels comprise all the natural fundamental sounds which are produced by the vocal cords. These sounds, as we have already mentioned, are produced according to natural laws. Examples :—

kapı and not *kapi*. *konak* and not *konek*.
sıkıntı and not *sikıntı*. *sürme* and not *sürma*.

It is only by the well-proportioned balance that the most melodious harmony in the sounds of the language has come forth. It is really the natural result of the smooth working of the laws of phonetics.

There are, however, some combinations of vowels, ***a-i, u-i, a-e, u-e,*** which appear, in some foreign words, to deviate from this rule (see 34*a*).

The subject is very vast, and I shall just give the very elementary points which it is necessary for the student to know to enable him to grasp the process of word-formation. To help him to understand what is about to be explained I shall put the sounds under two headings, " rise " and " drop ".

(20) The ***wide*** vowel sounds ***a, e, o, ö*** will be the *rise* and the ***narrow*** vowel sounds ***ı, i, u, ü*** will be the *drop*, irrespective of where they appear in the word.

NOTE.—**Rise** and **drop** cannot really be definitely defined, but to put it in a simple way we can say that when two sounds come together the weaker one will be the ***drop*** and the stronger one the ***rise.***

(21) These sounds may be ***grouped*** together either in a **consecutive** or in an **alternate** manner (see 22–23).

(22) The basis of the sounds in word formation is repetition that is that each of the sounds ***a, ı, u*** ("hard") and ***e, i, ü*** ("soft") is followed by itself. Examples :—

REPETITION.—***Tapa*** (stopper), ***sıkı*** (tight), ***kılıf*** (cover), ***kuru*** (dry), ***sene*** (year), ***cici*** (pretty), ***sini*** (tray), ***sallanma*** (swinging), ***çalkalama*** (shaking), ***kırıntı*** (piece), ***kuruntu*** (delusion), ***zemberek*** (latch), ***kertenkele*** (lizard), ***silinti*** (erasion), ***süprüntü*** (sweepings).

(23) Where a sound is not followed by itself it is followed by one of the other sounds in its own group, forming a "variation". When there is variation there are, generally speaking, no more than two vowel sounds in one word.

(23*a*) These are either in the form of a "drop" from a high tone, as :—
arı (bee), ***boru*** (tube), ***barut*** (gunpowder), ***tabur*** (battalion),

(23*b*) or a "rise" from a low tone, as :—
kısa (short), ***sıcak*** (warm).

(23*c*) or, in both cases, rise or drop, afterwards reverting to the first sound, as :—
salıncak (swing), ***sarımtrak*** (yellowish), ***kırlangıç*** (swallow) ***sıcaklık*** (warmth).

NOTE.—There are a few words which have more than two vowel sounds of a kind, but these are of foreign origin.

(24) Then again we find the two processes brought together in the form of a repetition of the first sound, followed by a "drop" or "rise", as :—

Repetition and drop ..	***kenevir*** (hemp seed).
Repetition and rise ..	***girişken*** (pushful).

(25) Or, again, from a drop to a rise with the repetition of the latter, as :—***yıkanmak*** (to bathe).
sıvamak (to plaster).

(26) The two sounds **o** and **ö** have a special feature in the formation of words. They do not repeat themselves. Where there would be repetition in other words, in the case of a

word containing either **o** or **ö** this letter will be followed by **u** and **ü**, as :—

koku (odour)	***kötü*** (bad)
topuk (heel)	***köprü*** (bridge)
soğuk (cold)	***gönül*** (affection)
doğru (straight)	***körük*** (bellows)

(27) In the case of variation in words containing **o** and **ö** the *drop* is made with the sounds **u** and **ü** respectively, instead of **ı** and **i**, and a *rise* with **a** and **e**, Examples :—

konak (residence)	***kötek*** (thrashing)
sokak (street)	***börek*** (pastry)

The same principle applies to the longer words, **repetition** and **rise** or **drop**, etc. Examples :—

Zonguldak (town of that name).
Safranbolu (town of that name).
korkuluk (scarecrow).
İnebolu (town of that name).

MUTATION

(28) The most outstanding point to be borne in mind is that in the Turkish language there are **two main divisions**, i.e. **hard** words and **soft** words. The application of this fundamental law, i.e. by the grouping together of the **hard sounds** and the grouping together of the **soft sounds**, is very far reaching. It controls the process of word formation, the verb conjugation, the declension cases of the noun, etc. In other words it actually brings about the law of Mutation. For instance, **when a suffix commencing with a consonant (*ci, ki, li, kun, lık, süz*,** etc.) is added to a word, either consonant or vowel ending, **the vowel in the suffix must be in harmony with the last vowel in the word.** Examples :—

*Kir-**li*** (dirty), *coş-**kun*** (excited), *temiz-**lik*** (cleanliness), *sür-**üm-süz*** (unsaleable), *şapka-**cı*** (hat-maker), *koru-**cu*** (keeper), *günde-**lik*** (daily pay).

(28*a*) **When a suffix commencing with a vowel, (*ık, ak, in, un*,** etc.) is added to a word, **the vowel of the suffix must be in harmony with the last vowel in the word.** Examples :—

*Kır-**ık*** (broken), *kork-**ak*** (coward), *kesim-**in*** (of the cut)

(28*b*) Suffixes are, in their turn, divided into two main groups :—

(*a*) those containing a ***wide*** vowel, and
(*b*) those containing a ***narrow*** vowel (see Ph. 7*c* and *d*).

(*a*) As out of the four ***wide*** vowels, ***a, e, o, ö,*** only ***two*** are used, ***a*** and ***e,*** these are used in **pairs, the hard *a* for hard words,** and **the soft *e* for soft words,** as for instance, ***ca*** (hard), and ***ce*** (soft), ***lar*** (hard), and ***ler*** (soft), etc. (see T. Gr. 4 and 33).

(*b*) Of the ***narrow*** vowels, ***all four are used,*** as for instance, ***lık, lik, luk, lük,*** (see T. Gr. 28*g*), and from these the one which harmonises most accurately with the last vowel in the word will be chosen.

(28*c*) When a suffix is in the form of a single letter (***k, m, s,***) a vowel in harmony with the last vowel in the word is inserted between the root-word and the suffix, as some consonants cannot be pronounced together. (This will be better understood if the student studies the English word "sarcasm" where, between the "s" and "m" there is a sound as if a vowel were there.) Examples :—

*Yaz-**ı-s*** (manner of writing), *bak-**ı-m*** (outlook), *dil-**i-m*** (a slice), *dik-**i-m*** (sewing), *gör-**ü-m*** (insight), *yür-**ü-k*** (active).

ASSIMILATION

This successiveness of natural sounds, which is called "fluidity" plays a great part in the Turkish words.

(29) When two consonants come together, one being the ending letter of the root word, and the second one the beginning letter of an "ending" (such as ***-dan*** and ***-den*** of the Ablative case) a "sharp" consonant will assimilate in sound the "flat" one, and change it to its equivalent "sharp" one, as explained further on (Ph. 15*b*) (See also T. Gr. 19.) Examples :—

*Kap-**dan*** becomes *Kap-**tan.*** *Ağaç-**dan*** becomes *Ağaç-**tan.***
*Kaş-**dan*** becomes *Kaş-**tan.*** *Raf-**dan*** becomes *Raf-**tan,*** etc.

Taking the two (Ablative case) endings ***-dan*** for hard words and ***-den*** for soft words again as an example, I would point out the fact that these actually are the two real endings and the student would not be exactly wrong if he used only these, but here again comes the matter of more euphonious pronunciation. It was found that *d* was not easy to say directly following *t* as *tokat-**dan*** and *iskelet-**den***, and so, in such words, the *d* was changed to *t* thus making the words *tokat-**tan*** and *iskelet-**ten***. Even if this letter had not been changed the student will find that in the ordinary quickness of conversational speech the ***d*** would sound very much like a ***t***.

(30) The words to which the ***-tan*** will be added will be HARD words, i.e. containing the vowels ***a, o, ı***, or ***u***, ending in ***k, t, p, s, ş, ç, f, h***. Examples :—

*Konak-**tan**, Kaput-**tan**, Çorap-**tan**, Makas-**tan**, savaş-**tan**, tıkaç-**tan**, yulaf-**tan**, Allah-**tan**.*

(30*a*) The ***-ten*** will be added to SOFT words, i.e. containing the vowels ***e, i, ö, ü***, ending in the same consonants. Examples :—*böbrek-**ten**, süt-**ten**, çöp-**ten**, kümes-**ten**, çiriş-**ten**, pirinç-**ten**, Şeref-**ten**.*

(30*b*) The actual endings ***-dan*** and ***-den*** will be added to all the other letters. (***ğ, l, m, n, r, y***, 15*c*) (***v, g, z, j***, 15*a*).

(30*c*) Verb roots and tense suffixes in verb conjugation, etc., are also subject to Graduation, Mutation, and Assimilation rules.

(30*d*) In some cases, the harmony causes one of the consonants to be dropped altogether, but this does not happen very often (see 33*c*).

(31) Again, when the "sharp" consonants, ***p, t, ç, k***, are at the end of the root word and come in contact with any suffix ***commencing with a vowel*** (in word forming and declension cases) they are changed to ***b, d c, ğ***, which are their equivalents in the "flat" and "neutral" groups (see also 31*cc*–32, 36, 37).

Examples :— *Çorap* becomes *Çora**bın*** (Gen. case).
Kabak becomes *Kaba**ğa*** (Dat. case).
Kireç becomes *Kire**ci*** (Obj. case).

This only happens if the word had originally ended with a FLAT consonant, and had been made SHARP when brought into the language (see also 31*cc* to 32). An up-to-date dictionary must be consulted when conjugating, as this will show the required letter.

(31*a*) The above rule (Ph. 31), with the exception of the verbs ***etmek*** (to do), ***gitmek*** (to go), ***gütmek*** (to bear), does not apply to verb roots in the formation of the Present,

Indefinite, and Future tenses, the Optative Mood, and the gerundial moods. Examples :—

				(*İtmek* = to push)	(*Kaçmak* = to run away)
(Pres.)	*Ediyor*	*Gidiyor*	*Güdüyor*	*İtiyor*	*Kaçıyor*
(Ind.)	*Eder*	*Gider*	*Güder*	*İter*	*Kaçar*
(Fut.)	*Edecek*	*Gidecek*	*Güdecek*	*İtecek*	*Kaçacak*
(Opt.)	*Ede*	*Gide*	*Güde*	*İte*	*Kaça*

(31*b*) When a suffix commencing with (***c, g, b, d***) is to be added to a word ending with a sharp consonant (***ç, k, p, t, f, h, s, ş***) (Ph. 15*b*) the latter will force the former to change to (***ç, k, p, t***). See (T. Gr. 12*f–h*, 18*b*, 19*b*, 29*b*).

(31*c*) The **graduation of sounds, assimilation, mutation,** and the insertion of ***y, n,*** and ***s,*** between the **main word** and the **suffixes** (expl. in the Grammar) are great factors in the maintenance of the fluidity of the language. This fluidity and the fact of the **accent being laid on the last syllable** necessitates that **when a word ends in a consonant** this latter should be a " **sharp** " one.

(31*cc*) This will be found to be the case in most Turkish words, and, should any foreign word taken into the language end in a " flat " consonant, this will be changed to its equivalent " sharp " one. This is incidental, however, when the word is modified (declension, etc.) for the original letter is put back, see Ph. 31 (see also T.Gr., 16*c*, 17*c*, 23*c*, and verbs.

Examples :—

çorab becomes *çorap* — *kiremid* becomes *kiremit*
kitab ,, *kitap* — *Ahmed* ,, *Ahmet*

(31*d*) When foreign words ending with **sharp consonants** are taken into the language they are not altered at all, and are not subject to alteration, their consonants having all the power of a Turkish sharp consonant (see T. Gr. 23*d*).

(32) Rule 31*cc* has an exception when the words are of only one syllable, as :—

Ok . . . *Okun, Oka, Oku* — *Sap* . . . *Sapın, Sapa, Sapı*
At . . . *Atın, Ata, Atı* — *Saç* . . . *Saçın, Saça, Saçı*

Thus we can see that the ending letters of words (nouns, adjectives, and others) are subject to direct vowel and consonant influence, and undergo changes. We must also remember, as we have mentioned before, that the utterance of certain vowels forces the utterance of certain consonants (Ph. 18–18*a*).

(32*b*) NOTE.—There are now very few Turkish words ending in ***c, b, d, v, z, j, g***.

INFLUENCE OF HARD AND SOFT SOUNDS ON FOREIGN WORDS

(33) The fundamental rule of "*hard*" and "*soft*" sounds has, throughout the life of the language, exercised its assimilatory power in the matter of shaping into the Turkish mould of word-formation, by way of every-day common usage, every foreign word brought into the language. Thus, in a word where a hard sound had existed together with two soft sounds, one sound had influenced the other and made it conform to the rule. For instance:—

Hoce	(Persian)	became	*Hoca*
Çarçive	"	"	*Çerçeve*
Çarşenbe	(Persian)	became	*Çarşamba*
Station	(French)	"	*İstasyon*
Mehmed	(Arabic)	"	*Memet*
Fire up	(English, Nautical)		*Fayrap*, etc.
Maaden	(Arabic)	became	*Mağden*

(34) Any exceptions to this rule will also be found to be of foreign origin, and even their pronunciation has been more or less Turkicised. Although they have retained their structure they have lost their original pronunciation and are to-day subject to the Turkish euphony. For example:—

i'mar	or	*İimar*	(Arabic)	became	*îmar*
ma'rifet	"	*maarifet*	"	"	*mârifet*
mi'de	"	*miide*	"	"	*mîde*, etc.

NOTE.—There is a tendency to drop the signs wherever possible, and eventually they will be written in the simple manner, as :—*imar, marifet, mide.*

(34*a*) A divergence of sound is sometimes caused by the hard vowels ***a*** and ***u*** coming in contact with the soft ***e*** and ***i***, as in :—

şimal	= north	*şamil*	= comprise
kitap	= book	*kâtip*	= clerk
Irak	= Irak	*harik*	= fire

merak = anxiety　　　***sadet*** = boundary
suret = copy　　　***mebus*** = M.P.

On the surface it might appear that they are forming an exception, but in reality they have been Turkicised in all respects, for the ***l*** in *şimal*, the ***p*** in *kitap*, the ***k*** in *İrak* and ***merak***, the ***ş*** in *şamil*, the ***k*** in ***kâtip***, the ***h*** in ***harik***, and the ***s*** in *sedet* have in their turn softened the ***a***, and the ***s*** in ***suret*** and ***mebus***, the ***u***.

In vowel-ending words of this type, or words where the last syllable contains a soft vowel, these ***soft*** vowels ***e*** and ***i*** have a softening effect on the ***hard*** ones ***a*** and ***u***, thereby making the word almost as soft as an original soft one, as in :—

nümune = sample　　　*rutubet* = damp
sühulet = ease　　　*duhuliye* = entrance fee

These words form the " hardish " and " softish " groups mentioned in (18).

A rule, which applies to these foreign words only, is that when the word ends with ***l*** it is considered to be " soft " irrespective of its vowel sounds, and will therefore take the various " soft " suffixes, as in :—

misâl　　***misâller***　　***rasûl***　　***rasûller***

LETTERS K, G

(35) There are no gutteral sounds in the language. All such sounds have gradually changed into " back palate sounds " which makes them a shade softer, and this would be where the previously mentioned " hardish " sounds would apply. Should this softening not be reverted to, the pronunciation would be too hard and cause a strain on the throat. Examples :—

Yigirmi becomes *yiğirmi*, ***saglam*** becomes ***sağlam***, ***dogru*** becomes *doğru*, ***egri*** becomes ***eğri***, ***igne*** becomes ***iğne***.

In these cases the ***ğ*** becomes almost mute and lost in the throat of the pronouncer, not heard by the listener, yet it is felt by the pronouncer. The words given above could almost be pronounced as if they were spelt :—

Yiirmi or *yîrmi*, ***saalam*** or ***sâlam***, ***dooru*** or ***dôru***, ***eeri*** or ***êri***, ***iine*** or ***îne***. (Alphabet 2, 4).

(36) The sound represented by the letter ***k*** is one which is subject to several changes. It retains its original sound when it

is at the beginning or in the middle of the word, but is subject to "softening" when being at the end of the word, and **preceded by a vowel,** it comes in contact with a suffix or termination beginning with a vowel. It then changes to a **ğ** in hard words (see Alph. 1) (see also T. Gr. 16, 17, 23, 74*a*).

For example :—***Kuyruk*** becomes ***Kuyruğu***(Obj. case)
Kabak „ ***Kabağı*** (Obj. case)

(37) In soft words where this seems to be still too hard it changes in the pronunciation to a very soft **ğ** or almost to the sound of **y** although still written **ğ**. (See Alph. Ğ (4).)
Examples :—

ördek becomes ***ördeği*** and is pronounced as if written ***ördeyi***
beşik „ ***beşiği*** „ „ „ „ ***beşiyi***

(37*a*) The **k** can actually be written "**y**" when subject to changes, but it is more correct to keep to **ğ.**

(37*aa*) When at the end of a word, hard or soft, and **preceded by a consonant,** the letter **k** changes to **g** and not to **ğ** when coming in contact with a suffix commencing with a vowel.

Examples :—

henk = harmony ***âhenge*** = to the harmony
ünk = earthenware pipe ***künge*** = to the e. pipe

In conclusion I must reiterate the following points :—

The Turkish word is a built-up structure consisting of the ***stem*** and ***various suffixes.*** In the case of ***verbs,*** the ***verb root acts as the stem.***

This stem is either ***hard*** or ***soft,*** and ends in either a ***consonant*** or a ***vowel.***

The suffixes, in their turn, are either ***"wide", in which case they are only in pairs, one for hard words and one for soft words,*** or ***"narrow", in which case they will contain any one of the four narrow vowels, the one harmonizing most accurately with the last vowel in the word to which it is being added, being chosen.*** Finally, in the pronunciation, great care must be taken to ***sound every letter in every word individually.*** This is particularly necessary in the case of the letters "**r**", "**n**", and "**h**" when they come at the end of a word, as otherwise, for reasons already explained, confusion will arise.

VOCABULARIES

(Lugatça**lar**)

Note 1.—To help the student and familiarize him with the "endings" affixed to the various words I have had these printed in heavy type, and where there is more than one affix a slight space has been left between them.

Note 2.—When a word is placed in one of the Oblique cases (See T.G. 16, 16*c*, 17, 18, 19, 23) the ending letter is subject to alteration. (Sharp consonants ***ç, k, p, t,*** sometimes change to ***c, ğ, b, d*** (see Ph. 31). To help the student I have, wherever possible, shown whether the ending changes or remains the same by placing a single letter showing the required form, after some of the words. (See also Phs. 28, 31*d*, 32, 32*b*).

The World and Nature

(Dünya ve tabiat)

English	Turkish	Pronunciation
Air	*hava*	huvu
climate	*iklîm*	ikle͡em
cloud	*bulut*	bo͡olo͡ot
cold	*soğ**uk***	sa͡ugho͡ok
darkness	*karan**lık***	kurunli(*r*)k
dew	*çiy*	chiy
earth	*toprak*	ta͡upruk
east	*şark, doğ**u***	shurk, da͡ugho͡o
eclipse of the sun	*güneş tutulma**sı**, küsuf*	ge͡wnesh to͡oto͡olmusi(*r*), ke͡wso͡of
eclipse of the moon	*ay tutulma**sı**, hüsuf*	uy to͡oto͡olmusi(*r*), he͡wso͡of
fire	*ateş*	utesh
fog	*sis*	sis
frost	*don* or *kırağı*	da͡un *or* ki(*r*)rughi(*r*)
hail	*dolu*	da͡ulo͡o
heat	*sıcak**lık***	si(*r*)jukli(*r*)k
ice	*buz*	bo͡oz
light	*ziya*	ziyu
lightning	*şimşek*	shimshek
moon	*ay*	uy
moonlight	*mehtap*	mehtup

English	Turkish	Pronunciation
north	*şimal, kuzey*	shimul, ko͡ozey
rain	*yağmur*	yughmo͡or
rainbow	*elimsâma*	elimsa͡amu
shade	*gölge*	ge͡ulge
shadow	*gölge*	ge͡ulge
sky	*gök*	ge͡uk
snow	*kar*	kur
south	*cenup, . . . b, güney*	jeno͡op, ge͡wney
star	*yıldız*	yi(*r*)ldi(*r*)z
sun	*güneş*	ge͡wnesh
thaw	*donlar çözülmesi, karın erimesi*	da͡unlur che͡uze͡wlmesi, kari(*r*)n erimesi
thunder	*gök gürlemesi*	ge͡uk ge͡wrlemesi
temperature	*dereceiharaet*	derejeihururet
to freeze	*donmak*	da͡unmuk
frosty weather	*don havası*	da͡un huvusi(*r*)
west	*garb, batı*	gurb, buti(*r*)
wind	*rüzgâr*	re͡wzgiur
warm	*sıcak*	si(*r*)*juk*

Land and Water
(Kara ve su)

English	Turkish	Pronunciation
Bay	*körfez*	ke͡urfez
beacon	*fener*	fener
beach	*kumsal*	ko͡omsul
brook	*dere*	dere
calm	*sâkin*	sa͡akin
canal	*kanal*	kunul
cape	*burun*	bo͡oro͡on
cliff	*yar, yalçın kaya*	yur, yulchi(*r*)n kuyu
coast	*sahil*	suhil
current	*akıntı*	uki(*r*)nti(*r*)
ebb	*cezir, deniz suyunun çekilmesi*	jezir, deniz so͡oyo͡ono͡on chekilmesi
flow	*med, deniz suyunun geri gelmesi,* or *kabarması*	med, deniz so͡oyo͡ono͡on geri gelmesi, *or* kuburmusi(*r*)
hill	*tepe*	tepe

English	Turkish	Pronunciation
island	*ada*	udu
lake	*göl*	geul
mainland	*kara*	kuru
marsh	*bataklık*	butukli(*r*)k
mountain	*dağ*	dugh
ocean	*dişdeniz*	dishdeniz
pebble	*çakıl taşı*	chuki(*r*)l tushi(*r*)
pier	*iskele*	iskele
plain	*ova*	auva
river	*nehir, ırmak*	nehir, i(*r*)rmuk
rock	*kaya*	kuyu
sand	*kum*	koom
sea	*deniz*	deniz
seashore	*deniz kenarı*	deniz kenuri(*r*)
shingle	*çakıl*	chuki(*r*)l
shore	*sahil*	suhil
storm	*fırtına*	fi(*r*)rti(*r*)nu
stream	*çay*	chuy
tides	*meddücezir*	meddewjezir
high tide	*med, kabarma*	med, kuburmu
low tide	*cezir, çekilme*	jezir, çekilme
valley	*vâdi*	vaadi
water	*su*	soo
fresh water	*tatlı* (sweet) *su*	tutli(*r*) soo
salt water	*deniz* (sea) *suyu*	deniz sooyoo
waterfall	*çağlıyan*	chughli(*r*)yun
wave	*dalga*	pulgn

Minerals and Metals
(Ham ve temizlenmiş mâdenler)

English	Turkish	Pronunciation
Brass	*pirinç*	pirinch
bronze	*tunç*	toonch
chalk	*tebeşir*	tebeshir
clay	*balçık*	bulchi(*r*)k
coal	*kömür*	keumewr
copper	*bakır*	buki(*r*)r
coral	*mercan*	merjun
crystal	*billur*	billoor
chrome	*krom*	kraum

English	Turkish	Pronunciation
glass	*cam*	jum
gold	*altın*	ulti(*r*)n
granite	*granit taşı*	grunit tushi(*r*)
gravel	*çakıllı kum*	chuki(*r*)lli(*r*) ko͡om
iron	*demir*	demir
lead	*kurşun*	ko͡orsho͡on
lime	*kireç*	kirech
marble	*mermer*	mermer
mercury	*civa*	jivu
nickel	*nikel*	nikel
silver	*gümüş*	ge͡wme͡wsh
slate	*kara taş* or *kaygan taşı*	kuru tush *or* kuygun tushi(*r*)
steel	*çelik*	chelik
stone	*taş*	tush
stones (precious)	*kıymetli taşlar*	ki(*r*)ymetli tushlur
diamond	*elmas*	elmus
emerald	*zümrüt*	ze͡wmre͡wt
pearl	*inci*	inji
ruby	*yâkut*	ya͡ako͡ot
tin	*teneke*	teneke
zinc	*çinko*	chinka͡u

Animals, Birds, Fish, etc.
(Hayvan*lar*, kuş*lar*, balık*lar*)

Bear	*ayı*	uyi(*r*)
bull	*boğa*	ba͡ughu
bat	*yarasa*	yurusu
calf	*dana*	dunu
cat	*kedi*	kedi
chicken	*piliç*	pilich
claw	*pençe, tırnak*	penche, ti(*r*)rnuk
crocodile	*timsah*	timsuh
cock	*horos*	ha͡ura͡us
cow	*inek*	inek
cod	*morina balığı*	ma͡urinu buli(*r*)ghi(*r*)
crab	*yengeç*	yengech

English	Turkish	Pronunciation
cries	*bağırmalar*	bughi(*r*)rmulur
barking	*havlama*	huvlumu
bleating	*meleme*	meleme
braying	*anırma*	uni(*r*)rmu
crowing	*horos ötmesi*	ha͡ura͡us e͡utmesi
growling	*hırlama*	hi(*r*)rlumu
howling	*uluma*	o͡olo͡omu
mewing	*mıyavlama*	mi(*r*)yuvlumu
neighing	*kişneme*	kishneme
deer	*geyik*	geyik
dog	*köpek*	ke͡upek
donkey	*eşek*	eshek
cuckoo	*guguk kuşu*	go͡ogo͡ok ko͡osho͡o
dove	*kumru*	ko͡omro͡o
duck	*ördek*	e͡urdek
eagle	*kartal*	kurtul
eel	*yılan balığı*	yi(*r*)lun buli(*r*)ghi(*r*)
elephant	*fil*	fil
feather	*tüy*	te͡wy
fox	*tilki*	tilki
goat	*keçi*	kechi
goose	*kaz*	kuz
gosling	*kaz palazı*	kuz puluzi(*r*)
grouse	*yaban horozu* or *horuzu*	yubun ha͡ura͡uzo͡o *or* ha͡uro͡ozo͡o
gull	*martı kuşu*	murti(*r*) ko͡osho͡o
hare	*tavşan*	tuvshun
hide	*deri*	deri
hen	*tavuk*	tuvo͡ok
herring	*ringa balığı*	ringu buli(*r*)ghi(*r*)
hoof	*hayvan tırnağı*	huyvun ti(*r*)rnughi(*r*)
horn	*boynuz*	ba͡uyno͡oz
horse	*at, beygir*	ut, beygir
lamb	*kuzu*	ko͡ozo͡o
lark	*çayır kuşu*	chuyi(*r*)r ko͡osho͡o
lion	*arslan* or *aslan*	urslun *or* uslun
lobster	*istakoz*	istuka͡uz
mane	*yele*	yele

English	Turkish	Pronunciation
monkey	*maymun*	muymo͡on
mouse	*fare*	fure
nightingale	*bülbül*	be͡wlbe͡wl
owl	*baykuş*	buyko͡osh
ox	*öküz*	e͡ukewz
oyster	*istiridiye*	istiridiye
parrot	*papağan*	pupughun
partridge	*keklik*	keklik
paw	*pençe*	penche
peacock	*tavus kuşu*	tuvo͡os ko͡osho͡o
pheasant	*sülün*	se͡wle͡wn
pig	*domuz*	da͡umo͡oz
pigeon	*güvercin*	ge͡wverjin
pike	*turna balığı*	to͡ornu buli(*r*)ghi(*r*)
quail	*bıldırcın*	bi(*r*)ldi(*r*)rji(*r*)n
rabbit	*ada tavşanı*	udu tuvshuni(*r*)
rat	*lağım sıçanı*	lughi(*r*)m si(*r*)chuni(*r*)
rook	*karga*	kurgu
salmon	*somon balığı*	sa͡uma͡un buli(*r*)ghi(*r*)
salt-fish	*tuzlu balık*	to͡ozlo͡o buli(*r*)k
sea-gull	*martı*	murti(*r*)
sheep	*koyun*	ka͡uyo͡on
snipe	*çulluk*	cho͡ollo͡ok
sparrow	*serçe*	serche
squirrel	*sincap*	sinjup
stork	*leylek*	leylek
swallow	*kırlangıç*	ki(*r*)rlungi(*r*)ch
swan	*kugu*	ko͡ogo͡o
sword-fish	*kılıç balığı*	ki(*r*)li(*r*)ch buli(*r*)ghi(*r*)
tail	*kuyruk*	ko͡oyro͡ok
thrush	*ardiç kuşu*	urdi(*r*)ch ko͡osho͡o
tiger	*kaplan*	kuplun
tortoise	*kara kaplumbağası* or *kaplumbağa*	kuru kuplo͡om-bughasi(*r*) *or* kuplo͡ombughu
trout	*ala balığı*	ulu buli(*r*)ghi(*r*)
turkey	*hindi*	hindi

English	Turkish	Pronunciation
turtle	*deniz kaplumbağası* or *kaplumbağa*	deniz kuplo͝om-bughusi(*r*) *or* kup-lo͝ombughu
whale	*balina balığı*	bulinu buli(*r*)ghi(*r*)
wing	*kanat*	kunut
wolf	*kurd*	ko͝ord
wren	*çalı kuşu*	chuli(*r*) ko͝osho͝o

Reptiles and Insects

(Yer***de*** sür***ünen*** hayvan***lar*** ve böcek***ler***)

English	Turkish	Pronunciation
Ant	*karınca*	kuri(*r*)nju
bee	*arı*	uri(*r*)
beetle	*kara böcek*	kuru be͡ujek
butterfly	*kelebek*	kelebek
caterpillar	*tırtıl*	ti(*r*)rti(*r*)l
flea	*pire*	pire
fly	*sinek*	sinek
frog	*kurbağa*	ko͝orbughu
insect	*böcek*	be͡ujek
maggot	*kurt*	ko͝ort
moth (clothes)	*güve*	ge͡wve
mosquito	*sivrisinek*	sivrisinek
snail	*sümüklü böcek*	se͡wme͡wkle͡w be͡ujek
snake	*yılan*	yi(*r*)lun
spider	*örümcek*	e͡ure͡wmjek
sting (wasp)	*sokma (eşek arısı)*	sa͡ukmu (eshek uri(*r*)si(*r*))
toad	*kara kurbağa*	kuru ko͝orbughu
wasp	*eşek arısı*	eshek uri(*r*)si(*r*)
worm	*solucan*	sa͡ulo͝onjun

Fruits, Trees, Flowers, and Vegetables

(Yemiş***ler***, ağaç***lar***, çiçek***ler***, sebze***ler***)

English	Turkish	Pronunciation
Almond	*badem*	budem
apple	*elma*	elmu
apricot	*kaysı*	kuysi(*r*)
ash tree	*dişbudak ağacı*	dishbo͝oduk ughuji(*r*)

English	Turkish	Pronunciation
asparagus	*kuş konmaz*	ko͡osh ka͡unmuz
bean(s)	*fasulya*	fuso͡olyu
beech tree	*gürgen ağacı*	ge͡wrgen ughuji(*r*)
beetroot	*pancar*	punjur
birch tree	*kayın ağacı*	kuyi(*r*)n ughuji(*r*)
branch	*dal*	dul
blackberry	*böğürtlen*	be͡ughe͡wrtlen
bunch (cluster)	*demet*	demet
cypress	*selvi ağacı*	selvi ughuji(*r*)
cabbage	*lahana*	luhunu
carnation	*karanfil*	kurunfil
carrot	*havuç*	huvo͡och
cherry	*kiraz*	kiruz
chestnut	*kestane*	kestune
cockscomb	*horos ibiği*	ha͡ura͡us ibighi
cucumber	*hıyar*	hi(*r*)yur
currants	*kuş üzümü*	ko͡osh e͡wze͡wme͡w
daffodils	*sarı zambak*	suri(*r*) zumbuk
dahlia	*yıldız çiçeği*	yi(*r*)ldi(*r*)z chicheghi
daisies (or daisy)	*papatya*	puputyu
date	*hurma*	ho͡ormu
elm	*kara ağaç*	kuru ughuch
fig	*incir*	injir
fir tree	*çam ağacı*	chum ughuji(*r*)
fruit tree	*yemiş ağacı*	yemish ughuji(*r*)
fuchsia	*küpe çiçeği*	ke͡wpe chicheghi
geranium	*sardunya çiçeği*	surdo͡onyu chicheghi
gooseberry	*ingiliz üzümü*	ingiliz e͡wze͡wme͡w
grape	*üzüm*	e͡wze͡wm
grape vine (bush)	*kütük*	ke͡wte͡wk
grape vine (climbing)	*asma*	usmu
hazel nut	*fındık*	fi(*r*)ndi(*r*)k
holly	*pırnal ağacı*	pi(*r*)rnul ughuji(*r*)
honeysuckle	*hanım eli*	huni(*r*)meli
horse-radish	*yaban turpu*	yubun to͡orpo͡o
hydrangea	*ortanca*	a͡urtunju

English	Turkish	Pronunciation
ivy	*hedera heliks sarmaşığı*	hederu heliks surmushi(*r*)ghi(*r*)
jasmin	*yasemin*	yusemin
laurel tree	*tefne ağacı*	tefne ughuji(*r*)
leaf	*yaprak*	yupruk
lemon	*limon*	lima͡un
lettuce	*mârul*	ma͡aro͡ol
lily	*zambak*	zumbuk
lime tree	*ıhlamur ağacı*	i(*r*)hlumo͡or ughuji(*r*)
melon	*kavun*	kuvo͡on
mint	*nane*	nune
mulberry	*dut ağacı*	do͡ot ughuji(*r*)
narcissus	*fulya*	fo͡olyu
oak	*meşe*	meshe
olive tree	*zeytun ağacı*	zeyto͡on ughuji(*r*)
onion	*soğan*	sa͡ughun
orange	*portakal*	pa͡urtukul
parsley	*maydanos*	muyduna͡us
peach tree	*şeftali ağacı*	sheftuli ughuji(*r*)
pear tree	*armut ağacı*	urmo͡ot ughuji(*r*)
peas	*bezelya*	bezelyu
pine	*çam ağacı*	chum ughuji(*r*)
plane tree	*çınar ağacı*	chi(*r*)nur ughuji(*r*)
plant	*fidan*	fidun
plum	*erik*	erik
pomegranate	*nar*	nur
poplar tree	*kavak ağacı*	kuvuk ughuji(*r*)
poppy	*gelincik*	gelinjik
potato	*patates*	pututes
radishes	*turp*	to͡orp
raisin	*kuru üzüm*	ko͡oro͡o e͡wze͡wm
raspberry	*ağaç çileği*	ughuch chileghi
roots	*kök*	ke͡uk
roots (seedlings)	*fide*	fide
rose	*gül*	ge͡wl
spinach	*ispanak*	ispunuk
stalk, stem	*sap*	sup
strawberry	*çilek*	chilek
sultana	*çekirdeksiz kuru üzüm*	chekirdeksiz ko͡oro͡o e͡wze͡wm

English	Turkish	Pronunciation
sunflower	*ay çiçeği*	uy chicheghi
tree trunk	*ağaç gövde**si***	ughuch ge͡uvdesi
tulip	*lâle*	la͡ale
turnip	*şalgam*	shulgum
violet	*menekşe*	menekshe
wallflower	*şebboy*	shebba͡uy
walnut	*ceviz*	jeviz
willow tree	*söğüt ağacı*	se͡ughe͡wt ughuji(*r*)

Colours

(Renk**ler**)

Auburn	*kumral*	ko͡omrul
black	*siyah*	siyuh
black (horse)	*yağız*	yughi(*r*)z
black (or brown) eyed	*kara göz**lü***	kuru ge͡uzle͡w
black-haired	*siyah saçlı*	siyuh suchli(*r*)
blue	*mavi*	muvi
— (saxe)	*çini mavi**si***	chini muvisi
— (royal)	*aç**ık** lacivert*	uchi(*r*)k lujivert
— (navy)	*lacivert*	lujivert
— (sky)	*aç**ık** mavi*	uchi(*r*)k muvi
blue-eyed	*mavi göz**lü***	muvi ge͡uzle͡w
bluish-grey-eyed	*çakır göz**lü***	chuki(*r*)r ge͡uzle͡w
brown (coffee colour)	*kahve rengi*	kuhve rengi
— (dark) ,, ,,	*koyu kahve rengi*	ka͡uyo͡o kuhve rengi
brown (horse)	*doru*	da͡uro͡o
chestnut	*kestane rengi*	kestune rengi
cream	*krem*	krem
crimson	*koyu kırmızı*	ka͡uyo͡o ki(*r*)rmi(*r*)zi(*r*)
dark (colour)	*koyu (renk)*	ka͡uyo͡o
dark (complexioned)	*esmer (beniz)*	esmer
faded (colour)	*sol**gun** (renk)*	sa͡ulgo͡on
fair-haired (blonde)	*lepiska saçlı*	lepisku suchli(*r*)
flame	*ateş rengi*	utesh rengi
green	*yeşil*	yeshil

English	Turkish	Pronunciation
green (bottle)	*nefti*	nefti
— (leaf)	*yaprak yeşili*	yupruk yeshili
grey	*kül rengi*	ke͡wl rengi
— (squirrel)	*sincâbî*	sinja͡abe͡e
hazel-eyed	*ela gözlü*	elu ge͡uzle͡w
light (colour)	*açık*	uchi(*r*)k
light (complexioned)	*buğday benizli*	bo͡oghduy benizli
mauve	*eflatun*	efluto͡on
orange	*turuncu*	to͡oro͡onjo͡o
pale (complexioned)	*solgun benizli*	sa͡ulgo͡on benizli
pink	*penbe*	penbe
purple	*mor*	ma͡ur
red	*kırmızı*	ki(*r*)rmi(*r*)zi(*r*)
rust colour	*pas rengi*	pus rengi
scarlet	*al*	ul
silver	*gümüşî*	ge͡wme͡wshe͡e
violet	*menekşe*	menekshe
white	*beyaz, ak*	beyuz, uk
white-haired	*ak saçlı*	uk suchli(*r*)
yellow	*sarı*	suri(*r*)
— (canary)	*kanarya sarısı*	kunuryu suri(*r*)si(*r*)

Things Seen in Town or Country

(Şehir ve sayfiye**de** göz**e** çarp**an** şey**ler**)

Bank (money)	*banka (para)*	bunku (puru)
— (of river)	*nehir kenarı*	nehir kenuri(*r*)
barley	*arpa*	urpu
barn	*ambar*	umbur
beehive	*arı kovanı*	ari(*r*) ka͡uvuni(*r*)
bridge	*köprü*	ke͡upre͡w
building	*binâ*	bina͡a
bush	*çalı*	chuli(*r*)
castle	*kal'e, hisar*	kul'e, hisur
cattle	*davar*	duvur
cow, ox	*inek, öküz*	inek, e͡uke͡wz
club (social)	*kulüp*	ko͡ole͡wp
corn	*hububat, zahire, tahıl*	ho͡obo͡obut, zuhire tuhi(*r*)l

English	Turkish	Pronunciation
cottage	***köşk*** **or** ***sayfiyelik***	ke͡ushk, suyfiyelik
countryside	***kır***	ki(*r*)r
courtyard	***avlu***	uvlo͡o
crop	***mahsul, verim, ürün***	muhso͡ol, verim, e͡wre͡wn
dairy farm	***mandıra***	mundi(*r*)ru
dining rooms	***lokanta***	la͡ukuntu
ditch	***hendek, arık***	hendek, uri(*r*)k
dust	***toz***	ta͡uz
factory	***fabrika***	fubriku
farm	***çiftlik***	chiftlik
farmer	***çiftçi***	chiftchi
fence (garden)	***tahta perde***	tuhtu (perde)
field	***tarla***	turlu
fisherman	***balıkçı***	buli(*r*)kchi(*r*)
flock, herd	***sürü***	se͡wre͡w
foot pavement	***ayak kaldırımı***	uyuk kuldi(*r*)ri(*r*)mi(*r*)
forest	***orman***	a͡urmun
garden	***bahçe***	buhche
gate (garden)	***bahçe kapısı***	buhche kupi(*r*)si(*r*)
grass (field)	***çayır***	chuyi(*r*)r
grass (lawn)	***çimen***	chimen
harvest	***mahsul***	muhso͡ol
hay	***kuru ot***	ko͡oro͡o a͡ut
hedge	***çit***	chit
hotel	***otel***	a͡utel
hut	***kulübe***	ko͡ole͡wbe
inn	***han***	hun
labourer	***işçi, amele***	ishchi, umele
lamp	***lamba***	lumbu
land	***arâzi, toprak***	ura͡azi, ta͡upruk
log	***kütük, odun***	ke͡wte͡wk, a͡udo͡on
maize	***mısır buğdayı***	mi(*r*)si(*r*)r bo͡oghduyi(*r*)
manure	***gübre***	ge͡wbre
market	***pazar***	puzur
meadow	***çayır, mer'a***	chuyi(*r*)r, mer-u
mill	***değirmen***	deghirmen
monument, statue	***âbide, heykel***	a͡abide, heykel

English	Turkish	Pronunciation
oats	*yulaf*	yo͡oluf
omnibus	*otobüs*	a͡uta͡ube͡ws
palace	*saray*	suruy
park	*park*	purk
path (footpath)	*keçi yolu*	kechi ya͡ulo͡o
peasant	*köylü*	ke͡uyle͡w
pavement	*kaldırım*	kuldi(*r*)ri(*r*)m
place (spot)	*mahal*	muhul
plough	*sapan*	supun
police	*polis*	pa͡ulis
prison	*ceza evi, hapisane*	cezu evi, hupisune
public-house	*meyhane*	meyhune
railway	*demir yolu*	demir ya͡ulo͡o
residence	*konak*	ka͡unuk
river	*nehir*	nehir
road	*yol*	ya͡ul
rye	*çavdar*	chuvdur
sheep	*koyun*	ka͡uyo͡on
school	*okul, mektep*	a͡uko͡ol, mektep
seed	*tohum*	ta͡uho͡om
sheep pen	*ağıl*	ughi(*r*)l
shepherd	*çoban*	cha͡ubun
shop	*dükkân*	de͡wkkian
soil	*toprak*	ta͡upruk
square	*meydan*	meydun
stable	*ahır*	uhi(*r*)r
straw	*saman*	sumun
street	*sokak*	sa͡ukuk
timber	*kereste*	kereste
town	*şehir*	shehir
tram	*tramvay*	trumvuy
university	*üniversite*	e͡wniversite
village	*köy*	ke͡uy
vineyard	*bağ*	bugh
wall	*duvar*	do͡ovur
well	*kuyu*	ko͡oyo͡o
wheat	*buğday*	bo͡oghduy
windmill	*yel değirmeni*	yel deghirmeni
wood	*odun*	a͡udo͡on

Times and Seasons
(Vakıt**lar**, mevsim**ler**)

English	Turkish	Pronunciation
Afternoon	*ikindi*	ikindi
beginning	*başlangıç, iptida, bidayet*	bushlungi(*r*)ch, iptidu, biduyet
Christmas	*Milâdı Îsa yortusu, Noel*	mila͡adi(*r*) isu ya͡urto͡oso͡o, na͡uel
dawn	*fecir, şafak, tan*	fejir, shufuk, tun
day	*gün*	ge͡wn
day after to-morrow	*öbürgün*	e͡ube͡wrge͡wn
day before yesterday	*evelsigün, evelkigün*	evelsige͡wn, evelkige͡wn
days of the week :—	*haftanın günleri*	huftuni(*r*)n ge͡wnleri
Sunday	*Pazar*	puzur
Monday	*Pazartesi*	puzurtesi
Tuesday	*Salı*	suli(*r*)
Wednesday	*Çarşamba*	churshumbu
Thursday	*Perşembe*	pershembe
Friday	*Cum'a* or *cuma*	jo͡om-u *or* jo͡omu
Saturday	*Cumartesi*	jo͡omurtesi
Easter	*Paskalya*	puskulyu
end	*nihayet, son*	nihuyet, sa͡un
evening	*akşam*	ukshum
fortnight	*ikihafta, ondört gün*	ikihuftu, a͡unde͡urt ge͡wn
half an hour	*yarım saat*	yuri(*r*)m suut
holiday	*tâtil*	ta͡atil
hour	*saat*	suut
Lent	*Büyük perhiz, (periz)*	be͡wye͡wk perhiz, (periz)
last week	*geçen hafta*	gechen huftu
midday	*ögle*	e͡ugle
midnight	*gece yarısı*	geje yuri(*r*)si(*r*)
minute	*dakika*	dukiku
month	*ay*	uy
months :—	*Aylar*	uylur
January	*İkincikânun*	ikinjikiano͡on
February	*Şubat*	sho͡obut

English	Turkish	Pronunciation
March	*Mart*	murt
April	*Nisan*	nisun
May	*Mayıs*	muyi(*r*)s
June	*Haziran*	huzirun
July	*Temmuz*	temmo͡oz
August	*Ağustos*	gho͡ostau͡s
September	*Eylül*	eyle͡wl
October	*Birinciteşrin*	birinjiteshrin
November	*İkinciteşrin*	ikinjiteshrin
December	*Birincikânun*	birinjikiano͡on
morning	*sabah*	subuh
next day	*ertesi gün*	ertesi ge͡wn
next week	*gelecek hafta*	gelejek huftu
next month	*gelecek ay*	gelejek uy
next year	*gelecek sene*	gelejek sene
night	*gece*	geje
quarter (3 months)	*üçaylık, doksan bir günlük*	e͡wchuyli(*r*)k, dau͡ksun bir ge͡wnle͡wk
quarter (hour)	*çeyrek (saat)*	cheyrek (suut)
seasons	*mevsimler*	mevsimler
spring	*ilk bahar*	ilk buhur
summer	*yaz*	yuz
autumn	*son bahar, güz*	sau͡n buhur, ge͡wz
winter	*kış*	ki(*r*)sh
second	*sâniye*	saa͡niye
sunrise	*güneş doğması, tulu'*	ge͡wnesh dau͡gh-musi(*r*) to͡olo͡o'
sunset	*güneş batması, gurub*	ge͡wnesh butmusi(*r*), go͡oro͡ob
to-day	*bu gün*	bo͡o ge͡wn
to-morrow	*yarın*	yuri(*r*)n
to-night	*bu gece*	bo͡o geje
this evening	*bu akşam*	bo͡o ukshum
twilight	*alaca karanlık, yatsıdan evvelki aydınlık*	uluju kurunli(*r*)k, yutsi(*r*)dun evvelki uydi(*r*)nli(*r*)k
week	*hafta*	huftu

English	Turkish	Pronunciation
Whitsuntide	*Pantekot*	punteka͡ut
year	*sene*	sene
yesterday	*dün*	de͡wn

Mankind, Relations
(Benibeşer, akraba***lar***)

English	Turkish	Pronunciation
One's father	*baba, peder*	bubu, peder
— father's father (paternal grandfather)	*dede*	dede
— father's brother (uncle)	*amca*	umju
— — brother's wife (aunt)	*yenge*	yenge
— — sister (aunt)	*hala*	hulu
— — sister's husband (uncle)	*enişte*	enishte
— — mother (paternal grandmother)	*baba-anne*	bubu-unne
— mother	*anne, ana, vâlde*	unne, unu, vaalde
— mother's brother (uncle)	*dayı*	duyi(*r*)
— — brother's wife (aunt)	*yenge*	yenge
— — sister (aunt)	*teyze*	teyze
— — sister's husband (uncle)	*enişte*	enishte
— — mother (maternal grandmother)	*anne-anne*	unne-unne
— — father (maternal grandfather)	*büyük baba*	be͡wye͡wk bubu
— brother	*birader, kardeş*	biruder, kurdesh
— brother's wife (sister-in-law)	*yenge*	yenge
— older brother	*âbey*	a͡abey

English	Turkish	Pronunciation
One's sister	*hemşire, kız kardeş*	hemshire, ki(*r*)z kurdesh
— sister's husband (brother-in-law)	*enişte*	enishte
— older sister	*abla*	ublu
— wife	*refika, karı, zevce*	refiku, kuri(*r*), zevje
— wife's sister (sister-in-law)	*baldız*	buldi(*r*)z
— — sister's husband (brother-in-law)	*bacanak*	bujunuk
— — brother (brother-in-law)	*kayınbirader*	kuyi(*r*)nbiruder
— — brother's wife (sister-in-law)	*yenge*	yenge
— husband	*koca*	ka͡uju
— husband's sister (sister-in-law)	*görümce*	ge͡ure͡wmje
— — sister's husband (brother-in-law)	*enişte*	enishte
— — brother (brother-in-law)	*kayın birader*	kuyi(*r*)n biruder
— — brother's wife (sister-in-law)	*elti*	elti
bachelor	*bekâr*	bekiar
boy	*oğlan, çocuk*	oghlun, cha͡ujook
bride	*gelin*	gelin
bridegroom	*güvey*	ge͡wvey
best man	*sağdıç*	sughdi(*r*)ch
brother-in-law	*kayın birader*	kuyi(*r*)n biruder
child (one's own)	*yavru, evlat, . . d çocuk*	yuvro͡o, evlut, cha͡ujo͡ok

English	Turkish	Pronunciation
child (any)	*çocuk*	chaujook
children (one's own)	*evlatlar, çocuklar*	evlutlur, chaujooklur
cousin	*kuzen, kardeş çocukları*	koozen, kurdesh chaujookluri(r)
daughter-in-law	*gelin*	gelin
father-in-law	*kaynata*	kuynutu
family	*familya, aile*	fumilyu, uile
gentleman	*mert, eradam, centilmen*	mert, erudum, jentilmen
girl	*kız*	ki(r)z
grandfather (general)	*dede, büyük baba*	dede, bewyewk bubu
grandmother (general)	*nine, büyük anne*	nine, bewyewk unne
grandchild (general)	*torun*	tauroon
lady	*bayan*	buyun
man	*adam, insan*	udum, insun
marriage	*evlenme, izdivaç*	evlenme, izdivuch
Miss, Mrs.	*Bayan*	buyun
mother-in-law	*kaynana*	kuynunu
Mr.	*Bay*	buy
nephew	*yeğen*	yeghen
niece	*yeğen*	yeghen
orphan	*öksüz*	euksewz
parents	*ebeveyn*	ebeveyn
son	*oğul*	aughool
spinster	*bâkire, bâkire kadın*	baakire, baakire kudi(r)n
son-in-law	*dâmat, . . . d*	daamut
widow	*dul*	dool
widower	*karısı ölmüş*	kuri(r)si(r) eulmewsh
woman	*kadın*	kudi(r)n

The Human Body
(İnsan vucudu)

English	Turkish	Pronunciation
Ankle	*kâb*	kiab
arm	*kol*	kaul
back	*arka*	urku

English	Turkish	Pronunciation
beard	*sakal*	sukul
blood	*kan*	kun
body	*vucut*	vo͡ojo͡ot
breast	*meme*	meme
bust	*göğüs, büst*	ge͡ughe͡ws, be͡wst
bosom	*bağır*	bughi(*r*)r
bones	*kemikler*	kemikler
bowels	*bağırsaklar*	bughi(*r*)suklur
brain	*beyin*	beyin
cheek	*yanak*	yunuk
chest	*göğüs*	ge͡ughe͡ws
chin	*çene*	chene
ears	*kulaklar*	ko͡oluklur
eyelid	*göz kapağı*	ge͡uz kupughi(*r*)
elbow	*dirsek*	dirsek
eyelashes	*kirpikler*	kirpikler
eye	*göz*	ge͡uz
eyebrows	*kaşlar*	kushlur
face	*yüz*	ye͡wz
fingers	*parmaklar*	purmuklur
foot	*ayak*	uyuk
forehead	*alın*	uli(*r*)n
gland	*bez, gudde*	bez, go͡odde
gums	*dişetleri*	dishetleri
hair	*saç, . . . ç*	such
hand	*el*	el
head	*baş*	bush
heart	*kalb (it is a very soft "l")*	kulb (this word is to be pronounced softly)
heel	*topuk*	ta͡upo͡ok
kidneys	*böbrekler*	be͡ubrekler
knee	*diz*	diz
leg	*bacak*	bujuk
limb	*a'za*	u-zu
lips	*dudaklar*	do͡oduklur
liver	*kara ciğer*	kuru jighér
lungs	*ciğer*, or *ak ciğer*	jigher, uk jigher
mouth	*ağız*	ughi(*r*)z
nails	*tırnaklar*	ti(*r*)rnuklur

English	Turkish	Pronunciation
neck	*boyun*	ba͡uyo͡on
nose	*burun*	bo͡oro͡on
shoulders	*omuz**lar***	a͡umo͡ozlur
side	*yan*	yun
skin	*deri*	deri
spine	*bel kemiği*	bel kemighi
stomach	*mi'de*	mi-de
throat	*boğaz*	ba͡ughuz
thumb	*baş parmak*	bush purmuk
toe	*ayak baş parmağı*	uyuk bush purmughi(*r*)
tongue	*dil*	dil
tooth	*diş*	dish
veins, artery	*damar, şiryan*	dumur, shiryun
whiskers	*sakal*	sukul
wrist	*bilek*	bilek
waist	*bel*	bel

Physical Qualities ; Bodily and Mental Powers

(Cismanî sifat**lar** ; Bedenî ve dımagî kuvvet**ler**)

Age (of persons)	*yaş*	yush
art	*hüner, erdem*	he͡wner, erdem
beginning	*başlan**gıç***	bushlungi(*r*)ch
cough	*öksürük*	e͡ukse͡wre͡wk
character	*ahlak*	uhluk
deceitful	*riyakâr*	riyukiar
dimensions	*büyük**lük ler**, eb'at**lar***	be͡wye͡wkle͡wkler, eb-utlur
breadth	*en*	en
depth	*derin**lik***	derinlik
height	*irtifa, yüksek**lik***	irtifu, ye͡wkseklik
length	*uzun**luk***	o͡ozo͡onlo͡ok
thickness	*kalın**lık***	kuli(*r*)nli(*r*)k
dishonest	*namus**suz***	numo͡osso͡oz
emotions	*teheyyücat*	teheyye͡wcut
anger	*dargın**lık***	durgi(*r*)nli(*r*)k
covetousness	*tamâ*	tuma͡a
dislike	[1] . . . ***dan** hoşlanmamak*	dun ha͡ushlunmumuk
emulation	*gıpta*	gi(*r*)ptu

[1] Preceding word will be in Abl. case.

English	Turkish	Pronunciation
envy	*haset, . . . d*	huset
hatred	*kin*	kin
jealousy	*kıskançlık*	ki(*r*)skunchli(*r*)k
pleasure	*zevk*	zevk
surprise	*tahayyür, şaşma*	tuhuyye͡wr, shushmu
end	*uç*	o͡och
feelings	*hissiyat*	hissiyut
fear	*korku*	ka͡urko͡o
suspicion	*sûizan*	sûizun
foolishness	*delilik, bönlük*	delilik, be͡unle͡wk
superstition	*bâtıl i'tikât, . . . d*	ba͡ati(*r*)l i-tikiut
gentleness	*nezaket*	nezuket
goodness	*iyilik*	iyilik
happiness	*saadet, kutluluk*	suudet, ko͡otlo͡olo͡ok
honesty	*namus*	numo͡os
honour	*onur*	a͡uno͡or
idea	*fikir, düsünce*	fikir, de͡wse͡wnje
intelligence	*akıl*	uki(*r*)l
judgment	*hüküm, sanı*	he͡wke͡wm, suni(*r*)
knowledge	*bilgi*	bilgi
laughter	*gülme*	ge͡wlme
middle	*orta*	a͡urtu
mind	*zihin, es*	zihin, es
patience	*sabır, çidama*	subi(*r*)r, chidumu
reason	*muhakeme*	mo͡ohukeme
sadness	*hüzün, üzüntü, acık*	he͡wze͡wn, e͡wze͡wnte͡w, aji(*r*)k
science	*fen*	fen
senses	*hisler*	hisler
feeling, (touch)	*duygu (dokunma, lems)*	do͡oygo͡o (da͡u-ko͡onmu, lems)
hearing	*işitme*	ishitme
seeing, sight	*görme*	ge͡urme
smell	*koklama*	ka͡uklumu
taste	*tat*	tut
side	*yan*	yun
smile, smiling	*tebessüm, gülümseyen*	tebesse͡wm, ge͡wle͡wmseyen

English	Turkish	Pronunciation
sneeze	*aksırma*	uksi(*r*)ı mu
sobbing	*hıçkıra hıçkıra ağla ma*	hi(*r*)chki(*r*)ru, hi(*r*)chki(*r*)ru, ughlumu
speaking	*konuşma*	ka͡uno͡oshmu
speech	*söylev, nutuk*	se͡ulev, no͡oto͡ok
strength	*kuvvet, güç . . . c, yet*	ko͡ovvet, ge͡wch, yet
thinking, thought	*düşünmek, düşünce*	de͡wshe͡wnmek, de͡wshe͡wnje
unhappiness	*mahzuniyet, durgunluk*	muhzo͡oniyet, do͡orgo͡onlo͡ok
unhappy	*mahzun, bezmen, karalı*	muhzo͡on, bezmen, kuruli(*r*)
voice	*ses, seda*	ses, sedu
weakness	*zaaf*	zuuf
weeping, to weep	*ağlama, ağlamak*	ughlumu, ughlumuk
wisdom	*hikmet, . . . t*	hikmet

Health
(Sıhhat)

Accident	*kaza*	kuzu
ambulance	*sıhhiye arabası*	si(*r*)hhiye urubusi(*r*)
appetite	*iştah*	ishtuh
bandage	*sargı*	surgi(*r*)
biliousness	*mi'de bulanması*	mi-de bo͡olun-musi(*r*)
bite	*ısırma*	i(*r*)si(*r*)rmu
blister	*kabarcık*	kuburji(*r*)k
bone-setter	*kırıkçı*	ki(*r*)ri(*r*)kchi(*r*)
bruise	*bere, çürük*	bere, che͡wre͡wk
burn	*yanık*	yuni(*r*)k
chemist	*ezacı*	ezuji(*r*)
chill	*hafif soğuk algınlığı*	hufif sa͡ugho͡ok ulghı(*r*)nli(*r*)ghi(*r*)
cholera	*kolera*	ka͡uleru
cold	*soğuk*	sa͡ugho͡ok
contagious, infectious	*sâri, bulaşıcı*	sa͡ari, bo͡olushi(*r*)ji(*r*)
constipation	*inkıbaz*	inki(*r*)buz

English	Turkish	Pronunciation
cough	*öksürük*	e͡ukse͡wre͡wk
cramp	*sinir gerginliği*	sinir gerginlighi
deaf	*sağır*	sughi(*r*)r
dentist	*dişçi*	dishchi
diarrhœa	*ishal, sürgün*	ishul, se͡wrge͡wn
diet	*perhiz* or *periz*	perhiz *or* periz
disease, illness	*illet, hastalık*	illet, hustuli(*r*)k
doctor, physician	*doktor, hekim*	dauktaur, hekim
draught (liquid)	*içim, doz* (*ilâç*)	ichim, da͡uz (ila͡ach)
— of air	*cereyan*	jereyun
dysentery	*dizanteri, buruntu*	dizunteri, bo͡oro͡onto͡o
exercise	*idman*	idmun
exhausted	*bitkin, bîtap*	bitkin, be͡etup
fainting	*bayılma*	buyi(*r*)lmu
fever	*nöbet, ateş, hümma, ısıtma*	ne͡ubet, utesh, he͡wmmu, i(*r*)si(*r*)tmu
fit	*ihtilaç*	ihtiluch
fracture	*kırık*	ki(*r*)ri(*r*)k
gout	*nıkrıs illeti*	ni(*r*)kri(*r*)s illeti
headache	*baş ağrısı*	bush ughri(*r*)si(*r*)
hoarseness (voice)	*kısıklık, boğukluk* (*ses*)	ki(*r*)si(*r*)kli(*r*)k, ba͡ugho͡oklo͡ok (ses)
hunchback	*kanbur*	kunbo͡or
hungry	*aç*	uch
hospital	*hastane*	hustune
ill	*hasta*	hustu
indigestion	*hazımsızlık*	huzi(*r*)msi(*r*)zli(*r*)k
inflammation	*iltihap, şişme*	iltihup, shishme
lame	*topal*	ta͡upul
medicine	*ilâç*	ila͡ach
nurse	*hasta bakıcısı, hemşire*	hustu buki(*r*)ji(*r*)si(*r*), hemshire
ointment	*melhem*	melhem
pain	*ağrı*	ughri(*r*)
pneumonia	*ak ciğerlerin iltihabı,* or *zatülree*	uk jigherlerin iltihubi(*r*), *or* zute͡wlree
paralysis	*inme*	inme

English	Turkish	Pronunciation
pill	*hap*	hup
pleurisy	*pilevranın iltihabı*, or *zatülcem*	pilevruni(*r*)n iltihubi(*r*), *or* zute͡wljem
poison	*zehir*	zehir
prescription	*reçete*	rechete
rheumatism	*romatizma*	ra͡umutizmu
remedy	*çare*	chure
rest	*istirahat*	istiruhut
scald	*haşlama*	hushlumu
scratch	*tırmalama*	ti(*r*)mulumu
sea-sickness	*deniz tutma sı*	deniz to͡otmusi(*r*)
sprain	*burkulma*	bo͡orko͡olmu
sting	*sokma*	sa͡ukmu
symptom	*âraz, alâmet*	a͡aruz, ula͡amet
surgeon	*operator*	a͡uperuta͡ur
temperature	*derecei hararet, . . . t*	derejei hururet
tired	*yorgun*	ya͡urgo͡on
tonic	*kuvvet ilacı*	ko͡ovvet iluji(*r*)
toothache	*diş ağrısı*	dish ughri(*r*)si(*r*)

Food, Drink, etc.
(Yiyecek, içecek, ilahanı)

English	Turkish	Pronunciation
Bacon	*domuz pastırması*	da͡umo͡oz pusti(*r*)r-musi(*r*)
beef	*sığır*	si(*r*)ghi(*r*)r
—, roast	*rostbif*	ra͡ustbif
— steak	*biftek*	biftek
bread	*ekmek*	eḱmek
—, brown	*tayın ekmeği*	tuyi(*r*)n ekmeghi
—, new, white	*taze, beyaz ekmek*	tuze, beyuz ekmek
—, rolls	*francala*	frunjulu
bread and (with) milk	*sütle ekmek*	se͡wtle ekmek
butter	*tere yağı*	tere yughi(*r*)
cake	*çörek*	che͡urek
cheese	*peynir*	peynir
chop, cutlet	*pırzola, külbastı*	pi(*r*)rza͡ulu, ke͡wl-busti(*r*)
cream	*kaymak*	kuymuk

English	Turkish	Pronunciation
cut, slice	*kesim, dilim*	kesim, dilim
dressing	*terbiye*	terbiye
drink	*içki*	ichki
brandy	*brendi, bir nevi konyak*	brendi, bir nevi ka͡unyuk
chocolate, cocoa	*çikolata, kakao*	chika͡ulutu, kukua͡u
coffee, black	*âdi kahve*	a͡adi kuhve
— with milk	*sütlü kahve*	se͡wtle͡w kuhve
fruit drinks	*meyve şerbetleri*	meyve sherbetleri
iced water	*buzlu su*	bo͡ozlo͡o so͡o
milk	*süt*	se͡wt
wine	*şarap, . . . b*	shurup
—, red, white	*kırmızı, beyaz şarap*	ki(*r*)rmi(*r*)zi(*r*), beyuz shurup
tea	*çay*	chuy
water	*su*	so͡o
egg	*yumurta*	yo͡omo͡ortu
—, hard-boiled	*lop yumurta*	la͡up yo͡omo͡ortu
—, boiled	*lafada yumurta*	lufudu yo͡omo͡ortu
—, fried	*sahanda yumurta*	suhundu yo͡omo͡ortu
fat	*iç yağı*	ich yughi(*r*)
flank (beast)	*döş*	de͡ush
flour	*un*	o͡on
fowl	*kümes hayvanları*	ke͡wmes huyvunluri(*r*)
game	*av eti*	uv eti
to grill, broil	*isgara*	isguru
ham	*jambon*	jumba͡un
honey	*bal*	bul
hunger, thirst	*açlık, susuzluk*	uchli(*r*)k, so͡oso͡o-zlo͡ok
ice	*buz*	bo͡oz
jam, marmalade	*reçel, turunç reçeli*	rechel, to͡oro͡onch recheli
joint (leg, shoulder)	(*but, kol*)	boot, ka͡ul
kidneys	*böbrek*	be͡ubrek

English	Turkish	Pronunciation
lamb	*kuzu*	ko͡ozo͡o
lean	*yavan*	yuvun
leg	*but*	bo͡ot
meal	*yemek*	yemek
meat	*et*	et
—, boiled	*sövüş eti*	se͡uve͡wsh eti
—, roast	*et kızartması*	et ki(*r*)zurtmusi(*r*)
meat with fat	*yağlı et*	yughli(*r*) et
lean meat	*yavan et, yağsız et*	yuvun et, yughsi(*r*)z et
mustard	*hardal*	hurdul
mutton	*koyun eti*	ka͡uyo͡on eti
oil	*yağ*	yugh
olive oil	*zeytun yağı*	zeyto͡on yughi(*r*)
pastry (work)	*hamur işi*	humo͡or ishi
pepper	*biber*	biber
pork	*domuz eti*	da͡umo͡oz eti
rib	*kaburga*	kubo͡orgu
rice	*pirinç*	pirinch
salt	*tuz*	to͡oz
sauce	*salça*	sulchu
sausage	*sucuk*	so͡ojo͡ok
seasoning	*baharat katılma*	buhurut kuti(*r*)lmu
shoulder	*kol*	ka͡ul
sirloin	*fileto*	fileto
to smoke	*tütün içmek*	te͡wte͡wn ichmek
— a cigar	*puro içmek*	po͡ora͡u ichmek
— a cigarette	*sigara içmek*	siguru ichmek
— a pipe	*pipo içmek*	pipa͡u ichmek
— tobacco	*tütün içmek*	te͡wte͡wn ichmek
soup	*çorba*	cha͡urbu
stuffing	*dolma*	da͡ulmu
sugar	*şeker*	sheker
under done	*az pişmiş*	uz pishmish
veal	*dana eti*	dunu eti
vegetables	*sebze*	sebze
vinegar	*sirke*	sirke
well done	*güzelce pişmiş*	ge͡wzelje pishmish

Turkish Dishes (Hot)
(*Türk Yemekleri* (*sıcak*))

English	Turkish	Pronunciation
young marrows stuffed with minced mutton, rice, and herbs.	*kabak dolma sı*	kubuk da͡ulmusi(*r*)
green vegetable braised in own juice with fried onion and tomato.	*bamya*	bumyu
runner beans	*çalı fasulyası*	chuli(*r*) fuso͡ol-yusi(*r*)
French beans	*ayşe kadın fasulyası*	uyshe kudi(*r*)n fuso͡olyusi(*r*)
mallow	*ebe gümeci*	ebe ge͡wmeji
purslain	*semiz otu*	semiz a͡uto͡o
egg on spinach	*yumurtalı ispanak*	yo͡omo͡ortuli(*r*) ispunuk
braised mutton, bamya, runner beans, marrow and aubergine.	*türlü*	te͡wrle͡w
minced meat and rice rissoles fried in egg batter.	*kadın budu*	kudi(*r*)n bo͡odo͡o
aubergine and chopped meat fried separately and braised together in own gravy.	*patlıcan orturtma sı*	putli(*r*)jun a͡urto͡ortmusi(*r*)
aubergine and cut up meat braised in little water and tomato con-centre and fried onion.	*patlıcan musakkası*	putli(*r*)jun mo͡osukkusi(*r*)
braised chicken	*piliç kızartma sı*	pilich ki(*r*)zurtmusi(*r*)

English	Turkish	Pronunciation
plain rice cooked in special way with butter added.	*pilav sade*	piluv sude
rice cooked as above with raisins, pine kernels and chopped liver added.	*kuzu içi*	ko͝ozo͝o ichi
rice cooked with tomato juice and butter.	*domatesli pilav*	da͡umutesli piluv
pieces of mutton and fat roasted on spit.	*döner kebap, . . . b*	de͡uner kebup
rice cooked together with pieces of meat, tomato and onion.	*etli pilav*	etli piluv
small pieces of mutton and fat grilled on charcoal, with chillies, or plain.	*şiş kebabı*	shish kebubi(*r*)
minced meat pressed round skewer and grilled, served with green chillies, or plain.	*şiş köftesi*	shish ke͡uftesi
a kind of pastry consisting of layers of cream cheese and layers of pastry.	*su böreği*	so͝o be͡ureghi
layers of pastry between a layer of onions, mince meat and fine kernel and baked in butter.	*boğaça*	ba͡ughuchu

English	Turkish	Pronunciation
cakebread covered with sesame seed in the shape of a ring	*simit*	simit
vine leaves stuffed with minced meat and rice cooked in butter	*etli yaprak dolma sı*	etli yupruk da͡ulmusi(*r*)
cabbage leaves stuffed as above	*etli lahana dolması*	etli luhunu da͡ulmusi(*r*)

Turkish Dishes (Cold)
(Türk yemek***leri*** (soğuk))

English	Turkish	Pronunciation
aubergine cut in long or round slices, fried in olive oil, served plain or with yoghourt	*patlıcan kızartma sı*	putli(*r*)jun ki(*r*)zurtmusi(*r*)
marrow, as above	*kabak kızartma sı*	kubuk ki(*r*)zurtmusi(*r*)
boiled chicken, served dry	*piliç söğüşü*	pilich se͡ughe͡wshe͡w
large chillies stuffed with rice, currants, and pine kernels, and cooked in olive oil	*zeytun yağlı biber dolma sı*	zeyto͡on yughli(*r*) biber da͡ulmusi(*r*)
young broad beans with pods, and little rice and onion, braised in own juice and olive oil	*zeytun yağlı bakla*	zeyto͡on yughli(*r*) buklu
aubergine stuffed with rice, currants, and pine kernels, cooked in olive oil	*patlıcan dolma sı*	putli(*r*)jun da͡ulmusi(*r*)

Turkish Sweet Dishes
(*Türk Tatlıları*)

English	Turkish	Pronunciation
quince, peaches, or plums boiled to syrupy state.	*ayva, şeftali, erik kompostosu*	uyvu, sheftuli, erik ka͡umpa͡u-sta͡uso͡o
rice pudding.	*sütlaç*	se͡wtluch
chicken-breast cooked to a pulp with milk and sugar.	*tavuk göğsü*	tuvo͡ok ge͡ughse͡w
blancmange.	*muhallebi*	mo͡ohullebi
ground almonds boiled down with milk and sugar.	*keşkülü fukara*	keshke͡wlle͡w fo͡okuru
bottom layer of blancmange 2 in. thick from bottom of cauldron.	*kazan dibi*	kuzun dibi
puff pastry with syrup.	*baklava*	bukluvu
¼ in. thick bread cakes cooked in butter and syrup.	*ekmek kadayıfı*	ekmek kuduyi(*r*)fi(*r*)
larger and thinner crumpets in syrup and butter.	*yassı kadayıfı*	yussi(*r*) kuduyi(*r*)fi(*r*)
shredded wheat baked in syrup and butter.	*tel kadayıfı*	tel kuduyi(*r*)fi(*r*)
a kind of plain fritter.	*şam baba*	shum bubu
a kind of doughnut	*lokma tatlısı*	la͡ukmu tutli(*r*)si(r)

Cooking and Table Utensils
(Mutbak ve sofra takımları)

English	Turkish	Pronunciation
Basin (pudding)	*kâse*	kiase
bowl	*liğen, el tası*	lighen, el tusi(*r*)
casserole	*kasrol*	kusra͡ul
colander	*süzgeç*	se͡wzgech

English	Turkish	Pronunciation
corkscrew	*tirbuşon*	tirbo͡osha͡un
cup	*fincan*	finjun
dish	*kap*	kup
eggspoon	*yumurta kaşığı*	yo͡omo͡ortū kushi(*r*)ghi(*r*)
fork	*çatal*	chutul
glass, tumbler	*bardak, kadeh*	burduk, kudeh
jug	*maşrapa*	mushrupu
kettle	*ibrik*	ibrik
knife	*bıçak*	bi(*r*)chuk
lid	*kapak*	kupuk
matches	*kibrit*	kibrit
pitcher	*testi*	testi
plate	*tabak*	tubuk
saucer	*fincan tabağı*	finjun tubughi(*r*)
saucepan	*tencere*	tenjere
spoon	*kaşık*	kushi(*r*)k
stove	*soba*	sa͡ubu
teaspoon	*çay kaşığı*	chuy kushi(*r*)ghi(*r*)
tea things	*çay takımı*	chuy tuki(*r*)mi(*r*)
tray	*tepsi*	tepsi

Dress and Toilet

(Elbise ve tuvalet)

English	Turkish	Pronunciation
Blouse	*biluz*	bilo͡oz
bath	*banyo, küvet*	bunya͡u, ke͡wvet
boots	*ayakabı*	uyukubi(*r*)
bracelet	*bilezik*	bilezik
braces	*askı*	uski(*r*)
brooch	*göğüş iğnesi*	ge͡ughe͡ws ighnési
brush	*fırça*	fi(*r*)rchu
button	*düğme*	de͡wghme
calico	*amerikan bezi* or *patiska*	umerikun bezi *or* putisku
cap	*kasket*	kusket
cloak	*pelerin*	pelerin
cloth (silk)	(*ipekli*) *kumaş*	(ipekli) ko͡omush
— (woollen)	(*yünlü*) *kumaş*	(ye͡wnle͡w) ko͡omush

English	Turkish	Pronunciation
coat	*kaput*	kupo͡ot
comb	*tarak*	turuk
combinations	*kombinezon*	ka͡umbineza͡un
cotton	*pamuk*	pumo͡ok
— (material)	*pamuklu (bez)*	pumo͡oklo͡o (bez)
drawers, knickers	*pantalon, don*	puntula͡un, da͡un
dress	*elbise*	elbise
elastic	*lastik kurdela*	lustik ko͡ordelu
evening dress (lady's)	*tuvalet*	to͡ovulet
— — (gent's)	*smokin*	sma͡ukin
flannels (gent's)	*fanela, yazlık pantalon*	funelu, yuzli(*r*)k puntula͡un
flannel (to wash with)	*el bezi*	el bezi
fur coat	*kürk*	ke͡wrk
garters	*çorap bağı, caritiyer*	cha͡urup bughi(*r*), juritiyer
gloves	*eldiven*	eldiven
hairpins	*firkete*	firkete
handkerchief	*mendil*	mendil
hat	*şapka*	shupku
jewellery	*mücevherat, . . . t*	me͡wjevherut
jumper (woollen)	*örme biluz, campır (yünlü)*	e͡urme bilo͡oz, jum-pi(*r*)r (ye͡wnle͡w)
lace	*dantela*	duntelu
lining	*astar*	ustur
looking-glass	*ayna*	uynu
neck-tie	*gravat, boyun bağı*	gruvut, ba͡uyo͡on bughi(*r*)
needle	*iğne*	ighne
overcoat	*palto*	pulta͡u
overcoat (light weight)	*pardösü*	purde͡use͡w
parasol	*şemşiye*	shemshiye
pins	*toplu iğne*	ta͡uplo͡o ighne
pocket	*ceb*	jeb
purse	*para çantası*	puruchuntusi(*r*)
razor	*ustura*	o͡osto͡oru
reel	*makara*	mukuru

English	Turkish	Pronunciation
ribbon	*kurdela*	ko͞ordelu
ring	*yüzük*	yew͡zew͡k
scissors (pair of)	*makas* (term not used)	mukus
sewing cotton	*tire*	tire
— silk	*ibrişim*	ibrishim
shawl	*şal*	shul
shoe	*kundura*	ko͞ondo͞oru
silk	*ipek*	ipek
skirt	*eteklik*	eteklik
sleeve	*kol*	ka͡ul
slippers	*terlik*	terlik
socks	*çorap, . . . b*	cha͡urup
stockings	*bayan* (or *kadın*) *çorabı*	buyun (*or* kudi(*r*)n) cha͡urubi(*r*)
soap	*sabun*	subo͞on
spectacles	*gözlük*	ge͡uzlew͡k
sponge	*sünger*	sew͡nger
stays, corsets	*korsa*	ka͡ursu
stud	*düğme*	dew͡ghme
suit	*elbise, kostüm*	elbise, ka͡ustew͡m
suiting (gent's)	*kumaş*	ko͞omush
tape	*şerit*	sherit
shirt	*gömlek*	ge͡umlek
tailor-made costume	*kostüm tayör*	ka͡ustew͡m tuye͡ur
thimble	*yüksük*	yew͡ksew͡k
thread	*tire*	tire
toothbrush	*diş fırçası*	dish fi(*r*)rchusi(*r*)
trousers (pair of)	*pantalon* (term not used)	puntula͡un
umbrella	*şemşiye*	shemshiye
veil	*peçe*	peche
waistcoat	*yelek*	yelek
watch	*saat*	sa͡at

Washing List
(Çamaşır listası)

English	Turkish	Pronunciation
Aprons, pinafores	*önlük ler*	e͡unlew͡kler
blanket	*battaniye*	buttuniye
bonnet	*başlık*	bushli(*r*)k

English	Turkish	Pronunciation
collar (men's)	*yakalık*	yukuli(*r*)k
combinations	*kombinezon*	ka͡umbineza͡un
coverlet	*örtü*	e͡urte͡w
cuff	*kolluk*	ka͡ullook
drawers (pair of)	*don, pantalon*	da͡un, puntula͡un
dress	*elbise*	elbise
dress shirt	*kolalı gömlek*	ka͡ululi(*r*) ge͡umlek
front	*göğüslük, önlük*	ge͡ughe͡wsle͡wk, e͡unle͡wk
handkerchief	*mendil*	mendil
pants	*don*	da͡un
petticoat	*eteklik*	eteklik
pillow slip	*yastık kılıfı*	yusti(*r*)k ki(*r*)li(*r*)fi(*r*)
shawl	*şal*	shul
shorts (men's)	*kısa don, şort*	ki(*r*)su da͡un, sha͡urt
shirt	*gömlek*	ge͡umlek
sheet	*çarşaf*	churshuf
towel	*havlu*	huvloo
vest	*fanile*	funile
waistcoat	*yelek*	yelek

The above can all be made *plural* by the addition of "lar" or "ler".

The House and Furniture

(Ev ve mobilya)

Ashes	*kül*	ke͡wl
basket	*sepet*	sepet
bath	*banyo*	bunya͡u
bed	*yatak*	yutuk
bedroom	*yatak odası*	yutuk a͡udusi(*r*)
bell	*çıngırak*	chi(*r*)ngi(*r*)uk
book	*kitap*	kitup
box	*kutu*	ko͡oto͡o
brick	*tuğla*	to͡oghlu
broom	*süpürge*	se͡wpe͡wrge
brush	*fırça*	fi(*r*)rchu
candle	*mum*	mo͡om
candlestick	*şamdan*	shumdun

English	Turkish	Pronunciation
carpet	*halı*	huli(*r*)
cellar	*kiler*	kiler
chair	*sandalya*	sundulyu
chest of drawers	*konsol*	ka͡unsa͡ul
clock	*saat*	sa͡at
coals	*kömür*	ke͡ume͡wr
couch	*sofa*	sa͡ufu
curtain	*perde*	perde
cushion	*yastık*	yusti(*r*)k
dining room	*yemek odası*	yemek a͡udusi(*r*)
door	*kapı*	kupi(*r*)
dressing table	*tuvalet*	to͡ovulet
drawer	*göz*	ge͡uz
divan	*sofa*	sa͡ufu
dresser (kitchen)	*çanak çömlek dolabı*	chunuk che͡umlek da͡ulubi(*r*)
electric lamp	*ampul, elektrik lambası*	umpo͡ol, elektrik lumbusi(*r*)
fire	*ateş*	utesh
flame	*alev*	ulev
floor	*döşeme*	de͡usheme
footstool	*basıncak, ayak minderciği*	busi(*r*)njuk, uyuk minderjighi
gas (cooking)	*hava gazı*	huvu guzi(*r*)
grate	*ocak*	a͡ujuk
hall	*aralık, sofa*	uruli(*r*)k, sa͡ufu
key	*anahtar*	unuhtur
kitchen	*mutbak*	mo͡otbuk
lavatory	*ayak yolu, helâ*	uyuk ya͡ulo͡o, hela͡a
lamp	*lamba*	lumbu
larder	*kiler*	kiler
library	*kütüphane*	ke͡wte͡wphune
lock	*kilit, . . . d*	kilit
mattress	*şilte*	shilte
mat	*paspas*	puspus
ornament	*süs*	se͡ws
passage	*koridor*	ka͡urida͡ur
piano	*piyano*	piyuna͡u
picture	*resim*	resim
pillow	*yastık*	yusti(*r*)k

English	Turkish	Pronunciation
roof	*dam*	dum
rug	*kilim*	kilim
room	*oda*	a͡udu
seat	*otur**acak** yer, yer*	a͡uto͡orujuk yer, yer
shelf	*raf*	ruf
shovel	*kürek*	ke͡wrek
sideboard	*büfe*	be͡wfe
smoke	*duman*	do͡omun
soot	*is*	is
staircase	*merdiven*	merdiven
stool	*iskemle*	iskemle
table	*masa*	musu
tongs	*maşa*	mushu
vase	*vazo*	vuza͡u
wall	*duvar*	do͡ovur
wireless (radio)	*radyo*	rudya͡u

Countries and Nations
(Memleket**ler**, millet**ler**)

English	Turkish	Pronunciation
Africa	*Afrika*	ufriku
America	*Amerika*	umeriku
American	*Amerika**lı***	umerikuli(*r*)
Asia	*Asya*	usyu
Australia	*Avustralya*	uvo͡ostrulyu
Belgium	*Belçika*	belchiku
Belgian	*Belçika**lı***	belchikuli(*r*)
Canada	*Kanada*	kunudu
China	*Çin*	chin
Chinese	*Çin**li***	chinli
country	*memleket*	memleket
Denmark	*Danimarka*	dunimurku
East Indies	*Doğu Hind*	da͡ugo͡o hind
Empire	*İmperator**luk***	i(*r*)mperuta͡urlo͡ok
English (language)	*İngiliz**ce***	ingilizje
Englishman	*İngiliz*	ingiliz
Englishwoman	*İngiliz bayanı* or *kadını*	ingiliz buyuni(*r*) *or* kudi(*r*)ni(*r*)
Estonian	*Estonyalı*	esta͡unyuli(*r*)
Europe	*Avrupa*	uvro͡opu
France	*Fransa*	frunsu

English	Turkish	Pronunciation
Frenchman	*Fransız*	frunsi(*r*)z
Frenchwoman	*Fransız kadını*	frunsi(*r*)z kudi(*r*)ni(*r*)
Finland	*Finlanda*	finlundu
Finnish (man)	*Fin, Finlandalı*	fin, finlunduli(*r*)
German (man)	*Alman*	ulmun
Germany	*Almanya*	ulmunyu
Holland	*Hollanda*	haullundu
Hungary	*Macar**istan***	mujuristun
Hungarian (man)	*Macar*	mujur
India	*Hind**istan***	hindistun
Indian (man)	*Hint**li***	hintli
Ireland	*İrlanda*	irlundu
Irish (man)	*İrlandalı*	irlunduli(*r*)
Italian (man)	*İtalyan*	itulyun
Italy	*İtalya*	itulyu
Japan	*Japonya*	jupaunyu
Japanese	*Japon, Japonyalı*	jupaun, jupaunyuli(*r*)
kingdom	*kral**lık***	krulli(*r*)k
Norway	*Norveç*	naurvech
republic	*cümhuriyet*	jewmhooriyet
Russia	*Rusya*	roosyu
Russian	*Rus*	roos
Scotland	*İskoçya*	iskauchyu
Scotsman	*İskoçyalı*	iskauchyuli(*r*)
Spain	*İspanya*	ispunyu
Spaniard	*İspanyol*	ispunyaul
Sweden	*İsveç*	isvech
Swede	*İsveç**li***	isvechli
Swiss	*İsviçre**li***	isvichreli
Switzerland	*İsviçre*	isvichre
Turkey	*Türkiye*	tewrkiye
Turk	*Türk*	tewrk

Travelling by Road and Rail
(Kara***dan*** ve şimendifer ile seyahat)

Apartments	*apartıman*	upurti(*r*)mun
arrival	*vusûl, varış*	voosûl, vuri(*r*)sh

English	Turkish	Pronunciation
bill	*hisap, . . . b*	hisup
boarding house	*pansiyon*	punsiyau͡n
brake	*fren*	fren
bridle	*baş*lık	bushli(*r*)k
cab	*araba*	urubu
chambermaid	*oda hizmet***çisi**	odu hizmetchisi
cloakroom	*gardörop*	gurdeu͡rau͡p
coach	*araba*	urubu
coffee room	*kahve*	kuhve
cushion	*yastık*	yusti(*r*)k
customs officer	*gümrük işyarı,* *gümrük me'muru*	gew͡mrew͡k ish-yuri(*r*), gew͡mrew͡k me-mo͡oro͡o
dining car	*lokanta***lı** *vagon*	lau͡kuntuli(*r*) vagau͡n
departure	*hareket, kalkış*	hureket, kulki(*r*)sh
engine	*makine*	mukine
excursion	*tenezzüh*	tenezzew͡h
fare	*ücret, . . . t*	ew͡jret
gentleman	*kibar adam, centilmen*	kibur udum, jentilmen
guard	*muhâfız*	mo͡ohaafi(*r*)z
guide	*kılavuz*	ki(*r*)luvo͡oz
hall porter	*kapıcı*	kupi(*r*)ci(*r*)
halter	*yular*	yo͡olur
hat box	*şapka kutu***su**	shupku ko͡oto͡oso͡o
hotel	*otel*	au͡tel
interpreter	*tercüman*	terjew͡mun
ladies	*bayan***lar**	buyunlur
lavatory	*aptesane, ayakyolu*	uptesune, uyukyau͡lo͡o
lift, elevator	*asansör*	usunseu͡r
lodgings, unfurnished	*kira***lık** *oda***lar**	kiruli(*r*)k, au͡dulur
luggage	*yol eşya***sı**	yau͡l eshyusi(*r*)
manager	*idare memuru, müdür*	idure memo͡oro͡o, mew͡dew͡r
motor-car	*otomobil*	au͡tau͡mau͡bil
newspaper	*gazete*	guzete
office	*yazıhane*	yuzi(*r*)hune
package	*paket, . . . t*	puket

English	Turkish	Pronunciation
payment	*te'diye, ödeme*	te-diye, e͡udeme
porter	*kapıcı*	kupi(*r*)ci(*r*)
porter (railway)	*hamal*	humul
railway (line)	*demiryolu*	demirya͡ulo͡o
railway station	*istasyon, gar*	istusya͡un, gur
receipt	*makpuz*	mukpo͡oz
reins	*dizgin*	dizgin
to ride (horse)	*ata binmek*	utu binmek
riding whip	*kamçı*	kumchi(*r*)
rug	*örtü, battaniye*	e͡urte͡w, buttuniye
saddle (for horse)	*eyer*	eyer
— (for donkey)	*semer*	semer
sleeping car	*yataklı vagon*	yutukli(*r*) vuga͡un
smoking room	*sigara salonu*	siguru sula͡uno͡o
subway	*tünel, yeraltı yolu*	te͡wnel, yerulti(*r*) ya͡ulo͡o
ticket	*bilet, . . . t*	bilet
first class	*birinci mevki*	birinji mevki
return	*gidip gelme*	gidip gelme
tip, gratuity	*bahşiş*	buhshish
train	*tren*	tren
electric tram	*elektrikli tramvay*	elektrikli trumvuy
waiter	*garson*	gursa͡un
waiting room	*bekleme salonu*	bekleme sula͡uno͡o
walk	*gezinti*	gezinti
whip	*kırbaç, . . . c*	ki(*r*)rbuch

Travelling by Sea

(Deniz seyahatı)

Aft	*kıç, . . . ç*	ki(*r*)ch
anchor	*demir*	demir
berth	*kamara*	kumuru
boat	*vapur*	vupo͡or
boat rowing	*kürek çekme*	ke͡wrek chekme
rowboat	*sandal*	sundul
boathook	*çengel*	chengel
boatman	*kayıkçı, sandalcı*	kuyi(*r*)kchi(*r*), sundulji(*r*)
boiler	*kazan*	kuzun

English	Turkish	Pronunciation
bow	*pruva*	pro͡ovu
bridge	*köprü*	ke͡uprew͡
buoy	*şamandıra*	shumundi(*r*)ru
— bell	*şamandıra çanı*	shumundi(*r*)ru chuni(*r*)
cabin	*kamara*	kumuru
cable	*kablo*	kubla͡u
captain	*kaptan*	kuptun
compass	*pusla*	po͡oslu
crew	*mürettebat, . . . t*	me͡wrettebut
deck	*güverte*	ge͡wverte
— lower	*alt güverte*	ult ge͡wverte
— upper	*üst güverte*	e͡wst ge͡wverte
dock	*havuz*	huvo͡oz
dry dock	*kuru havuz*	ko͡oro͡o huvo͡oz
to embark	*binmek*	binmek
engineer	*makinist*	mukinist
engine room	*makine dairesi*	mukine duiresi
fishing boat	*balıkçı kayığı*	buli(*r*)kchi(*r*) kuyi(*r*)ghi(*r*)
fishing net	*ağ*	ugh
flag	*bayrak*	buyruk
foghorn	*sis düdüğü*	sis de͡wde͡wghe͡w
fore	*geminin burnu, baş*	geminin bo͡orno͡o, bush
funnel	*baca*	buju
harbour, port	*liman*	limun
helm, rudder	*dümen, yeke*	de͡wmen, yeke
to land	*karaya çıkmak*	kuruyu chi(*r*)kmuk
landing stage	*iskele*	iskele
leeward	*ruzgâr istikametinde, ruzgâr altında*	roozgiar istikumetinde, ro͡ozgiar ulti(*r*)ndu
lifebelt	*can kurtaran kemeri*	jun ko͡orturun kemeri
lifeboat	*can kurtaran gemisi*	jun ko͡orturun gemisi
lifebuoy	*can kurtaran, simit*	jun ko͡orturun, simit
lighthouse	*fener*	fener

English	Turkish	Pronunciation
mast	*direk*	direk
first mate	*ikinci kaptan*	ikinji kuptun
oar	*kürek, . . . ğ*	ke͡wrek
pier	*iskele*	iskele
pilot	*kılavus, . . . z*	ki(*r*)luvo͡os
port side	*iskele*	iskele
pump	*tulumba*	to͡olo͡ombu
quay	*rıhtım*	ri(*r*)hti(*r*)m
rope	*halat, . . . d*	hulut
rudder	*dümen*	de͡wmen
sail	*yelken*	yelken
sailing ship	*yelken gemi***si**	yelken gemisi
saloon	*salon*	sula͡un
screw (propellor)	*pervane*	pervune
seaman	*deniz***ci**	denizji
sea-sickness	*deniz tutma***sı**	deniz to͡otmusi(*r*)
ship	*gemi, sefine*	gemi, sefine
skipper	*kaptan*	kuptun
signals, to make	*işaret (ver***mek***)*	ishuret (vermek)
starboard side	*sancak*	sunjuk
steamboat	*istimpot*	istimpa͡ut
steersman	*dümen***ci**	de͡wmenji
stern	*kıç, . . . ç*	ki(*r*)ch
steward	*kamarot, . . . t*	kumura͡ut
tug	*römorkör*	re͡uma͡urke͡ur
ventilator	*vantılatör*	vunti(*r*)lute͡ur
voyage	*seyahat*	seyuhut
watch	*nöbet***çi**	ne͡ubetchi
windward	*rüzgâr***a** *doğru, rüzgâr üzerinden*	re͡wzgiaru da͡ugh-ro͡o, re͡wzgiar e͡uzerinden

Amusements
Eğlenti**ler**)

English	Turkish	Pronunciation
Admission	*duhuliye*	do͡oho͡oliye
—, charge for	*duhuliye ücret***i**	do͡oho͡oliye e͡wjreti
ball (dancing)	*balo*	bula͡u
balloon	*balon*	bula͡un
cinematograph	*sinema*	sinemu
circus	*canbazhane*	junbuzhune

English	Turkish	Pronunciation
concert	*konser*	ka͡unser
accompanist	*piyanist, . . . t*	piyunist
chorus	*mugan**niler***	mo͡ogunniler
conductor	*şefdorkestır*	shefda͡ukesti(*r*)r
pianist	*piyanist, . . . t*	piyunist
piano	*piyano*	piyuna͡u
recital	*müsamere*	me͡wsumere
singer	*hânende, şarkı söyle**yen***	ha͡anende, shurki(*r*) se͡uyleyen
violin	*keman*	kemun
entrance	*giriş mahali (mahalli), methal, giriş yeri*	girish muhuli (muhulli), methul, girish yeri
entrance door	*giriş kapı**sı***	girish kupi(*r*)si(*r*)
exhibition, fair	*meşher, fuar*	meshher, fo͡our
exit	*mahreç, . . . c, çıkış yeri*	muhrech, chi(*r*)ki(*r*)sh yeri

Games and Pastimes

(Oyun ve eğlence***ler***)

English	Turkish	Pronunciation
Billiards	*bilardo*	bilurda͡u
boating	*sandal**la** gez**mek***	sundullu gezmek
chess	*satranç oyun**u***	sutrunch a͡uyo͡ono͡o
cricket	*kriket*	kriket
drawing	*resim*	resim
draughts	*dama oyun**u***	dumu a͡uyo͡ono͡o
dancing	*dans*	duns
fishing	*balık**çı lık***	buli(*r*)kchi(*r*)li(*r*)k
hunting	*av**cı lık***	uvji(*r*)li(*r*)k
races	*yarış*	yuri(*r*)sh
jockey	*cokey*	ja͡ukey
racecourse	*yarış meydanı*	yuri(*r*)sh meyduni(*r*)
rowing	*kürek çek**me***	ke͡wrek chekme
shooting	*avla**mak***	uvlumuk
swimming	***yüzücü lük***	ye͡wze͡wje͡wle͡wk
tennis	*tenis oyun**u***	tenis a͡uyo͡ono͡o
painting	*yağlı boya*	yughli(*r*) ba͡uyu

English	Turkish	Pronunciation
picture gallery	*Resim müzesi*	resim mew͡zesi
reading room	*mütalaa salonu, okuma salonu*	mew͡tuluu sula͡unoo͡, a͡ukoo͡mu sula͡unoo͡
subscription	*kaydiye parası*	kuydiye purusi(*r*)
theatre	*tiyatro*	tiyutra͡u
act (first)	*perde (birinci)*	perde (birinji)
actor	*aktör*	ukte͡ur
actress	*aktris, kadın aktör*	uktris, kudi(*r*)n ukte͡ur
dancing (ballet)	*bale, balet*	bule, bulet
walk	*gezinti*	gezinti
walking	*yürüyüş, dolaşma, dere tepe gitme*	yew͡rew͡yew͡sh, da͡ulushmu, dere tepe gitme
hiking	*dere tepe gitmek*	dere tepe gitmek
picnicking	*kırda yemek yimek*	ki(*r*)du yemek yimek
rambling	*kır gezintisi*	ki(*r*) gezintisi
music hall	*variyete*	vuriyete
museum	*müze*	mew͡ze
curtain	*perde*	perde
manager	*müdür*	mew͡dew͡r
opera	*opera*	a͡uperu
play	*oyun*	a͡uyoo͡n
refreshment room	*büfe*	bew͡fe
scene	*sahne*	suhne
gallery	*galeri*	guleri
reserved	*tutulmuş, rezerve*	too͡too͡lmoo͡sh, rezerve
stage	*sahne*	suhne

Cycling

(Bisiklete binme)

Axle	*dingil*	dingil
ball bearings	*biliya yatakları*	biliyu yutukluri(*r*)
bell	*çıngırak*	chi(*r*)ngi(*r*)ruk
bicycle	*bisiklet, t*	bisiklet

English	Turkish	Pronunciation
bolt	*civata*	jivutu
brake	*fren*	fren
caution	*ihtiyat, t, dikkat*	ihtiyut, dikkut
chain	*zincir*	zinjir
cone	*mahrut, . . . t, koni*	muhro͡ot, ka͡uni
connection	*irtibat, bağ,*	irtibut, bugh
cycle maker	*bisikletçi*	bisikletchi
— shop	*bisikletçi dükkânı*	bisikletchi de͡wkki͡ani(*r*)
— race	*bisiklet yarışı*	bisiklet yuri(*r*)shi(*r*)
— tour	*bisiklet gezintisi*	bisiklet gezintisi
— track	*yarış mahali (very soft "l") (mahalli)*	yuri(*r*)sh muhuli (muhulli)
danger	*tehlike*	tehlike
to dismount	*sökmek*	se͡ukmek
enamel	*vernik*	vernik
fork	*çatal*	chutul
frame	*çerçeve*	chercheve
friction	*delkütemas*	delke͡wtemus
handle	*sap*	sup
hub	*tekerlek başlığı*	tekerlek bushli(*r*)ghi(*r*)
indiarubber	*lastik*	lustik
inner tube	*iç lastiği*	ich lustighi
knapsack	*arka çantası*	urku chuntusi(*r*)
lamp	*lamba*	lumbu
lamp bracket	*lamba askısı*	lumbu uski(*r*)si(*r*)
link	*halka*	hulku
to lubricate	*yağlamak*	yughlumuk
map	*harita*	huritu
to mount	*bir araya getirmek*	bir uruyu getirmek
nut	*somun*	sa͡umo͡on
oil	*yağ*	yugh
oilcan	*yağdanlık*	yughdunli(*r*)k
outer cover	*dış lâstiği*	di(*r*)sh la͡astighi
pedal	*pedal, baskı*	pedul, buski(*r*)
pump	*tulumba*	to͡olo͡ombu
to pump up	*şişirmek*	shishirmek
rags	*paçavra*	puchuvru

English	Turkish	Pronunciation
removable	*çikarılabilir, gayri sabit, kabili nakil*	chikuri(*r*)lubilir, guyri subit, kubili nukil
to repair	*tâmir et**mek***	ta͡amir etmek
rim	*çenber*	chenber
saddle	*sele*	sele
screw	*vida*	vidu
spanner	*civata anahtarı*	jivutu unuhturi(*r*)
spoke	*tel*	tel
to start	*hareket et**mek***	hureket etmek
to steer	*kullan**mak**, idare et**mek***	ko͡ollunmuk, idure etmek
strap	*kayış*	kuyi(*r*)sh
to tighten up	*sıkış**tırmak***	si(*r*)ki(*r*)shti(*r*)r-muk
tricycle	*üç tekerlek**li** bisiklet*	e͡wch tekerlekli bisiklet
tyre	*lastik*	lustik
to unscrew	*vidayi sök**mek***	viduyi se͡ukmek
valve	*valv, supap*	vulv, so͡opup
wallet	*cüzdan*	je͡wzdun
wheels	*tekerlek**ler***	tekerlekler
front wheel	*ön tekerlek*	e͡un tekerlek
back wheel	*arka tekerlek*	urku tekerlek

Aeroplane Terms
(Tayyare istilahâtı)

English	Turkish	Pronunciation
Adjustable	*kabili tanzim*	kubili tunzim
aileron	*eleron*	elera͡un
airscrew	*pervane*	pervune
aerial navigation	*hava seyahatı*	huvu seyuhuti(*r*)
aerodrome	*tayyare istasyonu*	tuyyure istusya͡uno͡o
aeroplane	*tayyare*	tuyyure
aerostatics	*hava kanun**ları***	huvu kuno͡onluri(*r*)
ascent	*suut, yüksel**me***	so͡oo͡ot, ye͡wkselme
barograph	*hava ölçü**sü***	huvu e͡ulche͡wse͡w
bulkhead	*bölme*	be͡ulme
climbing tests	*suut tecrübe**leri***	so͡oo͡ot tejre͡wbeleri

English	Turkish	Pronunciation
cockardes	*kokart (lar)*	ka͡ukurt (lur)
cockpit	*pilot daire**si***	pila͡ut duiresi
communicating door	*ara kapı**sı***	uru kupi(*r*)si(*r*)
control wires	*idare ve sevk manivela**ları***	idure ve sevk muniveluluri(*r*)r
control column	*kontrol kolu*	ka͡untra͡ul ka͡ulo͡o
cylinder	*silindir*	silindir
cylinder head	*silindir baş**ı***	silindir bushi(*r*)
descent	*iniş*	inish
endurance test	*mukavemet tecrübe**si***	mo͡okuvemet tejro͡obesi
engine	*motör*	ma͡ute͡ur
engine cooling	*tebrit, motörün soğudul**ması***	tebrit, ma͡ute͡ure͡wn sa͡ugho͡odo͡ol-musi(*r*)
electrical installation	*elektrik te'sisat**ı***	elektrik te-sisuti(*r*)r
elevator	*elevatör*	elevute͡ur
engine mounting	*motör sehpa**sı***	ma͡ute͡ur sehpusi(*r*)
exhaust manifold	*ekzost boru**ları***	ekza͡ust ba͡uro͡oluri(*r*)
flying control	*uçuş kontrol**u***	o͡ocho͡osh ka͡untra͡ulo͡o
fuselage	*gövde, füzilaj*	ge͡uvde, fe͡wziluj
gap	*aralı**k***	uruli(*r*)k
interplane struts	*ara satıh dirsek**leri***	uru suti(*r*)h dirsekleri
inspection hole	*muayene göz**ü***	mo͡ouyene ge͡uze͡w
joystick	*sevk ve idare kontrol**u***	sevk ve idure ka͡untra͡ulo͡o
land turns	*yerde dönüş**ler***	yerde de͡une͡wshler
landing ground	*iniş meydanı*	inish meyduni(*r*)
landing run	*iniş cevelânı, iniş mesafe**si***	inish jevela͡ani(*r*), inish mesufesi
leading edge	*hücum kenar**ı***	he͡wjo͡om kenuri(*r*)
hangar	*hangar*	hungur
longerons	*motör tutamak**ları***	ma͡ute͡ur to͡otu-mukluri(*r*)
lower wing	*alt kanat, . . . d*	ult kanut

English	Turkish	Pronunciation
manœuvrability	*manevreye salihiyet, . . . t*	munevreye sulihiyet
oil tank	*yağ haznesi*	yugh huznesi
performance test	*performans tecrübesi*	perfaurmūns tejrew͡besi
petrol tank	*benzin haznesi*	benzin huznesi
petrol system	*benzin tertibatı*	benzin tertibuti(*r*)
pilot	*pilot, . . . t*	pila͡ut
port mainplane	*iskele esas kanadı*	iskele esus kunudi(*r*)
tail plane	*geri kanadı*	geri kunudi(*r*)
tail skid	*kuyruk tarağı*	ko͡oyro͡ok turughi(*r*)
take-off run	*suut cevelânı, suut mesafesi*	so͡oo͡ot jevela͡ani(*r*), so͡oo͡ot mesufesi
to taxi	*yer cevelânı*	yer jevela͡ani(*r*)
tare weight	*dara ağırlığı*	duru ughi(*r*)rli(*r*)ghi(*r*)
test flight	*muayene ve tecrübe uçuşu*	mo͡ouyene ve tejrew͡be o͡ocho͡osho͡o
trial flight	*imtihan uçuşu*	imtihun o͡ocho͡osho͡o
rudder	*dümen*	dew͡men
starboard mainplane	*sancak esas kanadı*	sunjuk esus kunudi(*r*)
steel ribs	*çelik kaburga parçaları*	chelik kubo͡orgu purchuluri(*r*)
struts	*dirsekler*	dirsekler
steel spar	*çelik direk*	chelik direk
undercarriage	*aterisaj, iniş tekerlekleri*	uterisuj, inish tekerlekleri
upper wing	*üst kanat, . . . d*	ew͡st kunut
vent pipe	*menfez*	menfez
wing	*kanat*	kunut
wiring	*elektrik tefrişatı*	elektrik tefrishuti(*r*)

Motoring

(Otomobil ile seyahat)

Carburettor	*karbüratör*	kurbew͡ruteu͡r
cross roads	*dört yol ağızı*	deu͡rt ya͡ul ughi(*r*)zi(*r*)

English	Turkish	Pronunciation
driver	*şoför*	shau͡feu͡r
elbow	*dirsek*	dirsek
electric	*elektrikli*	elektrikli
electricity	*elektrik*	elektrik
to evaporate	*tebahhur etmek*	tebuhhoor etmek
exhaust	*ekzost, motör yanığı*	ekzau͡st, mau͡teu͡r yuni(*r*)ghi(*r*)
to fill	*doldurmak*	dau͡ldo͡ormuk
flaw	*kusur, çatlak*	ko͡osoo͡r, chutluk
gas (fumes)	*gaz*	guz
gear	*vites, çark*	vites, churk
generator	*ceneratör, doğuray*	jeneruteu͡r, dau͡ghoo͡ruy
gradient	*yol meyli, rampa*	yau͡l meyli, rumpu
handle (turning)	*motör anahtarı*	mau͡teu͡r unuh-turi(*r*)
horn	*boru, düdük, korne*	bau͡roo͡, dew͡dew͡k, kau͡rne
horse-power	*beygir kuvveti*	beygir ko͡ovveti
ignition	*iş'al*	ish-ul
lever	*manivela*	munivelu
to light up	*lambayı yakmak*	lumbuyi(*r*) yukmuk
magneto	*mıknato, manyato*	mi(*r*)knutau͡, munyutau͡
motor	*motör*	mau͡teu͡r
packing	*salmastra*	sulmustru
petrol	*benzin*	benzin
pinion	*bisiklet gerisi*	bisiklet gerisi
pressure (high)	*yüksek tazyik, basınç, . . . c*	yew͡ksek tuzyik, busi(*r*)nch
— (low)	*alçak tazyık, basınç, . . . c*	ulchuk tuzyi(*r*)k, busi(*r*)nch
rack	*ağdan raf*	ughdun ruf
speed	*sür'at, hız*	sew͡r-ut, hi(*r*)z
— full	*tamyol, fulspit, t*	tumyau͡l, fo͡olspit
— high	*büyük sür'at, yarış sür'atı*	bew͡yew͡k sew͡r-ut, yuri(*r*)sh sew͡r-uti(*r*)
starting gear	*vites çarkı, hareket . . . t çarkı*	vites churki(*r*), hureket churki(*r*)

English	Turkish	Pronunciation
steering	*direksiyon, idare kolu*	direksiyaun, idure kauloo
Photography (Fotografçılık)		
Amateur	*amatör*	umuteur
background	*fon, zemin, manzura*	faun, zemin, munzuru
to burnish	*parlatmak*	purlutmuk
bulb	*ampul*	umpool
camera	*fotograf makinesi*	fautaugruf mukinesi
dark-room lamp	*kırmızı lamba*	ki(*r*)mi(*r*)zi(*r*) lumbu
developing	*develope, belirme*	develaupe, belirme
dishes	*küvet, t*	kewvet
dry plates	*kurucam*	kooroojum
enlargement	*agrandisman, büyültme*	ugrundismun, bewyewltme
exposure	*poz*	pauz
—, over	*fazla poz*	fuzlu pauz
—, snap	*enstantane, açıkta resim alma*	enstuntune, achi(*r*)-ktu resim ulmu
—, time	*tam poz*	tum pauz
—, under	*az poz*	uz pauz
faded	*solgun, solmuş*	saulgoon, saulmoosh
film	*filim*	filim
focus	*foküs, mihrak, ru'yet sahası*	faukews, mihruk, roo'yet suhusi(*r*)
funnel	*körük*	keurewk
glass measure	*ölçü bardağı*	eulchew burdughi(*r*)
half tone	*yarım ton, hafif*	yuri(*r*)m taun, hufif
negative	*negatif*	negutif
photographer	*fotografçı*	fautaugrufchi(*r*)
photograph	*fotograf*	fautaugruf
photographic	*fotografçılığa ait*	fautaugrufchi(*r*)-li(*r*)ghu uit
to photograph a person	*bir adamın fotografını almak*	bir udumi(*r*)n fautaugrufi(*r*)-ni(*r*) ulmuk

English	Turkish	Pronunciation
to photograph anything	*fotograf çekmek*	fa͡utau͡gruf chekmek
to have one's photo taken	*fotograf çıkartmak*	fa͡utau͡gruf chi(*r*)kūrtmuk
portrait	*resim*	resim
positive bath	*pozitiv banyo*	pa͡uzitiv bunya͡u
to print	*kağıda çekmek*	kughi(*r*)du chekmek
print	*kopya*	ka͡upyu
shutter	*objektif, f, kapak*	a͡ubjektif, kupuk
—, instantaneous	*enstantane kapağı*	enstuntune kupughi(*r*)
—, time	*poz kapağı*	pa͡uz kupughi(*r*)
silver bath	*tesbit banyosu*	tesbit bunya͡uso͡o
snaps	*enstantane resimler*	enstuntune resimler
speed indicator	*sür'at müş'iresi, gösterge*	se͡wr-ut me͡wsh-iresi, ge͡usterge
spirit level	*ruhlu tesviye*	roohloo tesviye
spot, stain	*benek, leke*	benek, leke
varnishing	*vernikleme, cilâlama*	vernikleme jila͡alumu
washing tank	*banyo*	bunya͡u

Post, Telegraph, and Telephone

(Posta, telegraf, ve telefon)

English	Turkish	Pronunciation
Book post (by)	*matbua postası (ile)*	mutbo͡ou pa͡ustusi(*r*) (ile)
called for (to be)	*post restan*	pa͡ust restun
collection	*toplama, devşirme*	ta͡uplumu, devshirme
contents	*muhteviyat*	mo͡ohteviyut
customs declaration	*gümrük beyannamesi*	ge͡wmre͡wk beyunnumesi
to deliver	*teslim etmek*	teslim etmek
delivery	*dağıtma, tevziat*	dughi(*r*)tmu, tevziut
description	*anlatma, tavsif*	unlutmu, tuvsif
destination	*varış yeri*	vuri(*r*)sh yeri
excess postage	*fazla ağırlık ücreti*	fuzlu ughi(*r*)rli(*r*)k e͡wjreti

English	Turkish	Pronunciation
insured value	*kıymeti mukad-dereli*	ki(*r*)ymeti mo͡okuddereli
letterbox	*posta kutusu*	pa͡ustu ko͡oto͡oso͡o
letter post	*mektup postası*	mekto͡op pa͡ustusi(*r*)
by letter	*yazı ile, tahriren*	yuzi(*r*) ile, tuhriren
money order	*para havalesi*	puru huvulesi
newspaper	*gazeta,* or *gazete*	guzetu, *or* guzete
postcard	*kartpostal*	kurtpa͡ustul
parcel	*paket*	puket
parcel post	*paket postası*	puket pa͡ustusi(*r*)
parcel post (by)	*paket postası ile*	puket pa͡ustusi(*r*) ile
postman	*postacı*	pa͡ustuji(*r*)
post office	*postâne*	pa͡usta͡ane
postmaster	*posta müdürü*	pa͡ustu me͡wde͡wre͡w
postage	*posta ücreti*	pa͡ustu e͡wjreti
postal order	*mandapost, posta havalenamesi*	mundupa͡ust, pa͡ustu huvulenumesi
to register	*taahhütlü yapmak*	tuuhhe͡wtle͡w yupmuk
reply paid	*cevaplı*	jevupli(*r*)
stamp	*pul*	po͡ol
to telegraph	*telgraf çekmek,* or *tellemek*	telgruf chekmek, *or* tellemek
telegraph	*telgraf*	telgruf
telegraph form	*telgraf varakası*	telgruf vuru-kusi(*r*)
telegram	*telgraf*	telgruf
—, wireless	*telsiz telgraf*	telsiz telgruf
telegraphy, wireless	*telsiz telgrafçılık*	telsiz telgruf-chi(*r*)li(*r*)k
to telephone	*telefon etmek*	telefa͡un etmek
to ring up	*telefon etmek*	telefa͡un etmek
telephone number	*telefon numarası*	telefa͡un no͡omurusi(*r*)
weight	*ağırlık*	ughi(*r*)rli(*r*)k
to weigh	*tartmak*	turtmuk

English	Turkish	Pronunciation
overweight	*nizamın***dan** *fazla ağır***lık**	nizumi(*r*)ndun fuzlu ughi(*r*)r-li(*r*)k

Correspondence
(Muhabere)

English	Turkish	Pronunciation
Address	*adres*	udres
to address	*adres***i** *yaz***mak**	udresi yuzmuk
to readdress	*yeni adres koy***mak**	yeni udres ka͡uymuk
blotting paper	*kurut***ma** *kâğıdı*	ko͡oro͡otmu ki͡aghi(*r*)di(*r*)
to copy	*kopiye et***mek**	ka͡upiye etmek
date	*tarih*	turih
enclosure	*mazruf*	muzro͡of
envelope	*zarf*	zurf
fountain pen	*mürekep***li** *kalem*	me͡wrekepli kulem
an immediate answer	*derhal cevap, . . . b müsta'cel cevap*	derhul jevup, me͡wstu-jel jevup
ink	*mürekkep, . . . b*	me͡wrekkep
inkstand	*hokka*	ha͡ukku
penknife	*çakı*	chuki(*r*)
letter	*mektup, bitik*	mekto͡op, bitik
note	*tezkere, not*	tezkere, na͡ut
paper	*kâğıt, . . . d*	ki͡aghi(*r*)t
pen	*kalem*	kulem
pencil	*kurşun kalem***i**	ko͡orsho͡on kulemi
quire	*kâğıt deste***si** (24 *yaprak*)	ki͡aghi(*r*)t destesi (24 yupruk)
seal	*mühür*	me͡whe͡wr
sheet	*yaprak*	yupruk
signature	*imza*	imzu
writing	*yazı*	yuzi(*r*)

Professions and Tradesmen
(Meslek***ler***, esnaf***lar***)

English	Turkish	Pronunciation
Artist	*artist*	urtist
author	*müellif, düzgen*	me͡wellif, de͡wzgen
baker	*ekmek***çi**	ekmekchi
banker	*banker*	bunker

English	Turkish	Pronunciation
barber	*berber*	berber
bookseller	*kitapçi*	kitupchi
bookbinder	*mücellit, . . . d*	me͡wjellit
brewer	*biracı*	biruji(*r*)
butcher	*kasap, . . . b*	kusup
carpenter	*dülger*	de͡wlger
cashier	*kasadar*	kusudur
clerk	*kâtip, yazıcı*	kiatip, yuzi(*r*)ji(*r*)
cook	*ahçı*	uhchi(*r*)
doorkeeper	*kapıcı*	kupi(*r*)ci(*r*)
draper	*tuhafiyeci*	to͡ohufiyeji
editor	*tâbi*	ta͡abi
engineer (general)	*mühendis*	me͡whendis
fishmonger	*balıkçı*	buli(*r*)kchi(*r*)
florist	*çiçekçi*	chichekchi
fruiterer	*manav*	munuv
glazier	*camcı*	jumji(r)
goldsmith	*kuyumcu*	ko͡oyo͡omjo͡o
governess	*mürebbiye*	me͡wrebbiye
grocer	*bakkal*	bukkul
hairdresser	*berber, perükâr*	berber, pere͡wkiar
hatter	*şapkacı*	shupkuji(*r*)
hosier	*çorapçı*	cha͡urupchi(*r*)
jeweller	*kuyumcu*	ko͡oyo͡omjo͡o
merchant	*tüccar*	te͡wjjur
messenger	*haberci*	huberji
messenger boy	*çocuk*	cha͡ujook
miller	*değirmenci*	deghirmenji
milliner	*şapkacı*	shupkuji(*r*)
child's nurse	*daya*	duyu
nursemaid	*dadı*	dudi(*r*)
physician, doctor	*doktor, hekim*	da͡ukta͡ur, hekim
policeman	*polis*	pa͡ulis
printer	*matbaacı*	mutbuuji(*r*)
professor	*profesör*	pra͡ufese͡ur
provision dealer	*zahire tüccarı*	zuhire te͡ujjuri(*r*)
publisher	*naşir*	nushir
saddler	*semerci*	semerji
servant	*hizmetçi*	hizmetchi
shoemaker	*kunduracı*	ko͡ondo͡oruji(*r*)

English	Turkish	Pronunciation
smith (black)	*nalbant*	nulbunt
stationer	*kâğıtçı*	kiaghi(*r*)tchi(*r*)
tailor	*terzi*	terzi
teacher	*öğretmen*	e͡ughretmen
tobacconist	*tütüncü*	te͡wte͡wnje͡w
tradesman	*esnaf*	esnuf
watchmaker	*saatçı*	suutchi(*r*)
workman	*işçi, amele*	ishchi, umele

Commercial Terms
(Tüccarî istilah**lar**)

English	Turkish	Pronunciation
Account	*hesap, . . . b*	hesup
—, to close	*hesabı kapatmak*	hesubi(*r*) kuputmuk
—, current	*hesabicarî, ağın hesap*	hesubijure͡e, ughi(*r*)n hesup
—, joint	*ortaklık hesabı, kapçıra hesabı, müşterek hesap*	a͡urtukli(*r*)k hesubi(*r*), kupchi(*r*)ru hesubi(*r*), me͡wshterek hesup
—, to settle	*hesabı ödemek, hesap kapamak*	hesubi(*r*) e͡udemek, hesup kupumuk
accountant	*muhasip, . . . b*	mo͡ohusip
acknowledgment	*cevap, ihbar*	jevup, ihbur
advance	*avans*	uvuns
to advertise	*ilân vermek*	ila͡an vermek
advertisement	*ilân*	ila͡an
advice	*ihbariye, bildirme*	ihburiye, bildirme
agent	*acanta*	ujuntu
agency	*acantalık*	ujuntuli(*r*)k
apprentice	*çırak*	chi(*r*)ruk
arrangement	*tertibat, uyuşma*	tertibut, o͡oyo͡oshmu
in arrears (he is)	*borcunu geciktirir*	ba͡urjo͡ono͡o gejiktirir
assets	*aktif, mevcudat*	uktif, mevjo͡odut
assistant	*muavin, yardımcı*	mo͡ouvin, yurdi(*r*)mji(*r*)
at three months	*üç ayda*	e͡wch uydu

English	Turkish	Pronunciation
to authorize	*salâhiyet vermek*	sula͡ahiyet vermek
average	*vasat, orta*	vusut, a͡urtu
balance	*bakiyye, geriye kalan*	bukiyye, geriye kulun
balance sheet	*bilanço*	biluncha͡u
bank	*banka*	bunku
bank-note	*bankonot*	bunka͡una͡ut
bankrupt	*müflis, batkın*	me͡wflis, butki(*r*)n
berth, situation	*hizmet, iş, vazife*	hizmet, ish, vuzife
bill	*hesap puslası*	hesup po͡oslusi(*r*)
business	*meşguliyet, iş*	meshgo͡oliyet, ish
buyer	*müşteri, alıcı*	me͡wshteri, uli(*r*)ji(*r*)
cargo	*hamûle, yük*	humûle, ye͡wk
cash	*peşin*	peshin
catalogue	*katalog, liste*	kutula͡ug, liste
— price	*katalog fiyatı*	kutula͡ug fiyuti(*r*)
charter	*imtiyaz, vesika*	imtiyuz, vesiku
to charter (vehicle)	*kiralamak*	kirulumuk
claim	*müddeiyat*	me͡wddeiyut
clearing house	*kliring bankası*	kiliring bunkusi(*r*)
clerk	*kâtip, yazıcı, bitigen*	kiatip, yuzi(*r*)-ji(*r*), bitigen
contract	*kontorat*	ka͡unta͡urut
contraband	*kaçak*	kuchuk
cost, insurance	*masraf, sigorta*	musruf, siga͡urtu
—, freightage	*navlun, nakliye ücreti*	nuvlo͡on, nukliye e͡wjreti
creditor	*alacaklı, dâyin*	ulujukli(*r*), da͡ayin
counting house	*vezne*	vezne
customs duty	*gümrük resmi*	ge͡wmre͡wk resmi
debit and credit	*alacak verecek, zimmet ve irat, . . d*	ulujuk verejek, zimmet ve irut
debt	*borç, c, deyin*	ba͡urch, deyin
debtor	*borçlu*	ba͡urchlo͡o
in debt	*medyun*	medyo͡on
declaration	*beyanname*	beyunnume
to deliver	*teslim etmek*	teslim etmek

English	Turkish	Pronunciation
delivery	*teslimat, tevdiat*	teslimut, tevdiut
demurrage	*istarya, tazminat*	isturyu, tuzminut
department	*daire*	duire
director	*müdür*	meŵdeŵr
discount	*iskonto, kırdırma payı*	iskaûntaû, ki(*r*)r-di(*r*)rmu puyi(*r*)
to discount	*iskonto et**mek**, baş al**mak***	iskaûntaû etmek, bush ulmuk
dividend	*temettü, kazanç payı*	temetteŵ, kuzunch puyi(*r*)
dues	*rüsum, vergi*	reŵsôom, vergi
duty	*vergi*	vergi
—, export	*ihracat resmi*	ihrujut resmi
—, import	*ithalat resmi*	ithulut resmi
estimate	*keşif, tahmin*	keshif, tuhmin
exchange	*borsa*	baûrsu
to export	*ihracet**mek***	ihruj etmek
guarantee	*te'minat*	te-minut
gross weight	*gayri safî ağır**lık***	guyri(*r*) sufee ughi(*r*)rli(*r*)k
to import	*ithal et**mek**, getirmek*	ithul etmek, getirmek
imports	*ithalat*	ithulut
information	*malûmat*	mulûmut
insolvent	*müflis, bat**kın***	meŵflis, butki(*r*)n
insurance	*sigorta*	sigaûrtu
to insure	*sigorta et**mek***	sigaûrtu etmek
interest	*faiz*	fuiz
introduction	*takdim, görüştür**me**, tanıt**ma***	tukdim, geûreŵshteŵrme, tuni(*r*)tmu
invoice	*fatura*	futôoru
lease	*iycar mukavelesi*	iyjur môokuvelesi
lessee	*müste'cir, kira**cı***	meŵste-jir, kiruji
lessor	*mûcir*	mûjir
liquidation	*likidasyon, tasfiye*	likidusyaûn, tusfiye
to load	*yük**lemek***	yeŵklemek
loss	*ziyan*	ziyun
manager	*idare âmiri*	idure aâmiri
market	*pazar*	puzur

English	Turkish	Pronunciation
market day	*pazar günü*	puzur ge͡wne͡w
negotiable	*cirolu, ciro edilir, sürülür*	jira͡ulo͡o, jira͡u edilir, se͡wre͡wle͡wr
nett	*sâfi*	sa͡afi
not negotiable	*cirosuz, havale edilemez*	jira͡uso͡oz, huvule edilemez
number	*adet, numara*	adet, no͡omuru
office	*yazıhane, büro*	yuzi(*r*)hune, be͡wra͡u
order	*havâle*	huva͡ale
to order	*emre, emrine*	emre, emrine
payable	*tesviyesi lâzım*	tesviyesi la͡azi(*r*)m
payment	*te'diye*	te-diye
prepaid	*peşinen*	peshinen
price	*fiyat*	fiyut
quotation	*fiyat verme*	fiyut verme
receipt	*makpuz*	mukpo͡oz
reduction	*tenzilat, indirme*	tenzilut, indirme
to register	*sicile geçirmek*	sijile gechirmek
registration	*kayıt, ...d*	kuyi(*r*)t
registered tonnage	*mukayyet ton, istiap haddi*	mo͡okuyyet ta͡un istiup huddi
remittance	*para yatırma, tevdiat, ...t*	puru yuti(*r*)rmu, tevdiut
rent	*kira*	kiru
representative	*mümessil*	me͡wmessil
retail	*perakende*	perukende
salesman	*satış adamı, satıcı*	sutish udumi(*r*), suti(*r*)ji(*r*)
secretary	*kâtip, b*	kiatip
settlement	*tesviye*	tesviye
shareholder	*hissedar*	hissedur
shares	*hisse senedatı*	hisse seneduti(*r*)
to ship	*yüklemek*	ye͡wklemek
shipper	*komisiyoncu*	ka͡umisiya͡unjo͡o
solvent	*iktidarlı, kudreti maliyesi düzgün*	iktidurli(*r*), ko͡odreti muliyesi de͡wzge͡wn
stock	*stok, mevcut mal*	sta͡uk, mevjo͡ot mul
stockholder	*hissedar*	hissedur

English	Turkish	Pronunciation
telegraphic address	*telgraf adresi*	telgruf udresi
towing	*yedek çek***me**	yedek chekme
trade (*commerce*)	*alışveriş* (*ticaret*)	uli(*r*)shverish (tijuret)
to trade in tobacco	*tütün ticareti yap***mak**	te͡wte͡wn tijureti yupmuk
traveller (commercial)	*seyyah tüccar, pılasiyer*	seyyuh te͡wjjur, pi(*r*)lusiyer
trustee	*mütevelli*	me͡wtevelli
to unload	*boşalt***mak**	ba͡ushultmuk
wholesale	*toptan*	ta͡uptun
wharf	*anbar*	unbur

Legal Terms

(adlî Istilâhat)

English	Turkish	Pronunciation
Acquittal	*beraat*	beruut
affidavit	*tahrirî ifade, beyanname*	tuhriree͡e ifude, beyunnume
agreement	*mukavele*	mo͡okuvele
allegation	*iddia—isnadat*	iddiu, isnudut
to allege	*iddia et***mek**	iddiu etmek
to arbitrate	*hakemlik* **etmek**	hukemlik etmek
arbitration	*tavassut*	tuvusso͡ot
arrangement	*uyuşma, i'tilaf*	o͡oyo͡oshmu, i-tiluf
to arrest	*tevkif et***mek**	tevkif etmek
to attest	*tastik et***mek,** *te'yidi beyanat et***mek**	tustik etmek, te-yidi beyunut etmek
attestation	*tastik, yemin***li** *beyanat*	tustik, yeminli beyunut
attorney	*müddei umumî*	me͡wddei o͡omo͡omhee
to authorize	*müsaede et***mek**	me͡wsuede etmek
award	*tazminat***a** *dair karar*	tuzminutu duir kurur
to award	*tazminatı ta'yinen hüküm ver***mek**	tuzminuti(*r*) tu-yinen he͡wke͡wm vermek
bail	*kefâlet*	kefa͡alet

English	Turkish	Pronunciation
bailiff	*icra me'muru*	ijra me'mo͡oro͡o
barrister, counsel	*dâva vekili, avukat*	daavu vekili, uvo͡okut
bond	*tahvilat*	tuhvilut
case	*dâva*	da͡avu
charge, accusation	*isnat, itham*	isnut, ithum
to charge	*itham etmek*	ithum etmek
complainant	*dâvacı*	da͡avuci(r)
conviction	*mahkûmiyet*	muhkiûmiyet
decision	*karar*	kurur
deed	*höccet, vesika, senedat*	he͡ujjet, vesiku, senedut
defence	*müdafaa*	me͡wdufuu
to defend	*müdafaa etmek*	me͡wdufuu etmek
defendant	*müddei aleyh*	me͡wddei uleyh
deposition	*ifade, takrir*	ifude, tukrir
discharge	*tebrie, serbest bırakılma*	tebrie, serbest bi(r)ruki(r)lmu
equity	*hakkaniyet*	hukkuniyet
evidence	*subut, delail*	so͡obo͡ot, deluil
execution	*icra*	ijru
executor (court)	*icra me'muru*	ijru me-mo͡oro͡o
fees	*ücret, masraf*	e͡wjret, musruf
fine	*para cezası*	puru cezusi(r)
fraud	*sahtekârlık*	suhtekia͡arli(r)k
imprisonment	*hapse konma*	hupse ka͡unmu
informer	*muhbir*	mo͡ohbir
injunction	*mudaheleyi âmir karar*	mo͡oduheleyi a͡amir kurur
inventory	*müfredat listesi*	me͡wfredut listesi
jail, gaol	*ceza evi, hapisane*	jezu evi, hupisune
judge	*hâkim*	ha͡akim
judgment	*hüküm*	he͡wke͡wm
to judge	*muhakeme etmek*	mo͡ohukeme etmek
jurisdiction	*salâhiyet*	sula͡ahiyet
jury	*hey'eti adul*	hey-eti udo͡ol
justice	*adâlet*	uda͡alet
law	*kanun*	kuno͡on
lawful, legal	*kanunî, meşru*	kuno͡one͡e, meshro͡o

English	Turkish	Pronunciation
lawyer	*avukat*	uvo͡okut
magistrate	*sulh hâkimi*	so͡olh ha͡akimi
to take oath	*yemin etmek*	yemin etmek
pardon	*af*	uf
penal servitude	*kürek cezası*	ke͡wrek jezusi(*r*)
perjury	*yalancı şahitlik*	yulunji(*r*) shuhitlik
petitioner	*müsted'i*	me͡wsted-i
plaintiff	*müddei*	me͡wddei
police station	*polis merkezi, karakol*	pa͡ulis merkezi, kuruka͡ul
police officer	*polis me'muru*	pa͡ulis me-mo͡oro͡o
prisoner	*mevkuf*	mevko͡of
procedure	*muamele*	mo͡oumele
proof	*ispat, delil, vesaik*	isput, delil, vesuik
prosecution	*takibat ı kanuniye*	tukibuti(*r*) kuno͡oniye
prosecutor	*müddei*	me͡wddei
public prosecutor	*müdde i umûmî*	me͡wddei o͡omûme͡e
punishment	*ceza*	jezu
robbery	*hırsızlık*	hi(*r*)rsi(*r*)zli(*r*)k
seal	*mühür*	me͡whe͡wr
sentence	*hüküm*	he͡wke͡wm
to sign	*imzalamak*	imzulumuk
statement	*ifâde*	ifa͡ade
statute	*kanunumahsus, nızamname i dahilî*	kuno͡ono͡omuhso͡os, ni(*r*)zumnumei duhilee
to sue	*dâva etmek*	da͡avu etmek
summons	*celp,...b*	jelp
surety	*kefil, zâmin*	kefil, za͡amin
tenant	*kiracı*	kiruji(*r*)
testator	*vasiyetçi, musî*	vusiyetchi, mo͡ose͡e
theft	*sırkat, hırsızlık*	si(*r*)rkut, hi(*r*)rsi(*r*)zli(*r*)k
thief	*hırsız*	hi(*r*)rsi(*r*)z
unlawful, illegal	*gayrimeşru, gayrikanunî, usulsuz*	guyrimeshro͡o, guyrikuno͡one͡e, o͡oso͡olso͡oz

English	Turkish	Pronunciation
will	*vasiyetname*	vusiyetnume
witness	*şahit*	shuhit
writ	*ilâm*	e͡ela͡am
Ranks and Titles		
(Meratib (rütbeler) ve elkab (lakaplar))		
Council	*meclis*	mejlis
crown	*mîrî*	me͡ecre͡e
deputy	*mürahhas*	me͡wruhhus
M.P.	*saylav, mebus*	suyluv, mebo͡os
duke, duchess	*dük, düşes*	de͡wk, de͡wshes
earl, count	*kont*	ka͡unt
countess	*kontes*	ka͡untes
emperor	*imperator*	imperuta͡ur
empress	*imperatoriça*	imperuta͡urichu
government	*hükûmet*	he͡wkûmet
heir, heir apparent	*vâris, veliaht*	va͡aris, veliuht
heiress	*vârise*	va͡arise
king, queen	*kıral, kıraliçe*	ki(*r*)rul, ki(*r*)ruliche
mayor	*belediye reisi*	belediye reisi
lord mayor	*şehir emini*	shehir emini
minister	*nazır, bakan*	nuzi(*r*)r, bukun
ministry	*nezaret, bakan**lık***	nezuret, bukunli(*r*)k
nobility	*zadeğân*	zudegha͡an
parliament	*parlamento*	purlumenta͡u
president	*başkan, reis*	bushkun, reis
prince, princess	*prens, prenses*	prens, prenses
royalty	*hanedanlık*	hunedunli(*r*)k
secretary	*kâtip*	kiatip
senator	*âyan*	a͡ayun
throne	*taht*	tuht
treasurer, cashier	*haznedar, veznedar*	huznedur, veznedur
Naval and Military Titles		
(Bahrî ve askerî lakap**lar**)		
Adjutant	*muavin*	mo͡ouvin
admiral	*amiral*	umirul
captain	*yuzbaşı*	yo͡ozbushi(*r*)
colonel	*miralay, albay*	miruluy, ulbuy

English	Turkish	Pronunciation
commandant (navy)	*kumandan*	ko͡omundun
commandant (army)	*binbaşı*	binbushi(*r*)
corporal	*onbaşı*	a͡unbushi(*r*)
doctor	*doktor*	da͡ukta͡ur
drummer	*davulcu*	duvo͡oljo͡o
engineer	*istihkâm*	istihkiam
lance-corporal	*çavuş*	chuvo͡osh
lieutenant	*teğmen*	teghmen
lieut.-col.	*yarbay, kaymakam*	yurbuy, kuymukum
marine	*bahriyeli, deniz eri*	buhriyeli, deniz eri
mate	*küçük zabit*	ke͡wche͡uk zubit
midshipman	*küçük zabit*	ke͡wche͡wk zubit
nurse	*hasta bakıcı*	hustu buki(*r*)ji(*r*)
officer	*zabit, subay*	zubit, so͡obuy
pilot	*kılavuz*	ki(*r*)luvo͡oz
sailor	*bahriyeli, denizci*	buhriyeli, denizji
sergeant	*üst çavuş*	e͡wst chuvo͡osh
sergeant-major	*baş çavuş*	bush chuvo͡osh
staff officer	*erkânıharp, kurumay*	erkiani(*r*)hurp, ko͡oro͡omuy
trumpeter	*trampeteci*	trumpeteji
second lieutenant	*asteğmen*	usteghmen
brigadier	*tuğ general*	to͡ogh generul
major-general	*tüm general*	te͡wm generul
lieut.-general	*kor general*	ka͡ur generul
field marshal	*mareşal*	mureshul
general	*orgeneral*	a͡urgenerul

Naval and Military Terms

(Bahrî ve askerî ta'birat)

Ambulance	*sıhhiye otomobili*	si(*r*)hhiye a͡uta͡uma͡ubili
ammunition	*mühimmat, capane*	me͡whimmut, jupune
army	*ordu*	a͡urdo͡o
army corps	*kolordu*	ka͡ula͡urdo͡o
artillery	*topçu*	ta͡upcho͡o
barracks	*kışla*	ki(*r*)shlu

English	Turkish	Pronunciation
battalion	*tabur*	tubo͡or
battery	*batarya*	buturyu
battle	*muharebe, savaş*	mo͡ohurebe, suvush
bayonet (fixed)	*süngü*	se͡wnge͡w
brigade	*liva, tug*	livu, to͡ogh
camp (army)	*orduğâh, kamp, . . . p*	a͡urdo͡oghi͡ah, kump
cannon	*top, . . . p*	ta͡up
cartridge	*fişek*	fishek
cavalry	*suvari*	so͡ovuri
colours (foreign)	*bayrak*	buyruk
colours (Turkish)	*sancak*	sunjuk
column	*kol*	ka͡ul
crew (navy)	*mürettebat, personel*	me͡wrettebut, persa͡unel
defaulter	*kaçak, firarî*	kuchuk, firure͡e
defence	*müdafaa*	me͡wdufuu
detachment	*kıt'a*	ki(*r*)t-u
discipline	*inzibat*	inzibut
to dismiss	*tardetmek*	turdetmek
to dismount (horse)	*attan inmek*	uttun inmek
Division	*Fırka, tümen*	Fi*r*(r)ku, te͡wmen
dockyard	*tersane*	tersune
to drill	*tâlim etmek*	ta͡alim etmek
drum	*davul*	duvo͡ol
embarkation	*irkâp, . . . b*	irkiap
enemy	*düşman*	de͡wshmun
engagement	*harba tutuşma, çarpışma*	hurbu, to͡oto͡oshmu churpi(*r*)shmu
enlistment	*kur'a*	ko͡or-u
equipment	*teçhizat, . . . t*	techhizut
escort	*muhafız*	mo͡ohufi(*r*)z
expedition	*kuvvei seferiye*	ko͡ovvei seferiye
file, row	*sıra*	si(*r*)ru
flag (foreign)	*bandıra*	bundi(*r*)ru
flag (Turkish)	*sancak*	sunjuk
flank	*cenah, yan*	jenuh, yun
fleet	*donanma*	da͡ununmu
in formation	*kıt'a halinde*	ki(*r*)t-u hulinde
fort	*kale, tabya*	kule, tubyu

English	Turkish	Pronunciation
to fortify	*tahkim etmek*	tuhkim etmek
furlough, on	*sıla, izin*	si(*r*)lu, izin
garrison	*muhafız asker, garnizon*	mo͡ohufi(*r*)z-usker, gurniza͡un
gunner	*topçu neferi, topçu eri*	ta͡upcho͡o neferi, ta͡upcho͡o eri
infantry	*piyade*	piyude
knapsack	*çanta*	chuntu
lance	*mızrak*	mi(*r*)zruk
manœuvre	*manevre*	munevre
militia	*milis askeri*	milis uskeri
to muster	*yoklama etmek*	ya͡uklumu etmek
non-combatant	*gayri muharip*	guyri mo͡ohurip
parade	*yoklama*	ya͡uklumu
patrol	*devriye*	devriye
picket	*inzibat eri, askerî polis, inzibat zabiti*	inzibut eri, uskere͡e pa͡ulis, inzibut zubiti
prisoner-of-war	*harp esiri*	hurp esiri
rations	*tayın, erzak*	tuyi(*r*)n, erzuk
recruit	*kur'a neferi*	ko͡or-u neferi
regiment	*alay*	uluy
regulations	*nizamat*	nizumut
salute	*resmı selam*	resmi(*r*) selum
scout	*izci, keşşaf*	izji, keshsh͡uf
sentry	*nöbetçi*	ne͡ubetchi
shot, shell	*saçma,* mermi	suchmu, mermi
skirmish	*çarpışma, müsademe*	churpi(*r*)shmu, me͡wsudeme
soldier	*asker*	usker
spy	*casus*	juso͡os
squadron (cavalry)	*suvari bölüğü*	so͡ovuri be͡ule͡wghe͡w
submarine	*tahtelbahir, denizaltı gemisi*	tuhtelbuhir, denizulti(*r*) gemisi
sword	*kılıç*	ki(*r*)il(*r*)ch
trench	*siper*	siper
troops	*kıtaat, asker*	ki(*r*)tuut, usker
uniform	*üniforma*	e͡wnifa͡urmu
wounded	*yaralı*	yuruli(*r*)

Religious Terms
(dînî ta'birat)

English	Turkish	Pronunciation
Absolution	*kefaret*	kefuret
altar	*mihrap, . . . b*	mihrup
angel	*melek*	melek
baptism	*vaftiz*	vuftiz
bible	*incil*	injil
belief, faith,	*iyman, i'tikat, inanç*	iymun, i-tikut, inunch
believer	*mu'tekit*	mo͡o-tekit
breviary	*ibadet kitabı*	ibudet kitubi(r)
burial	*defin, gömme*	defin, ge͡umme
cathedral	*katedral, büyük kilise*	kutedrul, be͡wye͡wk kilise
cemetery	*mezarlık*	mezurli(r)k
chapel	*mâbet, . . . d*	ma͡abet
charity	*hayrat, umuru hayriye*	huyrut, o͡om o͡oro͡o huyriye
choir	*heyet i muganniye*	heyeti mo͡ogunniye
Christian	*hıristiyan*	hi(r)ri(r)stiyun
church	*kilise*	kilise
clergyman	*râhip, . . . b*	ra͡ahip
— (Protestant)	*protestan papazı*	pra͡utestun pupuzi(r)
— (Catholic)	*katolik papazı*	kuta͡ulik pupuzi(r)
Creator	*yaradıcı, hâlik*	yurudi(r)ji(r), ha͡alik
creed	*mezhep, . . . b*	mezhep
divine	*kudsî, ilâhî*	ko͡odse͡e, ila͡ahe͡e
eternal life	*hayat ı ebedî*	huyuti(r) ebede͡e
eternity	*ebediyet, . . . t*	ebediyet
everlasting	*ölmez, lâyemut*	e͡ulmez, la͡ayemo͡ot
faithful	*mü'min*	me͡w-min
faithfulness	*sedâkat*	seda͡akut
fear	*korku*	ka͡urko͡o
to forgive	*affetmek*	uffetmek
forgiveness	*af*	uf
God	*tanrı, çalap*	tunri(r), chulup
the Gospel	*menakib i isa*	menukibi isu
grave	*mezar*	mezur
heaven	*cennet*	jennet

English	Turkish	Pronunciation
hell	*cehennem*	jehennem
holiness	*kudsiyet, . . . t*	ko͡odsiyet
holy	*mukaddes*	mo͡okuddes
Holy Ghost	*Ruhül Kudüs*	ro͡ohe͡wl ko͡ode͡ws
hope	*ümit, umut*	e͡wmit, o͡omo͡ot
hymn book	*ilâhî kitabı*	ila͡ahe͡e kitubi(*r*)
Jesus Christ	*İsa Elmesih*	Isu Elmesih
joy	*sevinç, . . . c*	sevinch
lecture	*mev'ize, hitabe*	mev'ize, hitube
Lord	*Rab*	Rub
love	*sevgi*	sevgi
marriage	*izdivaç, evlenme*	izdivuch, evlenme
matins	*sabah âyini*	subuh a͡ayini
mercy	*merhamet, . . . t*	merhumet
mission	*misiyonerlik*	misiya͡unerlik
missionary	*misiyoner*	misiya͡uner
nave	*minber*	minber
offertory	*sadakat*	sudukut
organ	*org*	a͡urg
peace	*sulh, huzuru kalb*	so͡olh, ho͡ozo͡oro͡o kulb
penance	*riyazât, . . . t*	riyuza͡at
praise	*senâ, öğüş*	sena͡a, e͡ughe͡wsh
to pray	*dua etmek*	do͡ou etmek
prayer	*dua, niyaz*	do͡ou, niyuz
prayer book	*dua kitabı*	do͡ou kitubi(*r*)
to preach	*vaaz etmek*	vuuz etmek
preacher	*vaiz*	vuiz
priest	*papas*	pupus
Protestant	*Protestan*	pra͡utestun
pulpit	*minber*	minber
to repent	*pişman olmak, nedâmet etmek*	pishmun a͡ulmuk, neda͡amet etmek
repentance	*nedâmet*	neda͡amet
Roman Catholic	*Katolik*	kuta͡ulik
sacrament	*âyin*	a͡ayin
sacred	*mukaddes*	mo͡okuddes
salvation	*halâs*	hula͡as
Saviour	*Müncî, Kurtarıcı*	me͡wnjee, ko͡orturi(*r*)ji(*r*)

English	Turkish	Pronunciation
sin, to sin	*günah, günah işlemek*	gewnuh, gewnuh ishlemek
sinful	*günahkâr*	gewnuhkiar
sinner	*suçlu*, or *günahkâr adam*	soochloo, *or* gewnuh-kiar udum
sorrow	*keder*	keder
soul	*ruh*	rooh
to trust	*emniyet etmek*	emniyet etmek
truth	*hakikat*	hukikut
vesper	*gece duaları*	geje dooulurı(*r*)
to worship	*tapınmak, ibâdet etmek*	tupı(*r*)nmuk, ibaa-det etmek

Mohammedan Religious Terms and Festivals

(*Müslüman dînî istilahlar ile bayramlar*)

English	Turkish	Pronunciation
Cakes sold on occasion of religious ceremonies	*kandil çöreği*	kundil cheureghi
caretaker of mosque	*kayyum*	kuyyoom
call to prayer	*ezan*	ezun
caller to prayer	*müezzin*	mewezzin
chaplet of beads	*tesbih*	tesbih
to use chaplet of beads	*tesbih çekmek*	tesbih chekmek
dervish	*derviş*	dervish
dervish house	*tekke*	tekke
niche in mosque where Imam conducts prayers	*mihrap, ...b*	mihrup
leader of prayers	*imam*	imum
intercession	*şefaat*	shefuut
religious school	*medrese*	medrese
fasting, to fast	*oruç, oruç tutmak*	aurooch, aurooch tootmuk
to break fast	*oruç bozmak*	aurooch bauzmuk
minaret	*minâre*	minaare
Mohammedan church (mosque)	*câmi, mescit*	jaami, mesjit
religious order	*tarikat, ...t*	turikut

English	Turkish	Pronunciation
pulpit	*minber*	minber
prayers	*namaz*	numuz
Mohammedan holy book	*kur'an*	ko͡or-un
recital of Kur'an	*telâveti kur'an*	tela͡aveti ko͡or-un
religious degree	*icazet, . . . t*	ijuzet
animal slaughtered for sacrificial purpose	*kurbanlık, . . . ğ*	ko͡orbunli(*r*)k
to slaughter for sacrifice	*kurban kesmek*	ko͡orbun kesmek
teacher of mystic knowledge	*mürşit, . . . d*	me͡wrshit
seeker of mystic knowledge	*mürit, . . . d*	me͡writ
to perform prayers	*namaz kılmak*	numuz ki(*r*)lmuk
to perform ablutions	*apdest almak*	updest ulmuk
turban	*sarık, . . . ğ*	suri(*r*)k
vow	*adak, . . . ğ*	uduk
minaret illumination, on festival occasions	*kandil*	kundil
any night of minaret illumination in commemoration of a religious event	*kandil gecesi*	kundil gejesi
tenth of Muharem	*aşure*	usho͡ore
Anniversary of birth of prophet	*mevludu şerif*	mevlo͡odo͡o sherif
— of night of conception of the Prophet	*ragaip gecesi*	ruguip gejesi
— of Prophet's spiritual night-ascent to Heaven	*miiraç gecesi*	miiruch gejesi
The night of power	*kadir gecesi*	kudir gejesi
The night of promulgation of decrees	*berat gecesi*	berut gejesi

Ships and Shipping
(gemi***ler*** ve gemi***ci lik***)

English	Turkish	Pronunciation
Anchor	*çapa, demir*	chupu, demir
boat (large)	*gemi, vapur*	gemi, vupo͡or
bow	*pruva, baş*	pro͡ovu, bush
cabin	*kamara*	kumuru
cable	*kablo*	kubla͡u
captain	*kaptan*	kuptun
compass	*pusla*	po͡oslu
course	*rota, istikamet i seyir*	ra͡utu, istikumeti seyir
crew	*mürettebat, . . . t*	me͡wrettebut
deck	*güverte*	ge͡wverte
dock	*havuz*	huvo͡oz
flag (Turkish)	*sancak*	sunjuk
harbour, port	*liman*	limun
helm	*dümen*	de͡wmen
keel	*omurga*	a͡umo͡orgu
landing-stage	*iskele*	iskele
lighthouse	*fener*	fener
man-of-war	*harp gemisi*	hurp gemisi
mast	*direk*	direk
merchantman	*ticaret gemisi*	tijuret gemisi
oar	*kürek, . . . ğ*	ke͡wrek
pilot	*kılavuz*	ki(*r*)luvo͡oz
rope	*halat*	hulut
sail	*yelken*	yelken
sailor, seaman	*gemici, denizci, tayfa*	gemiji, denizji, tuyfu
ship	*gemi*	gemi
steersman	*dümenci*	de͡wmenji
stern	*geminin kıç tarafı, kıç*	geminin ki(*r*)ch turufi(*r*), ki(*r*)ch
tug	*römorkör*	re͡umа͡urke͡ur
wharf	*anbar*	unbur

Wireless and Electrical Terms
(Tel**siz** ve elektriğe ait istilâhat)

English	Turkish	Pronunciation
Accumulator	*akümülatör, teressüp ve teraküm kabı*	uke͡wme͡wlute͡ur, teresse͡wp ve teruke͡wm kubi(*r*)
aerial	*anten*	unten
alternating current	*mütenavip cereyan*	me͡wtenuvip jereyun
ampere	*amper*	umper
amplifier	*büyült***ücü**, *amplifikatör, müşeddide*	be͡wye͡wlte͡wje͡w, umplifikute͡ur, me͡wsheddide
atmospherics	*parazit*	puruzit
broadcasting	*radyo neşriyatı* or *difüzion*	rudya͡u neshriyuti(*r*) *or* dife͡wzia͡un
cable	*kablo*	kubla͡u
capacity	*kapasite, saa*	kupusite, su͡u
circuit	*devre*	devre
coil	*bobin, tel kangalı*	ba͡ubin, tel kunguli(r)
condenser	*müksife, biriktirici, kondansatör*	me͡wksife, biriktiriji, ka͡undunsute͡ur
conductor (of electricity)	*nâkil*	na͡akil
coupling	*kuplaj*	ko͡opluj
crystal detector	*sez***ici** *billur, kristal detektör*	seziji billo͡or, kristul detekte͡ur
current	*cereyan*	jereyun
detector	*sez***ici**, *detektör*	seziji, detekte͡ur
direct current	*mütemâdi cereyan*	me͡wtema͡adi jereyun
dynamo	*dinamo*	dinuma͡u
electricity	*elektrik, . . . k*	elektrik
electrode	*elektrot, pil, kömür*	elektra͡ut, pil, ke͡ume͡wr
ether	*eter*	eter
filament	*tel, filaman*	tel, filumun
frame aerial	*çerçeve anten*	chercheve unten
frequency	*frekans*	frekuns

English	Turkish	Pronunciation
generator	*müvellit, ceneratör*	me͡wvellit, jenerute͡ur
high frequency	*yüksek frekans*	ye͡wksek frekuns
high tension battery	*yüksek tevettür pili,* or *bataryası*	ye͡wksek tevette͡wr pili, *or* buturyusi(*r*)
hydrometer	*mikyas ı mayıat, kesafet ölçüsü*	mikyus i(*r*) muyi(*r*)ut, kesufet e͡ulche͡wse͡w
impedance	*empedans, mukavemeti zahiriye*	empeduns, mo͡o-kuvemeti zuhiriye
inductance	*endüktans*	ende͡wktuns
insulation	*tecrit, . . . d*	tejrit
insulator	*mücerrit, . . . d*	me͡wjerrit
interference	*müdahele*	me͡wduhele
jamming	*bozma, sıkışmaklık*	ba͡uzmu, si(*r*)ki(*r*)-shmukli(*r*)k
kilowatt	*kilovat, . . . t*	kila͡uvut
loading coil	*tahmil bobini, tahmil kangalı*	tuhmil ba͡ubini, tuhmil kunguli(*r*)
loose coupling	*gevşek kuplaj*	gevshek ko͡opluj
loud speaker	*hızlı konuşan, ho parlör*	hi(*r*)zli(*r*) ka͡uno͡o-shun, ha͡u purle͡ur
low frequency	*alçak frekans*	ulchuk frekuns
magnet, magnetism	*mıknatıs, mıknatisiyet*	mi(*r*)knuti(*r*)s, mi(*r*)knutisiyet
mast	*direk*	direk
megohm	*megohm*	mega͡uhm
metres	*metrolar*	metra͡ulur
microfarad	*mikrofarat, . . . t*	mikra͡ufurut
microphone	*mikrofon*	mikra͡ufa͡un
milliampere	*miliamper*	miliumper
modulation	*telhin, sesin ta'dili*	telhin, sesin tu-dili
morse code	*morse alfabesi*	ma͡urse ulfubesi
negative	*menfi*	menfi
ohm	*ohm*	a͡uhm
open circuit	*açık devre*	uchi(*r*)k devre
oscillate	*ihtizaz*	ihtizuz
phone (unit)	*fon*	fa͡un
plate	*lavha*	luvhu
plug	*fiş*	fish

English	Turkish	Pronunciation
positive	*müsbet*	mew͡sbet
power	*kuvvet*	ko͡ovvet
primary	*iptidaî*	iptidue͡e
radio	*radyo*	rudya͡u
reaction	*reaksiyon, aksülamel*	reuksiya͡un, uksew͡lumel
receiver	*âhize, alıcı*	a͡ahize, uli(*r*)ji(*r*)
rectifier	*redresör düzeltici*	redrese͡ur dew͡zeltiji
relay station	*mütevassıt istasyon*	mew͡tevussi(*r*)t istusya͡un
rheostat	*reosta*	rea͡ustu
self capacity	*istiabı bizzat*	istiubi(*r*) bizzut
self inductance	*tesiri bizzat*	tesiri bizzut
short circuit	*kısa devre*	ki(*r*)su devre
studio	*studiyo, atöliye*	sto͡odiya͡u, ute͡uliye
telephone	*telefon*	telefa͡un
television	*telsiz görüş, televiziyon*	telsiz ge͡urew͡sh, televiziya͡un
tight coupling	*sabit kuplaj*	subit ko͡opluj
time signal	*saat* or *fasıla işareti*	su͡ut *or* fusi(*r*)lu ishureti
transmission	*difüzyon, transmisiyon*	difew͡zya͡un, trunsmisiya͡un
transmitter	*mürsile*	mew͡rsile
tuning coil	*ayar bobini*	uyur ba͡ubini
unit	*vahit, . . . d*	vuhit
vacuum	*boşluk, halâ*	ba͡ushlo͡ok, hula͡a
variometer	*variometre*	vuria͡umetre
velocity	*sür'at, . . . t*	sew͡r-ut
valves	*lamba*	lumbu
vernier	*vernie ölçüsü, müşire*	vernie e͡ulchew͡sew͡, mew͡shire
volt	*volt, . . . t*	va͡ult
voltmeter	*voltametre*	va͡ultumetre
watt	*vat*	vut
waves	*dalga*	dulgu
wavelength	*dalga uzunluğu*	dulgu o͡ozo͡on-lo͡ogho͡o
wave meter	*dalga ölcüsü*	dulgu e͡uljew͡sew͡

English	Turkish	Pronunciation
wet battery	*yaş pil*	yush pil
wireless set	*telsiz takımı, radyo*	telsiz tuki(*r*)mi(*r*), rudya͡u
wireless telegraph	*telsiz telgraf*	telsiz telgruf
zero	*sıfır*	si(*r*)fi(*r*)

Radio Programme

(Radyo cedveli)

Music	*müzik*	me͡wzik
Symphony	*senfoni*	senfa͡uni
festival	*festival*	festivul
solo	*solo*	sa͡ula͡u
choir	*koro*	ka͡ura͡u
light concert	*hafif konser*	hufif ka͡unser
military band	*askeri bando*	uskere͡e bunda͡u
light music	*hafif musiki*	hufif mo͡osiki
opera, operetta	*opera, operet*	a͡uperu, a͡uperet
recital	*resital*	resitul
instrumental solo	*enstrümantal solo*	enstre͡wmuntul sa͡ula͡u
dance music	*dans musikisi*	duns mo͡osikisi
gypsy orchestra	*çigan orkestrası*	chigun a͡urkestrusi(*r*)
violoncello	*viyolonsel*	viya͡ula͡unsel
chamber music	*oda musikisi*	a͡udu mo͡osikisi
organ recital	*org resitalı*	a͡urg resituli(*r*)
song recital	*şarkı resitalı*	shurki(*r*) resituli(*r*)
soloist	*solist*	sa͡ulist
symphonic concert	*senfonik konser*	senfa͡unik ka͡unser
saxophone	*saksofon*	suksa͡ufa͡un
quartette concert	*kuartet konser*	ko͡ourtet ka͡unser
report (news)	*reportaj*	repa͡urtuj
light airs	*hafif havalar*	hufif huvulur
chamber sextet	*oda seksteti*	a͡udu seksteti

Turkish Holidays

(Tâtil günleri (resmî))

OFFICIAL

English	Turkish	Pronunciation
Festival to mark end of month of fasting—3 days	*Şeker bayramı*	sheker buyrumi(*r*)
Festival of Sacrifice —4 days	*Kurban bayramı*	ko͞orbun buyrumi(*r*)
New Year—1 day	*Yıl başı*	yi(*r*)l bushi(*r*)
anniversary of declaration of Republic, 28th, 29th and 30th Oct.—3 days	*cümhuriyet bayramı*	jew͡mho͞oriyet buyrumi(*r*)
anniversary of battle fought at Afiyon, which secured the Independence, (30th August) —1 day	*tayyare zafer bayramı*	tuyyure zufer buyrumi(*r*)
Childrens' Day, 23rd April	*çocuk bayramı*	chau͡jo͞ok buyrumi(*r*)
National Sovereignty 23rd April	*Hakimiyeti Milliye bayramı* (1920)	hukimiyeti milliye buyrumi(*r*)
1st May	*bahar* or *amele bayramı*	buhur *or* umele buyrumi(*r*)
Anniversary of Ataturk's first landing in Samsun 19th May (1919)	*idman* or *gençlik bayramı*	idmun *or* genchlik buyrumi(*r*)

If the last day of any holiday falls on a Friday the Saturday following is also proclaimed a holiday.

Unofficial Holidays

(Gayri resmî tâtiller)

First *İnönü* victory (1921) 10th January	*birinci İnönü zaferi* (1921)	birinji ineu͡new zuferi (1921)

English	Turkish	Pronunciation
Çanakkale victory 18th March	*Çanakkale zaferi*	chunukkule zuferi
Harvest Home 21st March	*toprak bayramı*	t̮au͡pruk buyru mi(*r*)
Second *İnönü* victory 30th March (1921)	*ikinci İnönü zaferi*	ikinji ineu͡new͡ zuferi
Lamb festival day 6th May	*Hıdırellez*	hi(*r*)di(*r*)rellez
Commemoration of the death of airmen in War of Independence, 15th May	*tayyare şehitleri ihtifali*	tuyyure shehitleri ihtifuli
Commencement of financial year, 1st June	*malî sene iptidası*	malee͞ sene iptidusi(*r*)
First victory of Dumlu Pinar 26th August (1922)	*Dumlu Pınar zaferi başlangıcı*	do͞oml o͞o pi(*r*)nur zuferi bushlungi(*r*)ji(*r*)
Victory of Sakarya 12th September (1921)	*Sakarya zaferi*	sukuryu zuferi
9th September	*İzmirin kurtuluş bayramı*	izmirin ko͞orto͞olo͞osh buyrumi(*r*)
6th October	*İstanbulun kurtuluş bayramı*	istunbo͞olo͞on ko͞orto͞olo͞osh buyrumi(*r*)

Cardinal Numbers

(A'dâtı asliye)

One	*bir*	bir
two	*iki*	iki
three	*üç, ... c*	ew͡ch
four	*dört, ... d*	deu͡rt
five	*beş*	besh
six	*altı*	ulti(*r*)
seven	*yedi*	yedi
eight	*sekiz*	sekiz
nine	*dokuz*	dau͡ko͞oz

English	Turkish	Pronunciation
ten	*on*	a͡un
eleven	*on bir*	a͡un bir
twelve	*on iki*	a͡un iki
thirteen	*on üç*	a͡un e͡wch
fourteen	*on dört*	a͡un de͡urt
fifteen	*on beş*	a͡un besh
sixteen	*on altı*	a͡un ulti(*r*)
seventeen	*on yedi*	a͡un yedi
eighteen	*on sekiz*	a͡un sekiz
nineteen	*on dokuz*	a͡un da͡uko͡oz
twenty	*yirmi*	yirmi
— -one	*yirmi bir*	yirmi bir
— -two	*yirmi iki*	yirmi iki
— -three (etc.)	*yirmi üç*	yirmi e͡wch
thirty	*otuz*	a͡uto͡oz
forty	*kırk*	ki(*r*)rk
fifty	*elli*	elli
sixty	*altmış*	ultmi(*r*)sh
seventy	*yetmiş*	yetmish
eighty	*seksen*	seksen
ninety	*doksan*	da͡uksun
[one][1] hundred	*yüz*	ye͡wz
— thousand	*bin*	bin
— million	*miliyon*	miliya͡un

Ordinal Numbers
(Sıra adet***leri***)

First	***birinci***	birinji
second	***ikinci***	ikinji
third	***üçüncü***	e͡wche͡wnje͡w
fourth	*dörd**üncü***	de͡urde͡wnje͡w
fifth	*beş**inci***	beshinji
sixth	*altı**ncı***	ulti(*r*)nji(*r*)
seventh	*yed**inci***	yedinji
eighth	*sekiz**inci***	sekizinji
ninth	*dokuz**uncu***	da͡uko͡ozo͡onjo͡o
tenth	*on**uncu***	a͡uno͡onjo͡o
eleventh	*on bir**inci***	a͡un birinji
twelfth	*on ik**inci***	a͡un ikinji

English	Turkish	Pronunciation
thirteenth	*on üçüncü*	a͡un e͡wche͡wnje͡w
twentieth	*yirminci*	yirminji
twenty-first	*yirmi birinci*	yirmi birinji
— -second	*yirmi ikinci*	yirmi ikinji
— -third	*yirmi üçüncü*	yirmi e͡wche͡wnje͡w
hundredth	*yüzüncü*	ye͡wze͡wnje͡w
hundred [and] first	*yüz birinci*	ye͡wz birinji
two hundred [and] twentieth	*iki yüz yirminci*	iki ye͡wz yirminji
three hundredth	*üç yüzüncü*	e͡wch ye͡wze͡wnje͡w
thousandth	*bininci*	bininji
thousand [and] first	*bin birinci*	bin birinji
five thousandth	*beş bininci*	besh bininji
five thousand five hundred [and] fifth	*beş bin beş yüz beşinci*	besh bin besh ye͡wz beshinji
millionth	*milionuncu*	milia͡uno͡onjo͡o

[1] The words within brackets are always left out in the Turkish transliteration.

Collective and Distributive Numbers

(Tevzi**i** ve cami**i** a det**ler**)

All	*hep*	hep
a couple	*bir çift, . . . t*	bir chift
double	*iki kat, iki misli*	iki kut, iki misli
a dozen	*bir düzine*	bir de͡wzine
a fifth	*beşte bir*	beshte bir
firstly	*evvela, birinci olarak, ilkönce*	evvelu, birinji a͡uluruk, ilke͡unje
the half	*yarım*	yuri(*r*)m
half a dozen	*yarım düzine*	yuri(*r*)m de͡wzine
the last one	*en son gelen*	en sa͡un gelen
once	*bir kerre*	bir kerre
a pair	*bir çift*	bir chift
a part (portion)	*bir parça (kısım)*	bir purchu (ki(*r*)si(*r*)m)
a quarter, fourth	*bir çeyrek, dörtte bir*	bir cheyrek, de͡urt-te bir

English	Turkish	Pronunciation
secondly	*saniyen, ikinci si*	suniyen, ikinjisi
singly	*tek olarak*	tek a͡uluruk
a third	*üçte bir*	e͡wchte bir
thirdly	*üçüncü olarak*	e͡wche͡wnje͡w a͡uluruk
treble	*üç kerre*	e͡wch kerre
triple	*üç kerre*	e͡wch kerre
twice	*iki kerre*	iki kerre
two-fold	*iki kerre, iki katlı*	iki kerre, iki kutli(*r*)

Adjectives
(Sıfat**lar**

English	Turkish	Pronunciation
Able	*kabiliyetli, becerebilen, becerikli*	kubiliyetli, bejerebilen, bejerikli
active	*faâl, yürük*	fua͡al, ye͡wre͡wk
agreeable	*hoş*	ha͡ush
angry	*dargın*	durgi(*r*)n
anxious	*coşkun, kaygulu*	ja͡ushkoon, kuygo͡olo͡o
awkward	*ters, biçimsiz*	ters, bichimsiz
bad	*fena, bozuk, kötü*	fenu, ba͡uzo͡ok, ke͡ute͡w
barren	*kısır*	ki(*r*)si(*r*)r
beautiful	*güzel*	ge͡wzel
bitter	*acı*	uji(*r*)
blind	*kör*	ke͡ur
blunt (knife)	*kör (bıçak)*	ke͡ur (bichuk)
bold	*gözü pek, alp*	ge͡uze͡w pek, ulp
brave	*cesaretli*	jesuretli
bright	*parlak*	purluk
broad	*geniş*	genish
busy	*işlek*	ishlek
calm	*sâkin*	sa͡akin
careful	*dikkatlı, özenen, abaylı*	dikkutli(*r*), e͡uzenen, ubuyli(*r*)
careless	*kaygusuz, çopar*	kuygo͡oso͡oz, cha͡upu(*r*)
certain, uncertain	*muhakkak, şüpheli*	mo͡ohukkuk, she͡wpheli

English	Turkish	Pronunciation
cheap	*ucuz*	o͡oj o͡oz
cheerful	*güler yüzlü*	ge͡wler ye͡wzle͡w
civil, uncivil	*terbiyeli, kaba*	terbiyeli, kubu
clean	*temiz*	temiz
clear	*berrak*	berruk
clever	*mâhir*	ma͡ahir
clumsy	*hantal, beceriksiz*	huntul, bejereksiz
cold	*soğuk*	sa͡ughho͡ok
cowardly	*korkakça*	ka͡urkukchu
comfortable (room)	*müreffeh*	me͡wreffeh
comfortable (to be)	*rahat, . . . t*	ruhut
common	*âdi*	a͡adi
complete	*tamam*	tumum
incomplete	*bitmemiş, yarım yamalak*	bitmemish, yuri(*r*)m yumuluk
content	*memnun*	memnoon
continual	*sürekli*	se͡wrekli,
cool (weather)	*serin*	serin
correct	*doğru*	da͡ughro͡o
cruel	*zâlim*	za͡alim
curious	*meraklı*	merukli(*r*)
disagreeable	*geçimsiz*	gechimsiz
damp	*rutubetli, cibü*	ro͡oto͡obetli, jibe͡w
dangerous	*tehlikeli*	tehlikeli
dark, gloomy	*karanlık, kasvetli*	kurunli(*r*)k, kusvetli
dead	*ölü*	e͡ule͡w
deceased	*müteveffa, ölü*	me͡wteveffu, e͡ule͡w
deaf	*sağır*	sughi(*r*)r
dear (costly)	*pahalı*	puhuli(*r*)
deep	*derin*	derin
different	*başka*	bushku
dirty	*kirli*, pis	kirli, pis
distinct	*farklı*	furkli(*r*)
dry	*kuru*	ko͡oro͡o
dull	*sönük*	se͡une͡wk
eager	*istekli, hahişger*	istekli, huhishger
early	*erken*	erken
easy	*kolay*	ka͡uluy

English	Turkish	Pronunciation
empty	*boş*	ba͡ush
equal	*muâdil, denk, bekteş*	mo͡oa͡adil, denk, bektesh
every	*her*	her
fair, just	*dürüst, doğru*	de͡wre͡wst, da͡ughro͡o
false	*kalp, sahte*	kulp, suhte
famous	*meşhur*	meshhoor
fashionable	*modaya muvafık*	ma͡uduyu mo͡ovufi(*r*)k
fast (speed)	*sür'atlı, çevik*	se͡wr-utli(*r*), chevik
fat, stout	*şişman*	shishmun
favourable	*müsait, uygun, elverişli*	me͡wsuit, o͡oygo͡on, elverishli
few	*az*	uz
fine, beautiful	*nefis, güzel*	nefis, ge͡wzel
firm	*metin*	metin
fit, unfit	*lâyık, yaramaz*	la͡ayi(*r*)k, yurumuz
flat	*düz*	de͡wz
foolish	*gülünç*	ge͡wle͡wnch
fortunate	*tâlili*	ta͡alili
free	*serbest*	serbest
fresh	*taze*	tuze
frequent	*sık*	si(*r*)k
full	*dolu*	da͡ulo͡o
gay	*şen*	shen
general	*genel*	genel
gentle	*nâzik*	na͡azik
glad	*mahzuz*	muhzo͡oz
good	*iyi*	iyi
grand	*âli*	a͡ali
great	*büyük*	be͡wye͡wk
handsome	*yakışıklı*	yuki(*r*)shi(*r*)kli(*r*)
happy	*mes'ut*	mes-o͡ot
hard	*katı*	kuti(*r*)
heavy	*ağır*	ughi(*r*)r
high	*yüksek*	ye͡wksek
hilly	*yokuşlu*	ya͡uko͡oshlo͡o
hollow	*boş*	ba͡ush
honest	*namuslu*	numo͡oslo͡o

English	Turkish	Pronunciation
hot	*çok sıcak*	cha͡uk si(*r*)juk
ill	*hasta*	hustu
important	*mühim*	me͡whim
incorrect	*yanlış*	yunli(*r*)sh
injurious	*muzır, yaralayıcı*	moozi(*r*)r, yuruluyi(*r*)ji(*r*)
interesting	*alâkalı, enteresan*	ula͡akuli(*r*), enteresun
kind, obliging	*müşfik, lûtufkâr*	me͡wshfik, lûto͡ofki͡ar
lame	*topal*	ta͡upul
late	*geç*	gech
light (weight)	*hafif*	hufif
little	*küçük*	ke͡wche͡wk
long	*uzun*	o͡ozo͡on
loose	*gevşek*	gevshek
loathsome	*iğrenç*	ighrench
loud (voice)	*yüksek*	ye͡wksek
low (position)	*alçak*	ulchuk
many	*bir çok*	bir cha͡uk
mild (weather)	*mülayim*	me͡wluyim
miserable	*bedbaht*	bedbuht
modern	*asrî*	usre͡e
muddy	*çamurlu*	chumo͡orlo͡o
narrow	*dar*	dur
nasty	*kötü*	ke͡ute͡w
necessary	*lâzım*	la͡azi(*r*)m
new (not old)	*yeni*	yeni
nice (to taste)	*güzel*	ge͡wzel
— (delightful)	*enfes*	enfes
noble, ignoble	*kibar, deni*	kibur, deni
numerous	*bir çok*	bir cha͡uk
old	*eski*	eski
open	*açık*	uchi(*r*)k
ordinary, extra-ordinary	*âdi, hârikülâde*	a͡adi, ha͡arı-ke͡wla͡ade
pale	*solgun*	sa͡ulgo͡on
patient, impatient	*sabırlı, sabırsız*	subi(*r*)rli(*r*), subi(*r*)rsi(*r*)z
perfect, imperfect	*mükemmel*	me͡wkemmel

English	Turkish	Pronunciation
plain (clear)	*basit*	busit
— (intelligible)	*vâzıh*	va͡azi(*r*)h
pleasant	*hoş*	ha͡ush
poisonous	*zehirli*	zehirli
polite	*terbiyeli*	terbiyeli
poor	*fakir, fukara*	fukir, fo͡okuru
possible	*mümkün*	me͡wmke͡wn
practical	*pratik*	prutik
present	*mevcut*	mevjo͡ot
pretty	*sevimli*	sevimli
private	*hususî*	ho͡oso͡ose͡e
probable	*muhtemel*	mo͡ohtemel
proud	*mağrur*	mughro͡or
public	*umumî*	o͡omo͡ome͡e
puny	*cılız*	ji(*r*)li(*r*)z
pure	*saf*	suf
queer	*tuhaf*	to͡ohuf
quick, rapid	*çabuk*	chubo͡ok
quiet	*sâkin*	sa͡akin
rare	*nâdir*	na͡adir
raw (uncooked)	*çiğ*	chigh
ready	*hazır*	huzi(*r*)r
real	*hakikî*	hukike͡e
reasonable	*akıllı, söz dinler*	uki(*r*)lli(*r*), se͡uz dinler
regular	*muntazam*	mo͡ontuzum
reliable	*güvenek*	ge͡wvenek
remarkable	*dikkata değer*	dikkuta degher
rich	*zengin*	zengin
right (correct)	*doğru*	da͡ughro͡o
ripe	*olmuş, olgun*	a͡ulmo͡osh, a͡ulgo͡on
rough (in manners)	*kaba*	kubu
— (uneven)	*pürüzlü*	pe͡wre͡wzle͡w
round	*yuvarlak*	yo͡ovurluk
rude	*kaba*	kubu
rural	*köyümsü, kıra mahsus*	ke͡uye͡wmse͡w, ki(*r*)ru muhso͡os
sad	*mağmum, gamlı*	mughmo͡om, gumli(*r*)
safe	*emin, inanılır*	emin, inuni(*r*)li(*r*)r

English	Turkish	Pronunciation
same	*ayni*	uyni
satisfactory	*sevindirici, muvâfık*	sevindiriji, mo͡ova͡afi(*r*)k
secure (safe)	*emin*	emin
serious	*ciddi*	jiddi
severe	*sert, şiddetli*	sert, shiddetli
sharp (instrument)	*keskin*	keskin
short	*kısa*	ki(*r*)su
silent	*sessiz, sâkit*	sessiz, sa͡akit
simple	*sade*	sude
single (one)	*tek*	tek
slight	*nahif, arık*	nuhif, uri(*r*)k
soft (to touch)	*yumuşak*	yo͡omo͡oshuk
solid	*katı*	kuti(*r*)
sound (healthy)	*sağlam*	sughlum
sour	*ekşi*	ekshi
square	*dört köşeli, murabba*	de͡urt ke͡usheli, mo͡orubbu
stormy	*fırtınalı*	fi(*r*)rti(*r*)nuli(*r*)
straight	*doğru, müstakim*	da͡ughro͡o, me͡w-stukim
strange	*tuhaf*	to͡ohuf
strong	*dinç, kuvvetli*	dinch, ko͡ovvetli
stupid	*beyinsiz*	beyinsiz
sufficient	*kâfi, yetesi*	kiafi, yetesi
insufficient	*gayri kâfi*	guyri kiafi
suitable	*yarar*	yurur
sure	*güvenilir, emniyetli*	ge͡wvenilir, emniyetli
sweet	*tatlı*	tutli(*r*)
tall	*uzun*	o͡ozo͡on
tender	*körpe, fıstık gibi*	ke͡urpe, fi(*r*)sti(*r*)k gibi
terrible	*müthiş*	me͡wthish
thick	*kalın*	kuli(*r*)n
thin	*ince*	inje
tight	*dar*	dur
tidy (person)	*kıvrak, intizamı sever*	ki(*r*)vruk, intizu-mi(*r*) sever
tidy (room)	*muntazam, toplu*	mo͡ontuzum, ta͡u-plo͡o

English	Turkish	Pronunciation
tiresome	*muz'iç, yorucu, usandırıcı*	mo͡oz'ich, ya͡uro͡ojo͡o, o͡osundi(*r*)ri(*r*)ji(*r*)
tough (of meat)	*sert*	sert
troublesome	*üzücü, belalı*	e͡wze͡wje͡w, beluli(*r*)
true	*doğru, sahih*	da͡ughro͡o, suhih
ugly	*çirkin*	chirkin
unable	*gayri muktedir eli yetmez*	guyri mo͡oktedir eli yetmez
unsettled (weather)	*belirsiz, kararsız*	belirsiz, kurursi(*r*)z
unsound	*sakat, . . . t*	sukut
uncomfortable	*rahatsız*	ruhutsi(*r*)z
uncommon	*nâdir*	na͡adir
unequal	*ayarsız*	uyursi(*r*)z
unfashionable	*demode, modası geçmiş*	dema͡ude, ma͡udusi(*r*) gechmish
unfortunate	*tâlisiz*	ta͡alisiz
unhappy	*me'yus*	me-yo͡os
unimportant	*ehemmiyetsiz*	ehemmiyetsiz
uninteresting	*cazibesiz*	juzibesiz
unnecessary	*lûzumsuz*	lûzo͡omso͡oz
urgent	*tezelden, müstacel*	tez elden, me͡wstujel
useful	*faydalı*	fuyduli(*r*)
usual	*usûle muvafık*	o͡osûle mo͡ovufi(*r*)k
unusual	*usûlden hariç*	o͡osûlden hurich
valuable	*kıymetli, değerli, abaylı*	ki(*r*)ymetli, degherli, ubuyli(*r*)
invaluable	*paha biçilmez, kıymeti gayri-muayen*	puhu bichilmez, ki(*r*)ymeti guyri-mo͡ouyen
valueless	*değersiz*	deghersiz
various	*müteaddit*	me͡wteuddit
violent	*sert, şiddetli*	sert, shiddetli
visible	*bâriz, zâhir, görünür*	ba͡ariz, za͡ahir, ge͡ure͡wne͡wr
invisible	*görünmez, gizli*	ge͡ure͡wnmez, gizli
warm	*sıcak*	si(*r*)juk

English	Turkish	Pronunciation
weak	*kuvvet**siz**, zaif*	ko͡ovvetsiz, zuif
well	*sıhhat**lı***	si(*r*)hhutli(*r*)
wet	*ısla**k***	i(*r*)sluk
wholesome	*besleyici*	besleyiji
unwholesome	*muzır*	mo͡ozi(*r*)
wicked	*fâsit*	fa͡asit
willing	*arzu**lu***	urzo͡olo͡o
unwilling	*istek**siz***	isteksiz
wise	*düşün**ce li**, ayık*	de͡wshe͡wnjeli, uyi(*r*)k
wonderful	*fevkelâde, şaşırt**an***	fevkela͡ade, shushi(*r*)rtun
wooden	*ahşap, tahta*	uhshup, tuhtu
worthless	*değer**siz***	deghersiz
wretched	*bağrı yanı**k***	bughri(*r*) yuni(*r*)k
wrong	*yanlış*	yunli(*r*)sh
young	*genc*	gench

Verbs

(Fiil***ler***)

English	Turkish	Pronunciation
To accept	*al**mak**, esle**mek**, kabul et**mek***	ulmuk, eslemek, kubo͡ol etmek
— admire	*şaşa kal**mak***	shushu kulmuk
— answer	*cevap ver**mek***	jevup vermek
— approve	*beğen**mek**, doğru bul**mak***	beghenmek, da͡ughro͡o bo͡olmuk
— arrive	*varmak, ulaş**mak**, kavuş**mak***	vurmuk, o͡olush-muk, kuvo͡oshmuk
— ascend	*yukarı çık**mak***	yo͡okuri(*r*) chi(*r*)kmuk
— ask	*sor**mak***	sa͡urmuk
— assure	*te'min et**mek** inan ver**mek***	te-min etmek, inun vermek
— awake	*uyandır**mak***	o͡oyundi(*r*)rmuk
— be	*ol**mak***	a͡ulmuk
— be able	*kabiliyet**inde** ol**mak***	kubiliyetinde a͡ulmuk

English	Turkish	Pronunciation
To be afraid	*korkmak*	ka͡urkmuk
— be angry	*darılmak, dargın olmak*	duri(*r*)lmuk, durgi(*r*)n a͡ulmuk
— be hungry	*acıkmak, aç olmak*	uji(*r*)kmuk, uch a͡ulmuk
— be ignorant of	*haberi olmamak*	huberi a͡ulmumuk
— be injurious	*zararlı olmak, zarar vermek*	zururli(*r*) a͡ulmuk, zurur vermek
— be mistaken	*yanlış düşüncede bulunmak*	yunli(*r*)sh de͡wshe͡wnjede bo͡olo͡onmuk
— be quiet	*tek durmak, yavaşımak*	tek do͡ormuk, yuvushi(*r*)muk
— be thirsty	*susamak*	so͡osumuk
— beat	*dövmek*	de͡uvmek
— begin	*başlamak*	bushlumuk
— believe	*inanmak*	inunmuk
— blame	*suçlu bulmak*	so͡ochlo͡o bo͡olmuk
— boil	*kaynatmak*	kuynutmuk
— borrow	*ödünç almak*	e͡ude͡wnch ulmuk
— breakfast	*kahvr altı etmek*	kuhve ulti(*r*) etmek
— bring	*getirmek*	getirmek
— build	*yapı yapmak*	yupi(*r*) yupmuk
— button	*düğmelemek*	de͡wghmelemek
— unbutton	*düğmeyi çözmek*	de͡wghmeyi che͡uzmek
— bury	*gömmek*	ge͡ummek
— buy	*satın almak*	suti(*r*)n ulmuk
— carry	*taşımak*	tushi(*r*)muk
— chat	*görüşmek*	ge͡ure͡wshmek
— compare	*karşılaştırmak*	kurshi(*r*)lushti(*r*)-muk
— consent	*uzlaşmak, razı olmak*	o͡ozlushmuk, ruzi(*r*) a͡ulmuk
— continue	*devam etmek, uzamak*	devum etmek, o͡ozumuk
— cook	*pişirmek*	pishirmek
— cough	*öksürmek*	e͡ukse͡wrmek

English	Turkish	Pronunciation
To cover	*örtmek*	eurtmek
— come	*gelmek*	gelmek
— dance	*dans etmek*	duns etmek
— decide	*karar vermek*	kurur vermek
— deny	*inkâr etmek*	inkiar etmek
— depart	*hareket etmek*	hureket etmek
— descend	*inmek*	inmek
— desire	*arzu etmek*	urzoo etmek
— dine	*yimek*	yimek
— do, make	*yapmak*	yupmuk
— doubt	*şuphe etmek*	shoophe etmek
— draw, pull	*çekmek*	chekmek
— dream	*rûya görmek*	rûyu geurmek
— dress	*giyinmek*	giyinmek
— drink	*içmek*	ichmek
— dwell, live	*dolaşmak, yaşamak*	daulushmuk yushumuk
— eat	*yimek*	yimek
— exchange	*değiştirmek*	deghishtirmek
— exclaim	*taacüple bağırmak*	tuujewple bughi(r)rmuk
— excuse	*ma'zur görmek*	mu-zoor geurmek
— explain	*anlatmak*	unlutmuk
— fall	*düşmek*	dewshmek
— feel	*hissetmek*	hissetmek
— find	*bulmak*	boolmuk
— finish	*bitirmek*	bitirmek
— follow	*ardı sıra gitmek*	urdi(r) si(r)ru gitmek
— forget	*unutmak*	oonootmuk
— get, obtain	*elde etmek*	elde etmek
— get up	*ayağa kalkmak*	uyughu kulkmuk
— give	*vermek*	vermek
— go	*gitmek*	gitmek
— — in	*içeri girmek*	icheri girmek
— — out	*dışarı çıkmak*	di(r)shuri(r) chi(r)kmuk
— grow	*büyümek*	bewyewmek
— hate	*nefret etmek*	nefret etmek
— have	*mâlik olmak*	maalik aulmuk

English	Turkish	Pronunciation
To hear	*işit***mek**	ishitmek
— hesitate	*tereddüt et***mek**	teredde͡wt etmek
— hide	*sakla***mak**	suklumuk
— hope	*ümil et***mek**	e͡wmit etmek
— imagine	*tahayyül et***mek,** *kuruntu et***mek**	tuhuyye͡wl etmek, ko͡oro͡onto͡o etmek
— hold	*tut***mak**	to͡otmuk
— intend	*fikrinde ol***mak**	fikrinde a͡ulmuk
— introduce	*görüştür***mek**	ge͡ure͡wshte͡wrmek
— jump	*sıçra***mak**	si(*r*)chrumuk
— know	*bil***mek**	bilmek
— laugh	*gül***mek**	ge͡wlmek
— learn	*öğren***mek**	e͡ughrenmek
— lend	*eğreti ver***mek**	eghreti vermek
— lie down	*yat***mak**	yutmuk
— live	*yaşa***mak**	yushumuk
— look	*bak***mak**	bukmuk
— lose	*kaybet***mek**	kuybetmek
— love	*sev***mek**	sevmek
— mend	*tâmir et***mek**	ta͡amiretmek
— marry	*evlen***mek**	evlenmek
— meet	*buluş***mak**	bo͡olo͡oshmuk
— mention	*zikret***mek**	zikretmek
— object	*i'tiraz et***mek,** *engel çıkar***mak**	i-tiruz etmek, engel chi(*r*)kurmuk
— obtain	*elde et***mek**	elde etmek
— offend	*tecavüz et***mek,** *gücendir***mek**	tejuve͡wz etmek, ge͡wjendirmek
— offer	*sun***mak**	so͡onmuk
— open	*aç***mak**	uchmuk
— order, command	*emir et***mek,** or *emret***mek**	emir etmek, *or* emretmek
— pack up	*top***lamak**	ta͡uplumuk
— paint	*boya***mak**	ba͡uyumuk
— pay	*te'diye et***mek**	te-diye etmek
— plant	*dik***mek**	dikmek
— play	*oyna***mak**	a͡uynumuk
— plough	*çift sür***mek**	chift se͡wrmek

English	Turkish	Pronunciation
To pluck	*kopar***mak**	ka͡upurmuk
— praise	*met* or *meth et***mek**	met *or* meth etmek
— present	*bağış***lamak**	bughi(*r*)shlumuk
— prove	*ispat et***mek**	isput etmek
— put	*koy***mak**	ka͡uymuk
— read	*oku***mak**	a͡ukoo͡omuk
— reap	*biç***mek,** *orak***lamak**	bichmek, a͡uruklumuk
— receive	*al***mak,** *kabul et***mek**	ulmuk, kubo͡ol etmek
— reckon	*say***mak**	suymuk
— refuse	*reddet***mek**	reddetmek
— regret	*teesüf et***mek**	teese͡wf etmek
— remember	*hatır***lamak**	huti(*r*)rlumuk
— repay	*öde***mek**	e͡udemek
— repeat	*tekrar***lamak**	tekrurlumuk
— reply	*cevap ver***mek**	jevup vermek
— rest	*rahat et***mek**	ruhut etmek
— return, come back	*dön***mek,** *geri gel***mek**	de͡unmek geri gelmek
— go back	*geri git***mek**	geri gitmek
— give back	*geri ver***mek,** *iade etmek*	gerivermek, iude etmek
— ring (bell)	*çal***mak**	chulmuk
— roast	*furun***da** *kızart***mak**	fo͡oro͡ondu ki(*r*)zurtmuk
— run	*koş***mak**	ka͡ushmuk
— say, tell	*söyle***mek**	se͡uylemek
— search	*ara***mak**	urumuk
— see	*gör***mek**	ge͡urmek
— sell	*sat***mak**	sutmuk
— serve (someone in any capacity)	**birisinin işini** *yap***mak**	birisinin ishini yupmuk
— sew (needlework)	*dik***mek**	dikmek
— seek one's own advantage	**kendi** *çıkarına* **bakmak**	kendi chi(*r*)kuri(*r*)nu bukmuk
— shave	*traş ol***mak**	trush a͡ulmuk
— shine	*parla***mak**	purlumuk
— show	*göster***mek**	ge͡ustermek

English	Turkish	Pronunciation
To sigh	*içini çek**mek***	ichini chekmek
— sign	*imzala**mak***	imzulumuk
— sit down	*otur**mak***	a͡uto͡ormuk
— sleep	*uyu**mak***	o͡oyo͡omuk
— sow	*tohum ek**mek***	ta͡uho͡om ekmek
— speak	*konuş**mak***	ka͡uno͡oshmuk
— spin	*topaç gibi dön**mek***	ta͡upuch gibi de͡unmek
— spoil	*boz**mak***	ba͡uzmuk
— steal	*çal**mak***	chulmuk
— study	*mütâlaa et**mek***	me͡wta͡aluu etmek
— swear	*yemin et**mek***	yemin etmek
— take	*al**mak***	ulmuk
— take off (clothes)	*çıkar**mak***	chi(*r*)kurmuk
— taste	*tat**mak***	tutmuk
— tell (a tale)	*anlat**mak***	unlutmuk
— thank (any one)	*teşekkür et**mek***	teshekke͡wr etmek
— thank (God)	*şükret**mek**, hamd-et**mek***	she͡wkretmek humdetmek
— think	*düşün**mek***	de͡wshe͡wnmek
— throw	*at**mak***	utmuk
— touch	*dokun**mak***	da͡uko͡onmuk
— translate	*tercüme et**mek***	terje͡wme etmek
— travel	*seyahat et**mek***	seyuhut etmek
— unpack	*boşalt**mak***	ba͡ushultmuk
— want	*arzu et**mek*** or *iste**mek***	urzo͡o etmek, istemek
— wash	*yıka**mak***	yi(*r*)kumuk
— weep	*ağla**mak***	ughlumuk
— weigh	*tart**mak***	turtmuk
— wish	*dile**mek***	dilemek
— work	*çalış**mak***	chuli(*r*)shmuk
— wrap up	*sar**mak***	surmuk
— write	*yaz**mak***	yuzmuk

Adverbs, Conjunctions, and Post-Positions

(Zarf**lar**, âtıfa ve cer harf**ları**)

English	Turkish	Pronunciation
About	*takriben*	tukriben
— (concerning)	*dair*	duir
above	*üstünde*	e͡wste͡wnde
— all	*hususen, her şey'in fevkinde*	ho͡oso͡osen, her shey-in fevkinde
according to	*göre*	ge͡ure
across	*arasından*	urusi(*r*)ndun
after, after this	*sonra, bundan sonra*	sa͡unru, bo͡ondun sa͡unru
afterwards	*bilâhara*	bila͡ahuru
again	*gene*	gene
against	*aleyhinde*	uleyhinde
all at once	*hep birden*	hep birden
almost (nearly)	*takriben*	tukriben
alone, solely	*yalnız, yalnız olarak*	yulni(*r*)z, yulni(*r*)z a͡uluruk
already	*akdemce, vaktiyle*	ukdemje, vuktiyle
also, too, besides	*dahi, de, bundan başka*	duhi, de, bo͡ondun bushku
although	*her ne kadar*	her ne kudur
always	*daima*	duimu
amidst	*ortasında*	a͡urtusi(*r*)ndu
among	*arasında*	urusi(*r*)ndu
and	*ve*	ve
anywhere	*her hangi bir yerde*	her hungi bir yerde
as . . . as	[2] . . . *a* or *e kadar*	. . . kudur
as soon as	*hemen, müteakip*	hemen, me͡wteukip
at	*de*	de
— first	*evvel emirde, ilkönce*	evvel emirde, ilke͡unje
— last	*nihayet, en son*	nihuyet, en sa͡un
— least	*en az*	en uz
at once	*birdenbire*	birdenbire
at present	*hâlen, şimdilik*	ha͡alen, shimdilik
badly	*fena bir surette*	fena bir so͡orette
beautifully	*lâtif bir surette*	la͡atif bir so͡orette

[2] Preceding word will be in Dat. case.

English	Turkish	Pronunciation
because	*çünkü*	che͡wnke͡w
before (time)	[1]. . . *dan*(*den*) *evvel*	. . . den evvel
before (state)	*önünde, huzurunda*	e͡une͡wnde, ho͡ozo͡oro͡ondu
behind the house	*evin arkasında*	evin urkusi(*r*)ndu
below	*altında, aşağısında*	ulti(*r*)ndu ushughi(*r*)si(*r*)ndu
besides, beyond	*bundan başka, ötesinde*	bo͡ondun bushku, e͡utesinde
better	*daha iyi*	duhu iyi
between	*arasında*	urusi(*r*)ndu
briefly	*kısaca*	ki(*r*)suju
but	*fakat*	fukut
by	*yanında, yakınında*	yuni(*r*)ndu, yuki(*r*)ni(*r*)ndu
calmly	*sükûnetle*	se͡wkûnetle
close to . . .	[2] . . . *a* or *e yakın*	. . . yuki(*r*)n
consequently	*netice itibariyle*	netije itiburiyle
daily	*her gün, gün begün*	her ge͡wn, ge͡wn bege͡wn
down, downwards	*aşağı, aşağıya doğru*	ushughi(*r*), ushu-ghi(*r*)yu da͡ughro͡o
during (a week)	(*bir hafta*) *esnasında*	(bir huftu) esnusi(*r*)ndu
early, betimes	*erken*	erken
either . . . or	*ya . . . ya*	yu . . . yu
elsewhere	*başka yerde*	bushku yerde
even, as	*hatta, gibi*	huttu, gibi
everywhere	*her yerde*	her yerde
exactly	*doğru olarak, tamamiyle*	da͡ughro͡o a͡uluruk, tumumiyle
exceedingly	*fazlasiyle*	fuzlusiyle
excellently	*pek hoşça*	pek ha͡ushchu
except	[1] . . . *dan* (*den*) *başka*	. . . dun (den) bushku
faithfully	*samimiyetle*	sumimiyetle
far from	[1]. . . *dan* (*den*) *uzak*	. . . dun (den) o͡ozuk
foolishly	*delicesine*	delijesine
for	*için*	ichin

[1] Preceding word will be in Abl. case; [2] in Dat. case.

English	Turkish	Pronunciation
formerly	*evvelce*	eyvelje
from	*dan, den*	dun, den
fully	*etrafiyle*	etrufiyle
further	*daha uzak*	duhu o͡ozuk
gladly, readily	*sevinçle*	sevinchle
hardly	*müşkülatla*	me͡wshke͡wlutlu
henceforth	*şimdiden tezi yok, bu andan i'tibaren*	shimdiden tezi ya͡uk, bo͡o undun i-tiburen
here	*burada*	bo͡orudu
herewith	*bununla beraber*	bo͡ono͡onlu beruber
honestly	*namuskârane*	numo͡oskiarune
honourably	*şerefle*	sherefle
how	*nasıl*	nusi(*r*)l
however	*her ne hal ise*	her ne hul ise
if	*eğer*	egher
immediately	*hemen, derhal*	hemen, derhul
in, within	*içinde, içerisinde*	ichinde, iche-risinde
in future	*istikbâlde*	istikbaalde
indeed	*hakikaten*	hukikuten
inside	*içeride*	icheride
instead of	*yerine*	yerine
kindly	*şefkatla*	shefkutlu
late	*geç*	gech
less	*daha az*	duhu az
like, as	*gibi*	gibi
little	*küçük*	ke͡wche͡wk
more	*daha ziyade*	duhu ziyudu
much	*çok*	cha͡uk
near	*yakın*	yuki(*r*)n
nearly	*az kaldı*	uz kuldi(*r*)
neither this nor that	*ne bu ne o*	ne bo͡o ne a͡u
never	*asla*	uslu
next to	[2] . . . *a* or *e yakın*	. . . yuki(*r*)n
not	*değil*	deghil
not at all	*hiç bir vakıt, asla*	hich bir vuki(*r*)t uslu
not yet known	*daha mâlum değil*	duhu maalo͡om deghil

[2] Preceding word will be in Dat. case.

English	Turkish	Pronunciation
now	*şimdi*	shimdi
nowhere	*hiç bir yer**de***	hich bir yerde
often	*ekseriya*	ekseriyu
on, upon	*üzer**ine**, üst**üne***	e͡wzerine, e͡wste͡wne
on the contrary	*bil'akis*	bil-ukis
on the left of	*sol**unda***	sa͡ulo͡ondu
on the opposite side	*karşı taraf**ta***	kurshi(*r*) turuftu
on the right	*sağ**da***	sughdu
on this side	*butaraf**ta***	bo͡oturuftu
only	*yalnız*	yulni(*r*)z
opposite to	[2] . . . *a* or . . . *e muarız*	. . . mo͡ouri(*r*)z
or	*yahut*	yuho͡ot
otherwise	*başka türlü, aksi takdir**de***	bushku te͡wrle͡w, uksi tukdirde
outside	*dışar**da***	di(*r*)shurdu
over	*üst**üne**, üst**ünde***	e͡wste͡wne, e͡wste͡wnde
perhaps	*belki*	belki
presently, soon	*yakın**da**, çabuk*	yuki(*r*)ndu, chubo͡ok
previously	*evvel**ce***	evvelje
purposely	*kasten*	kusten
quickly	*çabu**cak***	chubo͡ojuk
quite, altogether	*tamami**yle**, büsbütün*	tumumiyle, be͡wsbe͡wte͡wn
quietly	*sükûnet**le***	se͡wkûnetle
rather (preferably)	*tercihen*	terjihen
rather (somewhat)	*bir az*	bir uz
round (a)	*etraf**ında***	etrufi(*r*)ndu
scarcely	*nâdiren, ancak*	na͡adiren, unjuk
seldom	*nâdiren, nâdir olarak*	na͡adiren, na͡adir a͡uluruk
since (adv.)	*zamandanberi, denberi*	zumundunberi, denberi
since (conj.)	*mâdemki*	ma͡ademki
so (in a high degree)	*okadar . . . ki*	a͡ukudur . . . ki
so (on this account)	*şu takdir**de***	sho͡o tukdirde

[2] Preceding word will be in Dat. case.

English	Turkish	Pronunciation
so much, so many	*şu kadar, bu kadar*	sho͡o kudur, bo͡o kudur
somehow	*her hangi bir suret**te***	her hungi bir so͡orette
sometimes	*bâzan*	ba͡azun
soon	*yakın**da***	yuki(*r*)ndu
still	*daha*	duhu
suddenly	*birdenbire, vehleten*	birdenbire, vehleten
that	*ki*	ki
then	*o zaman*	a͡u zumun
thence	*oradan*	a͡urudun
thenceforth	*o zamandanberi*	a͡u zumundunberi
there	*orada*	a͡urudu
therefore	***onun** için*	a͡uno͡on ichin
thoughtfully	*kaygu ile, alâka ile*	kuygo͡o ile, ula͡aku ile
through	*arasından*	urusi(*r*)ndun
thus, so	*böylece*	be͡uylece
till, until	*ıncaya* or *inceye kadar*	i(*r*)njuyu *or* injeye kudur
till now	*şimdiye kadar*	shimdiye kudur
to	***a*** or *e* (Dat. case suffix)	u *or* e
together	*beraber*	beruber
too much	*çok fazla*	cha͡uk fuzlu
towards the house	*eve doğru*	eve da͡ughro͡o
under	*altın**da***	ulti(*r*)nda
undoubtedly	*şüphe**siz***	she͡wphesiz
unless	*tâ ki*	ta͡a ki
up, upwards	*yukarı, yukarı**ya** doğru*	yo͡okuri, yo͡o-kuri(*r*)yu da͡ughro͡o
upon	*üzer**ine**, üzer**inde***	e͡wzerine, e͡wzerinde
very	*pek*	pek
weekly	*her hafta*	her huftu
well	***iyice***	iyije
what	*ne*	ne
when	*ne vakıt*	ne vuki(*r*)t
whence	*nere**den***	nereden

English	Turkish	Pronunciation
where	*nerede*	nerede
whether (if)	*ise* (or . . . *sa*, . . . *se*) (*eğer*)	ise (*or* . . . su̲, . . . se (egher)
while	*esnada*	esnudu
whilst	*müddetince*	mew͡ddetinje
why	*neden*	neden
willingly	*ist(e)yerek* (see T.G. 70*cc*)	isteyerek
with ; without	*ile ; siz*	ile ; siz
within	*içinde*	ichinde
without	*haricinde*	hurijinde
yearly	*senelik*	senelik
yet, still	*daha, hâlâ*	duhu, ha͡ala͡a

Notes.

I have made a special point of giving in the Conversational Phrases which follow, a translation by which the student can make himself properly understood, and at the same time give him a foundation on which to build other similar phrases, which in many cases he would not be able to do if the actual colloquial translation had been given.

As in the early stages the various changing vowel sounds are apt to be confusing, I have not, in many of the following phrases, effected these changes, but have reminded the student of them by quoting numbers, particularly (59*l*) and (70*cc*). For convenience I hereunder summarize them :—

(70*cc*) When the *verb root* ends with the vowels *a* or *e* these latter are changed to *ı* and *i* respectively, when adding certain tense suffixes. The other vowels do not change.

(59*l*) In certain moods of some tenses the *negative* suffix *ma* (*me*) should be replaced by *mı*, *mi* or *mü* according to the vowel in the word to which it is being added. To avoid confusion, however, I have kept to *ma* (*me*).

I have also, in many cases, put the Personal Pronouns in brackets. This is to remind the student that, except for emphasis, they are seldom used, the personal suffix added to the verb being sufficient.

CONVERSATIONAL PHRASES AND SENTENCES

Greetings and Polite Expressions

(Iltifat*lar,* nezaket istilah*ları*)

English	Turkish	Pronunciation
Good morning Mr. — (on meeting, by both parties)	*Bay ... selamüaleyküm : Bay ... gün aydın : Bay ... merhaba*	Buy... selumewuleykewm : Buy... gewn uydi(r)n : Buy merhubu
Good morning, — day, — afternoon, — evening, — night (by departer only)	*Allah**a** ısmarla**dık***	Ulluhu i(r)smurludi(r)k
Reply to any of the preceding sentences	*Allah selâmet ver**sin** ; gül**e** gül**e***	Ulluh selaamet versin : gewle gewle
Good evening (on meeting, by both parties)	*tün aydın ; merhaba*	tewn uydi(r)n : merhubu
Host welcoming guest (any time of day)	*Buyurun, sefa gel**diniz***	Booyooroon, sefu geldiniz
Good night (when retiring for the night)	*Geceniz hayırlı ol**sun***	gejeniz huyi(r)rli(r) aulsoon
How are you ?	*Nasıl**sınız** ?*	nusi(r)lsi(r)ni(r)z ?
Are you quite well ?	*Hakikaten iyi **mi siniz** ?*	hukikuten iyimisiniz ?
Quite well, thank you	*Çok iyi**yim** teşekkür ed**erim***	chauk iyiyim teshekkewr ederim
How is Mr. — ?	*Bay . . . nasıl**dır** ?*	buy...nusi(r)ldi(r)r ?
I am so pleased to meet you	*Sizi**nle** buluştuğum dan çok memnun**um***	sizinle booloosh-tooghoom dun chauk memnoonoom
I hope we shall meet again	*İnşaallah gene görüşürüz*	inshuulluh gene geurewshewrewz

English	Turkish	Pronunciation
I must go now	*Şimdi* (or *artık*), *gitmeliyim*	shimdi (*or* urti(*r*)k), gitmeliyim
I hope to come again	*Tekrar gel-(e)ceğimi ümit ederim*	tekrur gelejeghimi e͡wmit ederim
Will you excuse me ?	*Beni mâzur görür müsünüz ?*	beni ma͡azo͡or ge͡ure͡wrme͡w-se͡wne͡wz ?
I am afraid I cannot stay any longer	*Korkarım ki bundan fazla kalamam*	ka͡urkuri(*r*)m ki bo͡ondun fuzlu kulumum
Thanks	*Teşekkür ederim*	teshekke͡wr ederim
No, sir, (I don't want) thanks	*Hayır, bay, (istemem) teşekkür ederim*	huyi(*r*)r, buy, istemem, teshekke͡wr ederim
If you please	*Lûtfen*	lûtfen
I thank you	*Size teşekkür ederim*	size teshekke͡wr ederim
Much obliged ; many thanks	*Minnetdarım* ; *çok teşekkürler ederim*	minnetduri(*r*)m cha͡uk teshekke͡wr-ler ederim
I am very much obliged to you	*Size pek çok minnetdarım*	size pek cha͡uk minnetduri(*r*)m
Excuse (pardon) me, sir	*Beni mâzur görünüz bayım*	beni ma͡azo͡or ge͡ure͡wne͡wz buyi(*r*)m
I beg your pardon	*Afınızı dilerim*	ufi(*r*)ni(*r*)zi(*r*) dilerim
I am sorry, miss	*Müteesirim, bayan*	me͡wteesirim, buyun
I am so sorry	*Okadar müteesirim ki*, or *fazlasiyle müteesirim*	a͡ukudur me͡wteesir-im ki, *or* fuzlusiyle me͡wteesirim
I am very sorry	*Çok müteesirim*	cha͡uk me͡w-teesirim
It is nothing	*Bir şey değil*	bir shey deghil
There is no harm done	*Bir zararı mucip olmadı*	bir zuruti(*r*) mo͡ojip a͡ulmudi(*r*)

English	Turkish	Pronunciation
I must apologize (I wish to)	*İstifayı kusur etmek isterim*	istifuyi(*r*) ko͡oso͡or etmek isterim
Make my apologies	*Benim için istifayı kusurda bulununuz*	benim ichin istifuyi(*r*) ko͡oso͡ordu bo͡olo͡ono͡ono͡oz
Permit me to apologize	*İstifayı kusur etmekliğime müsaede buyurunuz*	istifuyi(*r*) ko͡oso͡or etmeklighime me͡wsuede bo͡oyo͡oro͡ono͡oz
No apology is needed	*İ'tizara lûzum yoktur*	i-tizuru lûzo͡om ya͡ukto͡or
Do not apologize	*Beyanı i'tizar etmeyiniz*	beyuni(*r*) i-tizur etmeyiniz
It was my fault	*Kabahat benim idi*	kubuhut benim idi
Can I be of any assistance to you?	*Size bir yardımda bulunabilir miyim?*	size bir yurdi(*r*)mdu bo͡olo͡onubilirmiyim?
You are very kind	*Pek müşfiksiniz*	pek me͡wshfiksiniz
Not at all	*Estağfurullah, asla*	estughfo͡oro͡olluh, uslu
May I ask?	*Sorabilir mi yim?*	sa͡urubilirmiyim?
Can you tell me?	*Söyleyebilir mi siniz?*	se͡uyleyebilirmisiniz
Allow me	*Bana müsaede ediniz*	bunu me͡wsuede ediniz
With pleasure	*Memnuniyetle*	memno͡oniyetle
Yes, sir	*Evet, bayım*	evet, bayi(*r*)m
No, madam	*Hayır, bayan*	huyi(*r*)r, buyun
I have not the time	*Vaktım yoktur*	vukti(*r*)m ya͡ukto͡or
Anything particular?	*Şayanı dikkat bir şey var mı?*	shuyuni(*r*) dikkut bir shey vurmi(*r*)?

Useful and Necessary Expressions

(Faydalı ve lûzum*lu* tâbirat)

English	Turkish	Pronunciation
Upstairs	*Yukarı**da***	yo͞okuri(*r*)du
Downstairs	*Aşağı**da***	ushughi(*r*)du
On horseback	***Ata** bin**miş***	utu binmish
Up and down	*Bir aşağı bir yukarı*	bir ushughi(*r*) bir yo͞okuri(*r*)
From top to bottom	*Baştan aşağı**ye** kadar*	bushtun ushu-ghi(*r*)ye kudur
What is the matter ?	*Mesele **nedir,*** or *Ne var ?*	mesele nedir, *or* ne var ?
Nothing	*Hiç bir şey*	hich bir shey
Come here	*Bura**ya** gel**iniz***	bo͞oruyu geliniz
I want to know	***Bilmek** ist(e)**yorum*** (see T.G. 70cc)	bilmek isteya͡u-ro͞om
Do not confuse me	*Ben**i** şaşırt**mayı-nız***	beni shushi(*r*)rt-muyi(*r*)ni(*r*)z
Leave me alone	*Ben**i** yalnız bırak**ınız***	beni yulni(*r*)z.bi(*r*)-ruki(*r*)ni(*r*)z
Do you speak English ?	*İngiliz**ce** konu-şur **mu sunuz** ?*	ingilizje ka͡uno͞o-sho͞or mo͞oso͞ono͞oz?
Do you know English ?	*İngiliz**ce** bilir **mi siniz** ?*	ingilizje bilirmisiniz ?
I do not speak English	*İngiliz**ce** bil**mem** ; İngiliz**ce** bil**m(e)yorum*** (see T.G. 59*l*)	ingilizje bilmem ; ingilizje bilmeya͡uro͞om
Is there anyone here who speaks English ?	*Bura**da** Ingiliz**ce** bil**en** (konuş**an**) var **mıdır** ?*	bo͞orudu Ingilizje bilen (ka͡uno͞oshun) vurmi(*r*)di(*r*)r ?
He is being extravagant	*mîras yedili**ği** tuttu*	me͞erus yedilighi to͞otto͞o
He could not have stayed longer	*kal**a**cağı kadar kaldı* or *kal**mış***	kulujughi(*r*) kudur kuldi(*r*) *or* kulmi(*r*)sh
For a short time only	*Yalnız kısa bir zaman için*	yulni(*r*)z ki(*r*)su bir zumun ichin
Yes ; no	*Evet ; hayır*	evet ; huyi(*r*)r

English	Turkish	Pronunciation
Bring me —	*Bana getiriniz*	bunu getiriniz
I do not understand	*Anlam(a)yorum* (see T.G. 59*l*)	unlumuya͡uro͡om
What do you say ?	*Ne diyor sunuz ?*	ne diya͡urso͡ono͡oz ?
What do you mean by that ?	*Bundan ne kast ediyor sunuz ?*	bo͡ondun ne kust ediya͡urso͡ono͡oz ?
Don't you know ?	*Bilmeyor mu sunuz ?*	bilmeya͡urmo͡oso͡ono͡oz ?
Come here	*Buraya geliniz*	bo͡oruyu geliniz
Sit here	*Buraya oturunuz*	bo͡oruyu a͡uto͡oro͡ono͡oz
I will go and see	*Gidip görürüm ; Gider ve görürüm*	gidip ge͡ure͡wre͡wm ; gider ve ge͡ure͡wre͡wm
I don't quite remember	*Tamamiyle hatırlam(a)yorum* (see T.G. 59*l*)	tumumiyle huti(*r*)lumuya͡uro͡om
All at once	*Hep birden*	hep birden
Sooner or later	*Ergeç ; Şimdicik ve ya bilâhara*	ergech ; shimdijik ve ya bila͡ahuru
You are joking	*Şaka ed(i)yorsunuz*	shuku ediya͡urso͡ono͡oz
How do you know ?	*Nasıl biliyor sunuz ?*	nasi(*r*)l biliya͡urso͡ono͡oz ?
It is of no use	*İşe yaramaz*	ishe yurumuz
What do you believe ?	*Neye inanır sınız ?*	neye inuni(*r*)rsi(*r*)ni(*r*)z ?
Perhaps	*Belki*	belki
They forget the language	*Lisanı unutuyor lar*	lisuni(*r*) o͡ono͡oto͡oya͡urlur
By the way	*Bu meyanda*	bo͡o meyundu
This way	*Bu suretle*	bo͡o so͡oretle
Now and then	*Ara sıra*	uru si(*r*)ru
Till then	*O vakıta kadar*	au vuki(*r*)tu kudur
In the meantime	*Aynı zamanda*	uyni(*r*) zumundu
First of all	*Her şeyden evvel*	her sheyden evvel
With one mind	*Bir düşünce ile*	bir de͡wshe͡wnje ile
Of course ; certainly	*Hâli tabiisiyle ; Şüpesiz*	ha͡al i tubiisiyle ; she͡wpesiz

English	Turkish	Pronunciation
I have not said a word	*Ben bir söz söylemedim*	ben bir se͡uz se͡uylemedim
Since last month	*Geçen aydanberi*	gechen uydunberi
Don't you know ?	*Bilm(e)yor musunuz ?* (see T.G. 59*l*)	bilmeya͡urmo͡oso͡ono͡oz ?
Too soon	*Haddinden fazla erken*	huddinden fuzlu erken
Too late	*Haddinden fazla geç*	huddinden fuzlu gech
Did you ask him ?	*Ondan sordunuz mu ?*	a͡undun sa͡urdo͡ono͡oz mo͡o ?
Shall I tell you ?	*Sana söyleyeyim mi ?*	sunu se͡uyleyeyim mi ?
I cannot stay any longer	*Daha fazla kalamam*	duhu fuzlu kulumum
I can do without it	*Ben onsuz yapabilirim*	ben a͡unso͡oz yupubilirim
I have been told	*Bana söylediler*	bunu se͡uylediler
I have come to tell you	*Sana söylemeğe geldim*	sunu se͡uylemeghe geldim
As much as I can	*Elimden geldiği kadar*	elimden geldighi kudur
He is no longer in any hurry	*O artık acele etmiyor*	a͡u urti(*r*)k ujele etmiya͡ur
What do you mean ?	*Ne demek ist(e)yorsunuz* (see T.G. 70*cc*)	ne demek isteya͡urso͡ono͡oz
How do you know ?	*Neden* or *Nasıl biliyorsunuz*	neden *or* nusi(*r*)l biliya͡urso͡ono͡oz
Where was I ?	*(Ben) nerede idim ?*	(ben) nerede idim ?
It is not my fault	*Benim kabahatım değildir*	benim kubuhuti(*r*)m deghildir
He has just come in	*O şimdicik geldi*	a͡u shimdijik geldi
He has come back	*O avdet etti*	a͡u uvdet etti
(I) cannot see it	*(Ben) onu göremyorum* (see T.G. 59*l*)	ben a͡uno͡o ge͡uremeya͡uro͡om

English	Turkish	Pronunciation
Who is it calls me ?	*Beni çagıran kimdir ?*	beni chugi(*r*)run kimdir ?
Inquire after Mr. Rüştü	*Bay Rüştünün sıhhatı hakkında malûmat edininiz*	buy rewshtewnewn si(*r*)hhuti(*r*) hukki(*r*)ndu mulûmut edininiz
What is it ?	*Nedir ? ne ist(e)yorsunuz ?* (see T.G. 70cc)	nedir ? ne isteyaursoonooz ?
A little	*Azıcık, Bir az*	uzi(*r*)ci(*r*)k, bir uz
Anyhow	*Her ne suretle olursa olsun*	her ne sooretle aulоorsu aulsoon
I do not wish much	*Çok bir şey ist(e)meyorum*	chauk bir shey istemeyauroom
Never mind	*Üzülmeyiniz*	ewzewlmeyiniz
Listen	*Dinleyiniz*	dinleyiniz
We can still begin	*Gene de* or *daha da başlayabiliriz*	gene de *or* duhu du bushluyubiliriz
Why do you want it ? (that)	*Neden onu ist(e)yorsunuz ?*	neden aunoo isteyaursoonooz ?
Where is it ?	*Nerededir ?*	nerededir ?
What are you going to do ?	*Ne yapacaksınız ?*	ne yupujuksi(*r*)ni(*r*)z
I would like	*İsterim*	isterim
I don't know	*Bilm(e)yorum* (see T.G. 59*l*)	bilmeyauroom
I can't find it	*Onu bulamayorum*	aunoo boolumuyauroom
I shall look for it	*(Ben) onu arayacağım*	(ben) aunoo uruyujughi(*r*)m
I cannot see here	*Burada görem(e)yorum* (see T.G. 59*l*)	boorudu geuremeyauroom
At the end of this year	*Bu senenin nihayetinde*	boo senenin nihuyetinde
You came to-day	*(Siz) bu gün geldiniz*	siz boo gewn geldiniz
Did you know ?	*Biliyor mu idiniz ?*	biliyaurmoo idiniz ?

English	Turkish	Pronunciation
I cannot	*Yapamam*	yupumum
I knew it	*(Onu) bil(i)yor idim* (see T.G. 70ccc)	(a͡unǒo͡) biliya͡ur idim
You will be left alone	*(Siz) yalnız bırakılacaksınız*, or *kalacaksınız*	siz yulni(*r*)z bi(*r*)ruki(*r*)lujuksi(*r*)ni(*r*)z, *or* kulujuksi(*r*)ni(*r*)z
We will leave you alone	*Sizi yalnız bırakacağız*	sizi yulni(*r*)z bi(*r*)rukujughi(*r*)z
I will not take them	*(Ben) onları alm(a)yacağım* (see T.G. 50*l*)	ben a͡unluri(*r*) ulmuyujughi(*r*)m
When I saw you the last time	*Sizi geçen* (or *son*) *defa gördüğümde*	sizi gechen (*or* sa͡un) defu ge͡urde͡wghe͡wmde
Have you seen my wife ?	*Zevcemi gördünüz mü ?*	zevjemi ge͡urde͡wne͡wz me͡w ?
Come here	*Buraya geliniz*	bo͡oruyu geliniz
That remains to be seen	*O zuhurata bakar ;* or *Bakalım ;* or *Bu elde edilecek neticeye bakar*	a͡u zo͡oho͡orutu bukur, *or* bukuli(*r*)m, *or* bo͡o elde edilejek netijeye bukur
Say nothing	*Hiç bir şey söylemeyiniz*	hich bir shey se͡uylemeyiniz
I beg your pardon	*Affınızı istirham ederim*	uffi(*r*)ni(*r*)zi(*r*) istirhum ederim
Speak louder	*Daha yüksek sesle konuşunuz*	duhu ye͡wksek sesle ka͡uno͡osho͡ono͡oz
What is to be done ?	*Ne yapılacaktır ?*	ne yupi(*r*)lujukti(*r*)r ?
That depends on events	*O ahvale mutevakkıfdır*, or *Vukuata bakar*	a͡u uhvule me͡wtevukki(*r*)fdi(*r*)r, *or* vo͡oko͡outu bukur
We shall see	*Bakalım*	bukuli(*r*)m
Consequently	*Binnetice*	binnetije
After all	*Nihayetülemir*	nihuyete͡wlemir
Afterwards	*Bilahara*	biluhuru

English	Turkish	Pronunciation
As much again	*Iki katlı ol**arak***	iki kutli(*r*) a͡uluruk
At once	*Hemen*	hemen
For once	*Bir def**aya** mahsus ol**arak***	bir defuyu muhso͡os a͡uluruk
Everyone	*Herkes*	herkes
The other day	*Geç**en** gün*	gechen ge͡wn
Every other day	*Her iki gün**de** bir*	her iki ge͡wnde bir
Elsewhere	*Başka bir yer**de***	bushku bir yerde
Otherwise	*Aksi takdir**de***	uksi tukdirde
Between ourselves	*Ara**mızda***	urumi(*r*)zdu
Ever since	*O zaman**dan beri***	a͡u zumundunberi
You have a good accent	*Güzel bir aksanı**nız** var*	ge͡wzel bir uksuni(*r*)ni(*r*)z vur
Thanks	*Teşekkür ed**erim***	teshekke͡wr ederim
I thank you	*Si**ze** teşekkür ed**erim***	size teshekke͡wr ederim
Let us go in	*İçer**iye** gir**elim***	icheriye girelim

Expressions of Emotion
(Teheyyüç *or* Heyecan ifade**leri**)

English	Turkish	Pronunciation
What !	*Ne!*	ne !
Is it possible?	*Mümkün **müdür**?*	me͡wmke͡wn me͡wde͡wr ?
Indeed	*Sahih **mi**?, sahi mi?*	suhihmi ?, suhimi ?
That is impossible	*O gayri mümkün**dür**,* or *Olamaz*	a͡u guyri me͡wmke͡wnde͡wr, *or* a͡ulumuz
That cannot be my fault	*O ben**im** kabahat**ım** ol**amaz***	a͡u benim kubuhuti(*r*)m a͡ulumuz
Oh, it's nothing	*Bir şey değil**dir***	bir shey deghildir
I am sorry for it	***Bundan** çok müteessir**im***	bo͡ondun cha͡uk me͡wteessirim
What a pity !	*Ne kadar yazık!*	ne kudur yuzi(*r*)k !
It is a sad thing	*Acıklı bir hadise**dir***	uji(*r*)kli(*r*) bir hudisedir

English	Turkish	Pronunciation
It gives me much pleasure	*Bana çok zevk veri***yor,** or *Beni çok sevindiri***yor,** or *Çok hoşuma gid***iyor**	bunu cha͡uk zevk veriya͡ur, *or* beni cha͡uk sevindiriya͡ur, *or* cha͡uk ha͡usho͡omu gidiyor
I am very glad	*Çok mesrur***um**	cha͡uk mesro͡oro͡om
What a shame !	*Ne kadar ayıp !*	ne kudur uyi(*r*)p !
How could you do so ?	*Bu işi yapmanıza şaştım ?*	Bo͡o ishi yupmuni(*r*)-zu shushti(*r*)m ?
You are very much to blame	***Bundan** size pek çok muahaza terettüp ed***er**	bo͡ondun size pek cha͡uk mo͡ouhuzu terette͡wp eder
I am ashamed of you	*Sizin yap***tığınızdan** *ben utan(ı-)* **yorum** (see T.G. 70ccc)	sizin yupti(*r*)ghi(*r*)-ni(*r*)zdun ben o͡otuni(*r*)ya͡uro͡om
For shame !	*Utan***ınız!**	o͡otuni(*r*)ni(*r*)z !
Do not be angry	*Darıl***mayınız**	duri(*r*)lmuyi(*r*)-ni(*r*)z
I am quite vexed about it	*Buna çok şaş***tım**	bo͡onu cha͡uk shush-ti(*r*)m
How vexing !	*İnsanın ne kadar canını sıkıyor,* or *Ne kadar müziç bir şey*	insuni(*r*)n ne kudur juni(*r*)ni(*r*) si(*r*)-ki(*r*)ya͡ur, *or* ne kudur me͡wzich bir shey
How beautiful !	*Ne kadar güzel !*	ne kudur ge͡wzel !
Help !	*Aman ! imdat !*	umun ! imdut !

Making Inquiries
(Tahkikat*ta* bulun*ma*)

English	Turkish	Pronunciation
Where can I buy an English news-paper ?	*İngiliz***ce** *bir gazete nere***den** *alabili***rim**	ingilizje bir gazete nereden ulubi-lirim
Will you kindly tell me — ?	*Lûtfen* **bana** *söyler* **mi siniz** *?*	lûtfen bunu se͡uy-lermisiniz ?
Do you understand me ?	*Beni anla***yor musunuz** *?*	beni unluya͡ur mo͡oso͡ono͡oz ?

English	Turkish	Pronunciation
Do you hear me ?	*Beni işid(i)**yor musunuz**!*	beni ishidiya͡ur mo͡oso͡ono͡oz
Are you sure ?	*Emin **misiniz** ?*	emin misiniz ?
What is that ?	*O **nedir** ?*	a͡u nedir ?
What do you mean ?	*Ne demek ist(e)**yorsunuz** ?*	ne demek isteya͡urso͡ono͡oz ?
Can I speak to Mr. Saffet ?	*Bay Saffet**le** görüşebili**r miyim** ?* (see T.G. 70cc)	buy suffetle geu͡rew͡shebilir miyim ?
When does he return ?	*Ne vakıt avdet ede**r** ?*	ne vuki(*r*)t uvdet eder ?
What do you say to this ?	***Buna** ne der**siniz** ?*	bo͡onu ne dersiniz ?
What is that for ?	*O ne için**dir** ?*	a͡u ne ichindir ?
What does that mean ?	*O ne demek**tir** ?, mâna**sı** nedir ?*	a͡u ne demektir ?, ma͡anusi(*r*) nedir ?
Who is there ?	*Ora**da** kim var ?; **Kimdir** o ?*	a͡urudu kim vur ?; kimdir a͡u ?
Who is that ?	***Kimdir** o ?*	kimdir a͡u ?
Is that Mr. Ali ?	*Bay Ali **midir** ?*	buy uli midir ?
Which is the way ?	*Hangi yoldan gidilir* or *Tâkip edil**ecek** yol hangi**sidir** ?*	hungi ya͡uldun gidilir *or* ta͡akip edilejek ya͡ul hungisidir ?
How can I get to— ?	*. . . a* or *e nasıl gide**bilirim** ?*	. . . u *or* e nasi(*r*)l gidebilirim ?
Is there a conveyance ?	*Vasıt**ai** nakliye var **mıdır** ?*	vusi(*r*)tui nukliye vur mi(*r*)di(*r*)r ?
Where is — ?	*. . . nere**dedir** ?*	. . . nerededir ?

The Customs

(Gümrük)

Come to the custom-house	*Gümrüğ**e** gel**iniz***	gew͡mrew͡ghe geliniz
The custom-house officer	*Gümrük me'muru*	gew͡mrew͡k memo͡oro͡o

English	Turkish	Pronunciation
Have you your passport ?	*Pasaport**unuz** var **mıdır** ?*; *Pasaport**unuz** üzer**iniz de** **midir** ?*	pusupa͡urto͡ono͡oz vur mi(*r*)di(*r*) ? ; pusupa͡urto͡ono͡oz e͡wzerinizde midir ?
Open your bag	*Çanta**nızı** aç**ınız***	chuntuni(*r*)zi(*r*) uchi(*r*)ni(*r*)z
Unlock your box	*Sandığ**ınızın** kili**dini** aç**ınız***	sundi(*r*)ghi(*r*)ni(*r*)zi(*r*)n kilidini uchi(*r*)ni(*r*)z
Will you examine this trunk ?	*Bu bavul**u** muayene eder **misiniz** ?*	bo͡o buvo͡olo͡o mo͡ouyene eder misiniz ?
Here are the keys	*Anahtarlar bura**dadır***	unuhturlur bo͡orududi(*r*)r
Have you anything to declare ?	*Gümrük resmi**ne** tâbi bir şey**iniz** var **mı** ?* or *Ithali memnu eşyanız var **mı** ?*	ge͡wmre͡wk resmine ta͡abi bir sheyiniz vur mi(*r*) ? *or* ithuli memno͡o eshyuni(*r*)z vur mi(*r*) ?
Not that I know of	*Zannetmiyorum*, or *Bil**diğime** göre yok**tur***	zunnetmiya͡uro͡om, *or* bildighime ge͡ure ya͡ukto͡or
No, nothing but wearing apparel	*Hayır, giyi**lecek** eşya**dan** başka hiç bir şey yok**tur***	huyi(*r*)r, giyilejek eshyudun bushku hich bir shey ya͡ukto͡or
Have you any tobacco or cigars ?	*Tütün**ünüz** ve ya puro**nuz** var **mı** ?*	te͡wte͡wne͡wne͡wz ve yu po͡ora͡uno͡oz vur mi(*r*) ?
I have a few cigars	*Bir kaç puro**m** var*	bir kuch po͡ora͡um vur
Is that all ?	*Hepsi bu kadar **mı** ?*	hepsi bo͡o kudur mi(*r*) ?
Those are free	***Onlar** serbest**tir*** ; *Şun**lar** gümrükten muaf**tır***	a͡unlur serbesttir ; sho͡onlur ge͡wmre͡wkten mo͡oufti(*r*)r

English	Turkish	Pronunciation
What is the duty? *or* How much is the duty?	*Gümrük resmi **nedir**?* or *Gümrük resmi ne kadar**dır**?*	ge͡wmre͡wk resmi nedir? *or* Ge͡wmre͡wk resmi ne kudurdi(*r*)r
Is my luggage passed?	*Eşya**m** serbest **mi-dir**?*	eshyum serbest mi-dir?

Railway

(Demir yol**u**)

English	Turkish	Pronunciation
To the station	*İstasyon**a***	istusya͡unu
Here is my luggage	*Eşya**m** bura**dadır***	eshyum bo͡orududi(*r*)r
I wish to register my luggage (during the journey)	*Eşya**mı** furgon**a** vermek ist(e)**yorum*** (see T.G. 70cc)	eshyumi(*r*) fo͡orga͡unu vermek isteya͡uro͡om
Take it to the cloakroom	*Emanet oda**sına** götür**ünüz***	emunet a͡udusi(*r*)nu ge͡ute͡wre͡wne͡wz
Go and get my luggage	*Gidi**p** eşya**mı** getir**iniz**;* or *Gid**iniz**, eşya**mı** getir**iniz***	gidip eshyumi(*r*) getiriniz; *or* gidiniz, eshyumi(*r*) getiriniz
Have you the ticket?	*Bilet siz**de mi-dir**?*	bilet sizdemidir?
Yes, here it is	*Evet bura**dadır***	evet bo͡orududi(*r*)r
What luggage have you?	*Ne eşya**nız** var**dır**?*	ne eshyuni(*r*)z vurdi(*r*)r?
The luggage is over-weight	*Eşya**nın** ağırlı**ğı** nizamı**ndan** (or muayyen sıklet**ten**) fazla**dır***	eshyuni(*r*)n ughi(*r*)rli(*r*)ghi(*r*) nizumi(*r*)ndun (*or* mo͡ouyyen si(*r*)kletten) fuzludi(*r*)r
Where is the railway station?	*Şimendifer istasyon**u** nere**de dir**?*	shimendifer istusya͡uno͡o neredeedir?
Where is the booking office?	*Bilet mahall**i** nere**dedir**?*	bilet muhulli neredeedir?

English	Turkish	Pronunciation
Where is the ladies' waiting-room	*Bayan**lara** mahsus bekle**me** salon**u** nere**de dir** ?*	buyunluru muhsōōs bekleme sulâūnōō neredsdir ?
Where is the inquiry room ?	*İstihbarat oda**sı** nere**de dir** ?*	istihburut âūdusi(*r*) nerededir ?
Where is the train for Izmir	*İzmir'**e** gide**cek** tren nere**de dir** ?*	izmire gidejek tren nerededir ?
Where is the refreshment-room ?	*Büfe nere**de dir** ?*	bewfe nerededir ?
Where is the lavatory ?	*Aptestane nere**de dir** ?*	uptestune nerededir ?
Are you going by the express ?	*Ekspres**le** **mi** gide**cek siniz** ?*	ekspresle mi gidejeksiniz ?
Show me a time-table	*Ban**a** bir seyrüsefer cedvel**i ni** göster**iniz***	bunu bir seyrewsefer jedvelini geūsteriniz
When does the train start ?	*Tren ne vakıt hareket ed**iyor** ?*	tren ne vuki(*r*)t hureket ediyâūr
Can I book through to Ankara	*Ankara'**ya** kadar doğru bilet al**abilir miyim** ?*	unkuruyu kudur dâūghrōō bilet ulubilirmiyim ?
Do I change on the journey ?	*Esnay seyahat**ta** aktarma **ede cek miyim** ?*	esnuy seyuhuttu ukturmu edejek miyim ?
I want a first-class ticket to Ankara	*Ankara'**ya** kadar **birinci** sınıf bir bilet ist(e)**yorum*** (see T.G. 70cc)	unkuruyu kudur birinji si(*r*)ni(*r*)f bir bilet isteyâūrōōm
Second-class return	*Bir tane İk**inci** mevki gidip gelme*	bir tune ikinji mevki gidip gelme
Two third-class singles	*Üç tane üçün**cü** git**me***	ewch tune ewchewnjew gitme
What is the fare to Ankara	*Ankara'**ya** kadar bilet fiyatı **nedir** ?*	unkuruyu kudur bilet fiyuti(*r*) nedir ?
What class, sir ?	*Kaç**ıncı** mevki bay**ım** ?*	kuchi(*r*)nji(*r*) mevki buyi(*r*)m ?

English	Turkish	Pronunciation
For how long is it valid ?	*Bu ne zamana kadar mu'teberdir ?*	bo͡o ne zumunu kudur mo͡o'teberdir ?
We want sleeping places	*Biletleri yataklı olarak ist(e)yoruz* (see T.G. 70cc)	biletleri yutukli(*r*) a͡uluruk isteya͡uro͡oz
We want (let it be) a corridor carriage	*Koridorlu bir araba olsun*	ka͡urida͡urlo͡o bir urubu a͡ulso͡on
We want (let it be) a carriage for 6 persons (train)	*Altı kişilik bir kompartiman olsun*	ulti(*r*) kishilik bir ka͡umpurtimun a͡ulso͡on
We want (let it be) a smoking compartment	*Sigara içenlere mahsus bir kompartıman olsun* (see T.G. 70cc)	siguru ichenlere muhso͡os bir ka͡umpurti(*r*)mun a͡ulso͡on
We want platform tickets	*Peron biletleri almak ist(e)yoruz* (see T.G. 70cc)	pera͡un biletleri ulmuk isteya͡uro͡oz
The communication cord	*İmdat kordonu,* or *İmdat işareti*	imdut ka͡urda͡uno͡o *or* imdut ishureti
The dining car	*Vagon restoran,* or *Lokantalı vagon*	vuga͡un resta͡urun, *or* la͡ukuntuli(*r*) vuga͡un
Is this the train for Istanbul ?	*İstanbul'a giden tren bu mudur ?*	istunbo͡olu giden tren bo͡omo͡odo͡or ?
You will travel via Adana	*Adana tarikiyle seyahat edeceksiniz*	udunu turikiyle seyuhut edejeksiniz
Is this seat engaged ?	*Bu yerin sahibi var mıdır ?*	bo͡o yerin suhibi vur mi(*r*)di(*r*)r ?
There is no room	*Yer yoktur*	yer ya͡ukto͡or
Call the guard, *or* Where is the guard	*Şeftreni çağırınız,* or *Şeftren nerede ?*	sheftreni chughi(*r*)ri(*r*)ni(*r*)z, *or* sheftren nerede
The train is just going to start	*Tren hemen hareket etmek üzeredir*	tren hemen hureket etmek e͡wzeredir

English	Turkish	Pronunciation
Open the window	*Pençereyi açınız*	penchereyi uchi(*r*)-ni(*r*)z
Close the door	*Kapıyı kapayınız*	kupi(*r*)yi(*r*) kupu-yi(*r*)ni(*r*)z
Here is a station	*Şurada bir istasyon vardır*	sho͡orudu bir istus-ya͡un vurdi(*r*)r
Do we get out here ?	*Burada in(i)yor muyuz ?;* (see T.G. 70ccc)	bo͡orudu iniya͡ur mo͡oyo͡oz ? ;
	Burada inecek miyiz ?	bo͡orudu inejek miyiz ?
How long do we stop here ?	*Burada ne kadar duruyoruz ?*	bo͡orudu ne kudur do͡oro͡oya͡uro͡oz ?
Do we change carriages here ?	*Burada katar değiştir(i)yor muyuz ?* (see T.G. 70ccc)	bo͡orudu kutur deghishtiriya͡ur mo͡oyo͡oz ?
How long do we stop here ?	*Burada ne kadar duracağız*	bo͡orudu ne kudur do͡orujughi(*r*)z ?
Five minutes	*Beş dakika*	besh dukiku
All change	*Her kes inmelidir*	her kes inmelidir
Change for Izmir	*İzmir için aktarma*	izmir ichin ukturmu
Show your tickets	*Biletlerinizi gösteriniz*	biletlerinizi ge͡usteriniz
Tickets, please	*Biletleri lûtfen*	biletleri lûtfen
Give up your ticket	*Biletinizi teslim ediniz*, or *veriniz*	biletinizi teslim ediniz, *or* veriniz
When is the next train ?	*Bundan sonraki tren ne vakıttır ?*	bo͡ondun sa͡unruki tren ne vuki(*r*)t-ti(*r*)r ?
My luggage is lost	*Eşyam zayı olmuştur*	eshyum zuyi(*r*) a͡ul-mo͡oshto͡or
I shall claim for it	*Zarar ve ziyan talep edeceğim*	zurur ve ziyun tulep edejeghim
I left it on the train	*Şimendiferde bıraktım*	shimendiferde bi(*r*)rukti(*r*)m
What train did you travel by ?	*Hangi tren ile seyahat ettiniz ?*	hungi tren ile seyu-hut ettiniz
I have missed my train	*Trenimi kaçırdım*	trenimi kuchi(*r*)r-di(*r*)m

Air Travel

(Hava seyahatı)

English	Turkish	Pronunciation
I wish to travel by aeroplane	*Tayyare ile seyahat* ***etmek*** *ist(e)****yorum*** (see T.G. 70cc)	tuyyure ile seyuhut etmek isteyaûroõm
How could I go to the aerodrome?	*Tayyare istasiyon****una*** *nasıl gidebil****irim****?*	tuyyure istusiyaûnoõnu nusi(r)l gidebilirim?
What time does the plane start?	*Tayyare ne vakıt hareket ed****er****?*	tuyyure ne vuki(r)t hureket eder?
Where can I obtain my ticket?	*Bilet****imi*** ***nereden*** *tedarik ed****ebilirim****?*	biletimi nereden tedurik edebilirim?
Are we subject to custom examination?	*Gümrük muayene****sine*** *tâbi* ***miyiz****?*	geŵmreŵk moõuyenesine taâbimiyiz?
What luggage can we take with us?	*Yanı****mızda*** *ne gibi eşya götür****ebiliriz***	yuni(r)mi(r)zdu ne gibi eshyu geûteŵrebiliriz

Taxi, Bus, and Tram

(Otomobil, otobüs ve tramvay)

English	Turkish	Pronunciation
Call a taxi	*Bir otomobil çağır****ınız***	bir autaumaubil chughi(r)ri(r)ni(r)z
Closed; open	*Kapalı*; *açık*	kupuli(r); uchi(r)k
Put my luggage in the cab	*Eşya****mı*** *araba****ya*** *koy****unuz***	eshyumi(r) urubuyu kaûyoõnoõz
Drive me to ——	... *a* or ... *e götürü****nüz***	... u *or* ... e geûteŵreŵneŵz
What is the fare, driver?	*Arabacı, ücret****in*** ***nedir****?* or *ne kadar?*	urubuji(r), eŵjretin nedir? *or* ne kudur?
Show me your charges	*Bana tarife****nizi*** *göster****iniz***	bunu turifenizi geûsteriniz
Drive quickly	*Çabuk*, or *Süratlı gid****iniz***	chuboõk, *or* seŵrutli(r) gidiniz
Drive slower	*Daha yavaş gid****iniz***	duhu yuvush gidiniz

English	Turkish	Pronunciation
Stop ! Go on !	*Durunuz ! Yolunuza devam ediniz*	d͡oor͡oon͡ooz ! ya͡ul͡oon͡oozu devum ediniz
Wait !	*Bekleyiniz*	bekleyiniz

The Omnibus Station

(Otobüs durağı, otobüs bekleme yeri)

English	Turkish	Pronunciation
Is there a bus or tram to Eyup ?	*Eyub'a otobüs ve ya tramvay gidiyor mu ?*	ey͡oobu a͡uta͡ube͡ws ve yu trumvuy gidiya͡ur mu ?
Where does it start from ?	*Nereden hareket ediyor ?*	nereden hureket ediya͡ur ?
Where can I get a motor bus to Bebek ?	*Bebeğ'e gitmek için nerede bir otobüs bulabilirim ?*	bebeghe gitmek ichin nerede bir a͡uta͡ube͡ws b͡oolubilirim
Does this car go to Galata ?	*Bu araba Galata'ya gider mi ?*	B͡oo urubu gulutuyu gidermi ?
No, the next one	*Hayır, gelecek araba gider*	huyi(*r*)r, gelejek urubu gider
We will take a bus	*Otobüs ile gideriz*	a͡uta͡ube͡ws ile gideriz
Do you pass Taksim ?	*Taksim'den geçiyor musunuz ?*	tuksimden gechiya͡ur m͡oos͡oon͡ooz ?
Give me a ticket	*Bana bir bilet veriniz*	bunu bir bilet veriniz
Cars stop here	*Arabalar burada durur*	urubulur b͡oorudu d͡oor͡oor
Conductor	*Biletçi*	biletchi
Driver	*Şoför*	sha͡ufe͡ur
Full ; full inside, outside only	*Dolmuştur ; içerisi dolmuştur, yalnız dışarıya binilir*	da͡ulm͡oosht͡oor ; icherisi da͡ulm͡oosht͡oor, yulni(*r*)z di(*r*)shuri(*r*)yubinilir
I wish to get out	*İnmek ist(e)yorum*	inmek isteya͡ur͡oom
Wait until the car stops	*Araba duruncaya kadar bekleyiniz*	urubu d͡oor͡oonjuyu kudur bekleyiniz

English	Turkish	Pronunciation
Please change my ticket	*Lûtfen biletimi değiştiriniz*	lûtfen biletimi deghishtiriniz
Do not alight until the car has stopped	*Araba durmadıkça inmeyiniz*	urubu do͡ormu-di(*r*)kchu inmeyiniz

Hotel and Rooms (Otel ve oda**lar**)

(Direct request should be preceded by "lûtfen" = please)

English	Turkish	Pronunciation
Is there a good hotel here ?	*Buralarda iyi bir otel var mıdır ?*	bo͡orulurdu iyi bir a͡utel vur mi(*r*)-di(*r*)r ?
Which is the best hotel ?	*En iyi otel hangisidir ?*	en iyi a͡utel hun-gisidir ?
May I see your rooms ?	*Odalarınızı görebilir miyim ?*	a͡uduluri(*r*)ni(*r*)zi(*r*) ge͡urebilir miyim ?
I want a bedroom and sitting-room	*Bir yatak odası ve bir oturma odası ist(e)yorum* (see T.G. 70*cc*)	bir yutuk a͡udusi(*r*) ve bir a͡uto͡ormu a͡udusi(*r*) isteya͡ur-o͡om
Let me see the rooms	*Odaları bana gösteriniz*	a͡uduluri(*r*) bunu ge͡usteriniz
What is the charge for this room ?	*Bu odanın kirası nedir ?*	bo͡o a͡uduni(*r*)n kirusı(*r*) nedir ?
Does that include everything ?	*Buna her şey dahil midir ?*	bo͡onu her shey duhilmidir ?
That is too dear	*Bu pek pahalıdır*	bupekpuhuli(*r*)di(*r*)r
I want a cheaper room	*Daha ucuz bir oda isterim* (or *ist(e)-yorum*) (see T.G. 70*cc*)	duhu o͡ojo͡oz bir a͡udu isterim (*or* isteya͡uro͡om)
A double-bedded room	*İki kişilik bir oda*	iki kishilik bir a͡udu
Can you recommend me a boarding-house ?	*Bana bir pansiyon tavsiye edebilir misiniz ?*	bunu bir punsiya͡un tuvsiye edebilir misiniz ?
On boarding terms	*Yimek ve yatmak dahil olduğu halde*	yimek ve yutmuk duhil a͡uldo͡ogho͡o hulde
What rooms have you to let ?	*Kiralık odalarınız hangileridir ?*	kiruli(*r*)k a͡uduluri(*r*)-ni(*r*)z hungileridir ?

English	Turkish	Pronunciation
What rooms do you want ?	*Hangi* ***odaları*** *ist(e)****yor sunuz*** *?* (see T.G. 70cc)	hungi a͡uduluri(*r*) isteya͡ursoͦonoͦoz ?
We will take these rooms	*Bu* ***odaları*** *tuta-* ***cağız***	boͦo a͡uduluri(*r*) toͦotujughi(*r*)z
How long do you want them for ?	*Ne kadar zaman için ist(e)****yor su-*** ***nuz*** *?* (see T.G. 70cc)	ne kudur zumun ichin isteya͡ur-soͦonoͦoz ?
We shall stay a week	*Bir hafta* ***kalacağız***	bir huftu kulujug-hi(*r*)z
Are the beds well aired ?	*Yatak****lar*** *iyice* ***havalandırıldı*** ***mı*** *?*	yutuklur iyije huvulundi(*r*)r-i(*r*)ldi(*r*)mi(*r*) ?
What is my number ?	*Numaram kaçtır ?*	noͦomurum kuch-ti(*r*)r ?
Go up by the lift	*Yukarı****ya*** *asan-sör****le*** *çık****ınız***	yoͦokuri(*r*)yu usun-se͡url chi(*r*)ki(*r*)-ni(*r*)z
Where is the lift ?	*Asansör nere****de-*** ***dir*** *?*	usunse͡ur nerede-dir ?
Show this gentle-man —	*Bay****a*** *ik****inci*** *katı* *göster****iniz***	buyu ikinji kuti(*r*) ge͡usteriniz
The second floor	*İk****inci*** *kat*	ikinji kut
Send the chamber-maid to me	*Ban****a*** *hizmet****çiyi*** *gönder****iniz***	bunu hizmetchiyi ge͡underiniz
Call the waiter	*Garson****u*** *çağ****ırınız***	gursa͡unoͦo chug-hi(*r*)ri(*r*)ni(*r*)z
Let me have my shoes ; boots	*Potinler****imi,*** *aya-kap****larımı*** *getir****iniz***	pa͡utinlerimi, uyukupluri(*r*)-mi(*r*) getiriniz
What is the number of my room	*Odam****ın*** *numarası* *kaçtır* or ***nedir*** *?*	a͡udumi(*r*)n noͦomu-rusi(*r*) kuchti(*r*)r *or* nedir ?
Let us have supper soon	*Akşam yemeğ****ini*** *erken* ***yiyelim***	ukshum yemeghini erken yiyelim
Give me my change	*Paran****ın*** *üstünü* *ver****iniz***	puruni(*r*)n e͡wste͡w-ne͡w veriniz
Take my luggage down	*Eşyamı aşağı****ya*** *indir****iniz***	eshyumi(*r*) ushug-hi(*r*)yu indiriniz

English	Turkish	Pronunciation
Are our rooms ready ?	*Oda**larımız** hazır**mıdır** ?*	a͡uduluri(*r*)mi(*r*)z huzi(*r*)rmi(*r*)di(*r*)r?
Give me the key of my room	*Oda**mın** anahtar**ını** bana ver**iniz***	a͡udumi(*r*)n unuhturi(*r*)ni(*r*) bunu veriniz
Have you a table d'hôte ?	*Bura**da** tablödot var **mıdır** ?*	o͡orudu tuble͡uda͡ut vurmi(*r*)di(*r*)r ?
If someone calls for me	*Ben**im** için bir**isi** geli**rse** ?*	benim ichin birisi gelirse ?
Call me at seven	*Beni yedi**de** uy**andırınız***	beni yedide o͡oyundi(*r*)ri(*r*)ni(*r*)z
We will take our coffee at eight	*Kahve**mizi** saat sekiz**de** iç**eriz***	kuhvemizi suut sekizde icheriz
Are there any letters for me ?	*Ben**im** için hiç mektup var **mı** ?*	benim ichin hich mekto͡op vurmi(*r*) ?
Where is the w.c. ?	*Yuz numara nere**dedir** ?*	yo͡oz no͡omuru neredeldir ?
Can I have a warm bath ?	*Yıkan**mak** için sıcak su hazır edebili**r misiniz**?*	yi(r)kunmuk ichin si(*r*)juk so͡o huzi(*r*)r edebilir misiniz ?
I should like a cold bath	*Soğuk su ile yıkan**mak** ister**im***	sa͡ugho͡ok so͡o ile yi(*r*)kunmuk isterim
The bathroom is on this floor	*Hamam bu kat**tadır***	humum bo͡o kuttudi(*r*)r
At the end of the corridor	*Koridor**un** nihayet**indedir***	ka͡urida͡uro͡on nihuyetindedir
A swimming bath	*Yüz**me** havuzu*	ye͡wzme huvo͡ozo͡o
A bathing dress	*Mayo*	muya͡u
Bring me some warm water	***Bana** bir az sıcak su getir**iniz***	bunu bir uz si(*r*)juk so͡o getiriniz
Give me a candle, please	*Lûtfen **bana** bir mum ver**iniz***	lûtfen bunu bir mo͡om veriniz
There are no matches	*Bura**da** kibrit yok**tur,*** or *kibrit yok*	bo͡orudu kibrit ya͡ukto͡or, *or* kibrit ya͡uk

English	Turkish	Pronunciation
We leave early to-morrow morning	*Yarın sabah erken-den* ***gidiyoruz***	yuri(*r*)n subuh erkenden gidi-ya͡uro͡oz
I want an extra blanket	*Fazla bir battaniye ist(e)***yorum** (see T.G. 70*cc* or ***isterim***	fuzlu bir buttuniye isteya͡uro͡om *or* isterim
Cut my hair	*Saçımı kesiniz*	suchi(*r*)mi(*r*) kesiniz
A shampoo	*Başımı şampuan ile yıkayınız*	bushi(*r*)mi(*r*) shum-po͡oun ile yi(*r*)ku-yi(*r*)ni(*r*)z
My bill, please	*Hisabımı lûtfen veriniz*	hisubi(*r*)mi(*r*) lût-fen veriniz
I want a shave	*Tıraş ol***mak** *ist(e)-***yorum**	ti(*r*)rush a͡ulmuk isteya͡uro͡om
There is a mistake in my bill	*Hisabımda bir yanlışlık var*	hisubi(*r*)mdu bir yunli(*r*)shli(*r*)k vur
I am sure you will find it is correct	*Hisabı doğru bulacağınızdan eminim*	hisubi(*r*) da͡ughro͡o bo͡olujughi(*r*)ni(*r*)z-dun eminim
I did not dine here on Tuesday	*Salı günü burada yemek yimedim*	sali(*r*) ge͡wne͡w bo͡o-rudu yemek yimedim
You have charged a day too much	*Bir gün fazla olarak hisap edilmiştir*	bir ge͡wn fuzlu a͡ulu-ruk hisup edil-mishtir
This is an over-charge	*Bu fahiş bir ücret-***tir,** or *Bu ücret fahiştir*	bo͡o fuhish bir e͡wjrettir, *or* bo͡o e͡wjret fuhishtir

(Direct request should be preceded by "lûtfen" = please

Dinner
(Akşam yemeği)

Waiter	*Garson*	gursa͡un
What time is dinner ?	*Yemek saat kaçta hazırdır ?*	yemek suut kuchtu huzi(*r*)rdi(*r*)r ?
We dine at six o'clock	*Saat altıda yemek yiyoruz*	suut ulti(*r*)du yemek yiya͡u-ro͡oz

English	Turkish	Pronunciation
Table d'hôte is at 2 o'clock	*Tablödot saat* ***ikidedir***	tubleũdaũt suut ikidedir
Reserve this table for me	*Bu masayı* ***benim*** *için* ***tutunuz***	bo͝o musuyi(*r*) benim ichin to͝oto͝ono͝oz
That table is reserved	*O masa tu**tulmuştur***	aũ musu to͝oto͝olmo͝oshto͝or
We expect a friend	*Bir dos**tumuzu** bekl(e)**yoruz*** (see T.G. 70cc)	bir daũsto͝omo͝ozo͝o bekleyaũro͝oz
Have you a large table?	*Büyük bir masa**nız** var **mı**?*	bew̃yew̃k bir musuni(*r*)z vurmi(*r*)?
Here is a table for two	*Bura**da** iki kişi**lik** bir masa var(**dır**)* (see T.G. 68 and 68a)	bo͝orudu iki kishilik bir musu vardi(*r*)r
We are a party of four	*Biz dört kişiyiz* or *Biz dört **kişiden** ibaret**iz***	biz deũrt kishiyiz *or* biz deũrt kishiden iburetiz
This way, madam	*Bu taraf**tan** buyu**runuz**, bayan*	bo͝o turuftun bo͝oyo͝oro͝ono͝oz, buyun
Take my coat	*Palto**mu** al**ınız***	pultaũmo͝o ali(*r*)ni(*r*)z
The dinner is at a fixed price	*Yemek fiyatı muayyen**dir***	yemek fiyuti(*r*) mo͝ouyyendir
What is the price?	*Fiyatı **nedir**?*	fiyuti(*r*) nedir?
Is wine included?	*Şarap dahil **midir**?*	shurup duhilmidir?
Will you give me the menu please?	*Bana liste**yi** verir **misiniz**?*	bunu listeyi verir misiniz
Show me the bill-of-fare	*Bana yemek liste**sini** gösterin**iz**,* or *gösterir **misiniz**?*	bunu yemek listesini geũsteriniz, *or* geũsterir misiniz?
A serviette	*Peçete*	pechete
This is not clean	*Bu temiz değil**dir***	bo͝o temiz deghildir
What have you ready?	*Hazır ol**arak** ne var**dır**?*	huzi(*r*) aũluruk ne vurdi(*r*)r?
I will take soup	*Çorba iste**rim***	chaũrbu isterim
I will take pea soup	*Bezelya çorba**sı** iste**rim***	bezelyu chaũrbusi(*r*) isterim

English	Turkish	Pronunciation
I will take tomato soup	*Domates çorba**sı** ister**im***	da͡umutes cha͡urbu-si(*r*) isterim
I will take vegetable soup	*Sebze çorba**sı** ister**im***	sebze cha͡urbusi(*r*) isterim
. . . some broth	*Azıcık et suy**u***	uzi(*r*)ci(*r*)k et so͡oyo͡o
What shall I help you to ?	*Siz**e** ne ver**eyim** ?*	size ne vereyim ?
Will you have some fish ?	*Bir az balık yer **misiniz** ?*	bir uz buli(*r*)k yer misiniz ?
What fish have you ?	*Ne balı**ğı** var ?*	ne buli(*r*)ghi(*r*) vur ?
No, thank you	*Hayır, teşekkür ede**rim***	huyi(*r*)r, teshekke͡wr ederim
See, here is the menu	*Buyur**un,** liste bura**da***	bo͡oyo͡oro͡on, liste bo͡orudu
We have fried fish	*Balık kızart**mamız,*** (or *kızartması*) *var*	buli(*r*)k ki(*r*)zurt-mumi(*r*)z (*or* ki(*r*)-zurtmusi(*r*)) vur
We have fresh herrings	*Taze balı**ğımız,*** (or *balık*) *var*	tuze buli(*r*)ghi(*r*)-mi(*r*)z (*or* buli(*r*)k) vur
Have you any boiled mutton ?	*Sövüş**ünüz** var **mı** ?*	se͡uve͡wshe͡wne͡wz vurmi(*r*) ?
Have you roast beef ?	*Rostbif**iniz*** or *rostbif var **mı** ?*	ra͡ustbifiniz *or* ra͡ust-bif vur mi(*r*) ?
Have you mutton ?	*Koyun et**iniz*** (or *eti*) *var **mı** ?*	ka͡uyo͡on etiniz (or eti) vur mi(*r*) ?
Have you roast lamb ?	*Kuzu kızart**manız*** (or *kızartması*) *var **mı** ?*	ko͡ozo͡o ki(*r*)zurt-muni(*r*)z (*or* ki(*r*)zurtmusi(*r*)) vur mi(*r*) ?
What do you drink ?	*Ne içe**r siniz** ?*	ne ichersiniz ?
Bring me the wine list	*Şarap liste**sini** getir**iniz***	shurup listesi-ni getiriniz
Here is the list	*Liste bura**da***	liste bo͡orudu
What wine will you have ?	*Ne cins şarap içe**r-siniz** ?*	ne jins shurup ichersiniz ?
I will have a bottle	*Bir şişe şarap ister**im***	bir shishe shurup isterim

English	Turkish	Pronunciation
I will have a half-bottle	*Bir yarım şişe**lik** iste**rim***	bir yuri(*r*)m shishelik isterim
I will have dinner wine	*(Ben) sofra şarabı iste**rim***	(ben) sa͡ufru shurubi(*r*) isterim
I will have whisky	*(Ben)* * *viski iste**rim***	ben viski isterim
I will have brandy *or* give me a brandy	*Brendi iste**rim*** or *Ban**a** bir brendi veriniz*	brendi isterim *or* Bunu bir brendi veriniz
I do not like this wine	*Bu şarabı beğen**m**(**e**)-**yorum*** (see T.G. 59*l*)	bo͡o shurubi(*r*) beg-henmeya͡uro͡om
Some ice	*Dondur**ma***	da͡undo͡ormu
Help yourself	*Lûtfen buyuru**nuz***	lûtfen bo͡oyo͡oro͡o-no͡oz
It is excellent	*Gayet güzel**dir***	gayet ge͡wzeldir
Bring me a salad	*Ban**a** bir salata getir **iniz***	bunu bir sulutu getiriniz
Bring me some mixed fruit	*Ban**a** karış**ık** meyve getir**iniz***	bunu kuri(*r*)shi(*r*)k meyve getiriniz
Bring me boiled potatoes	*Ban**a** haşlan**mış** patates getir**iniz***	bunu hushlun-mi(*r*)sh pututes getiriniz
Bring me green peas	*Ban**a** taze bezelye getir**iniz***	bunu tuze bezelye getiriniz
Remove the plates	*Tabak**ları** götürü**nüz*** or *kaldırınız*	tubukluri(*r*) ge͡ute͡w-re͡wne͡wz *or* kuldi(*r*)ri(*r*)ni(*r*)z
Bring me some roast chicken (*or* will you bring)	*Ban**a** tavuk kızart**ması** getiriniz,* (or *Getirir **misiniz***)	bunu tuvo͡ok ki(*r*)-zurtmusi(*r*) geti-riniz, *or* getirir misiniz
Bring me some boiled fowl	*Ban**a** haşlan**mış** tavuk getir**iniz***	bunu hushlun-mi(*r*)sh tuvo͡ok getiriniz
What sweet dishes have you ?	*Ne tatlı**larınız** var ?*	ne tutli(*r*)luri(*r*)ni-(*r*)z vur ?

* (*Ben*) = (*I*). The mention of *I* is not necessary in Turkish. (See T.G., 50 and 58)

English	Turkish	Pronunciation
We have omelettes	*Omelet**lerimiz*** var	a͡umeletlerimiz vur
We have omelettes with cheese	*Peynir**li** omelet**imiz** var*	peynirli a͡umeletimiz vur
Give me a clean fork	*Ban**a** temiz bir çatal ver**iniz***	bunu temiz bir chutul veriniz
Will you take some more ?	*Bir az daha al**ır** **mısınız** ?*	bir uz duhu ali(*r*)r mi(*r*)si(*r*)ni(*r*)z ?
Pass the salt, please	*Tuzu lûtfen ver**ir** **misiniz** ?*	to͡ozo͡o lûtfen verir misiniz
— — pepper „	*Biberi lûtfen ver**ir** **misiniz** ?*	biberi lûtfen verir misiniz
— — mustard „	*Hardal**ı** lûtfen ver**ir** **misiniz** ?*	hurduli(*r*) lûtfen verir misiniz
— — vinegar „	*Sirke**yi** lûtfen ver**ir** **misiniz** ?*	sirkeyi lûtfen verir misiniz
— — oil „	*Zeytun yağ**ını** lûtfen ver**ir** **misiniz** ?*	zeyto͡on yughi(*r*)ni(*r*) lûtfen verir misiniz
I am very thirsty	*Çok susad**ım** ; Çok hararet**im** var*	cha͡uk so͡osudi(*r*)m; cha͡uk hururetim vur
There is some fruit tart	*Bir az* or *azıcık yemiş**li** turta var*	bir uz *or* uzi(*r*)ci(*r*)k yemishli to͡ortu vur
There is some rice and plums	*Azıcık sütlaç ile erik kompostosu var*	uzi(*r*)ci(*r*)k se͡wtluch ile erik ka͡umpa͡usta͡uso͡o vur
What dessert have you ?	*Ne yemiş**leri** **niz** var ?*	ne yemishleriniz vur ?
We have only stewed fruits	*Yalnız komposto**lar** var,* or *vardır*	yulni(*r*)z ka͡umpa͡usta͡ulur vur, *or* vurdi(*r*)r
We have only apples	*Yalnız elma**mız** var**dır**,* or *var*	yulni(*r*)z elmumi(*r*)z vurdi(*r*)r, *or* vur
We have only peaches	*Yalnız şeftali**miz** var*	yulni(*r*)z sheftulimiz vur
Some black coffee	*Süt**süz** kahve*	se͡wtse͡wz kuhve
Some cigarettes	*Bir kaç sigara*	bir kuch siguru
Do you smoke a pipe ?	*Pipo iç**er** **misiniz** ?*	pipa͡u icher misiniz ?

English	Turkish	Pronunciation
Waiter, the bill	*Garson, hisabı getiriniz*	gursa͡un, hisubi(*r*) getiriniz
Pay for me	*Hisabı siz benim yerime tesviye ediniz*	hisubi(*r*) ¯siz benim yerime tesviye ediniz
You can keep the change	*Paranın üstünü kendinize alıkoy-unuz*	puruni(*r*)n e͡wste͡w-ne͡w kendinize uli(*r*)ka͡uyo͡ono͡oz

Breakfast
(Kahve altı)

(Direct request should be preceded by "lûtfen" = please)

English	Turkish	Pronunciation
Is breakfast ready?	*Kahve altı hazır mı?*	kuhve ulti(*r*) huzi(*r*)rmi(*r*) ?
Breakfast is ready	*Kahve altı hazırdır*	kuhve ulti(*r*) huzi(*r*)rdi(*r*)r
Is the tea made?	*Çay yapıldı mı?*	chuy yupi(*r*)ldi(*r*) mi(*r*) ?
Do you drink tea or coffee?	*Çay mı yoksa kah-ve mi içersiniz?*	chuy mi(*r*) ya͡uksu kuhve mi icher-siniz ?
Coffee without milk	*Sütsüz kahve*	se͡wtse͡wz kuhve
Coffee with milk	*Sütlü kahve*	se͡wtle͡w kuhve
Do you take milk and sugar?	*Süt şekerli mi olsun?*	se͡wt shekerli mi a͡ulso͡on ?
No sugar, thanks	*Şekeri olmasın, teşekkür ederim*	shekeri a͡ulmu-si(*r*)n, teshekke͡wr ederim
This cream is sour	*Bu kaymak ekşidir*	bo͡o kuymuk ekshi-dir
Will you take an egg?	*Yumurta ister mi-siniz?*	yo͡omo͡ortu ister-misiniz ?
Yes, please	*Evet, rica ederim, lûtfen*	evet, riju ederim, lûtfen
These eggs are hard	*Bu yumurtalar çok katı olmuştur*	bo͡o yo͡omo͡ortulur cha͡uk kuti(*r*) a͡ul-mo͡oshto͡or
Give me the salt	*Bana tuzu veriniz*	bunu to͡ozo͡o veriniz

English	Turkish	Pronunciation
Pass me the butter	(*Bana*) *tere yağını uzatınız*, or *uzatır mısınız?*	bunu tere yughi(*r*)-ni(*r*) o͡ozuti(*r*)-ni(*r*)z, *or* o͡ozuti(*r*)r mi(*r*)si(*r*)ni(*r*)z?
This butter is not fresh	*Bu tere yağı taze değildir*	bo͡o tere yughi(*r*) tuze deghildir
Bring me more	(*Bana*) *bir az daha getiriniz*	bunu bir uz duhu getiriniz
The coffee is not strong enough	*Bu kahve kâfi derecede kaynamamıştır*	bo͡o kuhve kiafi derejede kuynumumi(*r*)shti(*r*)r
We want more cups	*Bir kaç fincan daha ist(e)yoruz* (see T.G. 70*cc*)	bir kuch finjun duhu isteya͡u-ro͡oz
Some hot rolls	*Bir iki taze francala*	bir iki tuze frunjulu
A piece of toast	*Bir parça tost*	bir purchu ta͡ust
A rasher of bacon	*Bir dilim domuz pastırması*	bir dilim da͡umo͡oz pusti(*r*)rmusi(*r*)
Nothing more, thanks	*Başka bir şey istememem teşekkür ederim*	bushku bir shey istemem teshek-ke͡wr ederim

Tea

(Çay)

English	Turkish	Pronunciation
Afternoon (5 o'clock) tea	*Fayf oklok çayı* or *öğleden sonraki çay*	Fuyf a͡ukla͡uk chuy-i(*r*) *or* e͡ughleden sa͡unruki chuy
Will you come to tea?	*Çaya gelir misiniz?*	chuyu gelir misi-niz?
Tea is quite ready	*Çay tamamiyle hazırdır*	chuy tumumiyle huzi(*r*)rdi(*r*)r
Pour out the tea	*Fincanlara koyunuz*, or *fincanları doldurunuz*	finjunluru ka͡uyo͡o no͡oz, *or* finjun-luri(*r*) da͡uldo͡o-ro͡ono͡oz
Do you like strong tea?	*Koyu çay sever misiniz?*	ka͡uyo͡o chuy sever misiniz?
Not too strong	*Fazla koyu olmasın*	fuzlu ka͡uyo͡o a͡ulmu-si(*r*)n

English	Turkish	Pronunciation
I like it rather weak	*Çayı hafifçe olarak severim*	chuyi(*r*) hufifche a͡ulurук severim
Do you take cream ?	*Kaymak yer misiniz ?*	kuymuk yermi-siniz ?
Bring some tea-cakes	*Bir kaç tane çay çöreği* or *pasta getiriniz*	bir kuch tune chuy che͡ureghi *or* pustu getiriniz
Some toast	*Bir az tost*	bir uz ta͡ust
Some biscuits	*Bir iki bisküvi*	bir iki biske͡wvi
Some cakes	*Bir kaç pasta*	bir kuch pustu
Ring, if you please	*Zili lûtfen çalınız*	zili lûtfen chuli(*r*)-ni(*r*)z
A piece of bread and butter	*Bir parça ekmek ile tere yağı*	bir purchu ekmek ile tere yughi(*r*)
Will you take some cake ?	*Bir parça kek ister misiniz ?*	bir purchu kek ister misiniz ?
A small piece	*Küçük bir parça*	ke͡wche͡wk bir purchu
Another cup of tea ?	*Bir fincan çay daha ister misiniz ?*	bir finjun chuy duhu ister misiniz
A little more milk ?	*Bir az daha süt ister misiniz ?*	bir uz duhu se͡wt ister misiniz ?
Is your tea sweet enough ?	*Çayınız kâfi derecede tatlı mıdır ?*	chuyi(*r*)ni(*r*)z kiafi derejede tutli(*r*) mi(*r*)di(*r*)r ?
I should like rather less sugar	*Tercihen daha az şeker isterim* or *Tercihen o kadar şeker istemem*	terjihen duhu uz sheker isterim *or* terjihen a͡u kudur sheker istemem

Supper
(Akşam yemeği)

Come and have some supper	*Geliniz, yemeğe buyurunuz*	geliniz yemeghe bo͡oyo͡oro͡ono͡oz
This is a nice place	*Burası güzel bir yerdir*	bo͡orusi(*r*) ge͡wzel bir yerdir
It is all ready	*Her şey hazırdır*	her shey huzi(*r*)r-di(*r*)r

English	Turkish	Pronunciation
It will not be long	*Çok uzamı**yacaktır***	cha͡uk o͡ozumi(*r*)yujukti(*r*)r
Thank you, I will only have a cup of tea (of coffee)	*Teşekkür eder**im,** yalnız bir fincan çay (kahve) iç**erim***	teshekke͡wr ederim, yulni(*r*)z bir finjun chuy (kuhve) icherim
A glass of beer	*Bir bardak bira*	bir burduk biru
A fruit drink	*Şerbet*	sherbet
I should like a drink and a smoke	*Bir iç**ki** ile sigara iç**mek** ister**im***	bir ichki ile siguru ichmek isterim
No thanks, I must get home	*Hayır, teşekkür ede**rim,** eve git**meliyim***	huyi(*r*)r, teshekke͡wr ederim, eve gitmeliyim
My car is waiting	*Otomobil beni bekl(e)**yor*** (see T.G. 70*cc*)	a͡uta͡uma͡ubil beni bekleya͡ur
I can go by train	*Tren**le** gidebili**rim***	trenle gidebilirim

In Town
(Şehir**de**)

English	Turkish	Pronunciation
Which way shall we go ?	*Hangi taraf**tan** gide**lim** ?*	hungi turuftun gidelim ?
Which is the way ?	*Hangi yol**dan** gidi**lecektir** ?*	hungi ya͡uldun gidilejektir ?
Where does this road lead ?	*Bu yol nereye çık**ar** ?*	bo͡o ya͡ul nereye chi(*r*)kur ?
To the right ; left	*Sağ**a ;** sol**a***	sughu ; sa͡ulu
About a mile	*Takriben bir mil*	tukriben bir mil
Go up the street	*Bu sokak**tan** yukarı**ya** doğru gidi**niz***	bo͡o sa͡ukuktun yo͡okuri(*r*)ya da͡ughro͡o gidiniz
Is it far from here ?	*Bura**dan** uzak **mıdır** ?*	bo͡orudun o͡ozukmi(*r*)di(*r*)r ?
How far is it to Adana ?	*Adana **buradan** ne kadar uzak**tır** ?*	udunu bo͡orudun ne kudur o͡ozukti(*r*)r ?
Straight on	*Dos doğru*	da͡us da͡ughro͡o

English	Turkish	Pronunciation
Straight before you	*Tam ilerinizde*	tum ilerinizde
Let us go	*Gidelim*	gidelim
Show me the way	*Bana yolu gösteriniz*	bunu yaulōō geusteriniz
I am going to walk	*Yürüyerek gideceğim*	yewrewyerek gidejeghim
Turn to the right	*Sağa dönünüz*	sughu deunewnewz
Keep to the left	*Solu tâkip ediniz*	saulōō taakip ediniz
Take the first to the left, then the second to the right	*(Evvela) soldan birinci sokağa, sonra sağdan ikinci sokağa sapınız*	(evvelu) sauldun birinji saukughu, saunru sughdun ikinji saukughu supi(r)ni(r)z
Could you tell me where is there —	*. . . nerede olduğunu söyleyebilir misiniz?*	. . . nerede auldōōghōōnōō seuyleyebilirmisiniz ?
—The Ladies' toilet	*Bayanlara mahsus apdestane(nin) . . .*	buyunluru muhsōōs updestunenin
—The bus stop	*Otobüs durağı(nın) . . .*	autaubews dōōrughi(r)ni(r)n
—The tram stop	*Tramvay durağı(nın) . . .*	trumvuy dōōrughi(r)ni(r)n
—The chemist (on night duty)	*(Nöbetçi) eczanenin . . .*	neubetchi ejzunenin
—A restaurant	*Bir lokanta(nın) . . .*	bir laukuntuni(r)n
—The Anglican Church	*Anglikan kilisesinin . . .*	unglikun kilisesinin
—The dentist here	*Buradaki dişçinin . . .*	bōōruduki dishchinin
—The passport office	*Pasaport dairesinin . . .*	pusupaurt duiresinin
—A high-class hotel	*İyi bir otelin . . .*	iyi bir autelin
—A cheap hotel	*Ucuz bir otelin . . .*	ōōjōōz bir autelin
Cross the street	*Sokağın karşı tarafına geçiniz*	saukughi(r)n kurshi(r) turufi(r)nu gechiniz

English	Turkish	Pronunciation
In what street ?	*Hangi soka**kta**?*	hungi sa͡ukuktu ?
Is this the way to Galata ?	*Galata**ya** gid**en** yol bu **mudur**?*	gulutuyu giden ya͡ul bo͡omo͡o-do͡or ?
Is the road easy to find ?	*Yol**u** bul**mak** kolay **mıdır**?*	ya͡ulóo bo͡olmuk ka͡uluy mi(*r*)-di(*r*)r ?
Do you know Mr. Nadir ?	*Bay Nâdir'**i** tanır **mısınız**?*	buy na͡adiri tuni(*r*) mi(*r*)si(*r*)ni(*r*)z ?
I do not know any-one of that name	*O isim**de** kimse**yi** bil**m**(e)**yorum***	a͡u isimde kimseyi bilmeya͡uro͡om
I know him very well	*Onu çok iyi tanı **yorum***	a͡uno͡o cha͡uk iyi tani(*r*) ya͡uro͡om
He is a friend of mine	*(O) dost**larımdan** bir**idir***	a͡u da͡ustluri(*r*)mdun biridir
Where does he live ?	*Nere**de** ikamet edi-**yor**?*	nerede ikumet edi-ya͡ur ?
Close by (near here)	*Şura**cık ta** (bura**ya** yakın)*	sho͡oruji(*r*)ktu (bo͡oruyu yaki(*r*)n)
Can you direct me to his house ?	***Bana** ev**ini** tarif edebil**ir mi siniz**?*	bunu evini turif edebilirmisiniz ?
Is Mr. Izzet at home ?	*Bay İzzet ev**de mi-dir**?*	Buy Izzet evdemi-dir ?
Can I see Mr. Izzet ?	*Bay İzzet'**i** gör**ebili r miyim**?*	Buy Izzeti ge͡ure-bilirmiyim ?
He is out just now	***Şimdilik** ev**de** değil**dir***	shimdilik evde deghildir
Does he expect you ?	***Sizi** bekl(i)**yor mu idi**?* (see T.G. 70ccc)	sizi bekliya͡urmo͡o idi ?
Have you an appointment ?	*Kendi**siyle** rande-vu**nuz** var **mı**?*	kendisiyle runde-vo͡ono͡oz vur-mi(*r*) ?
When does he return ?	*Ne vakıt avdet ede-**cek**?*	ne vuki(*r*)t uvdet edejek ?
When could I see him ?	*Kendi**sini** nevakıt gör**ebili rim**?*	kendisini nevaki(*r*)t ge͡urebilirim ?
I will call on Monday	*Pazarte**si** günü geli**rim***	puzurtesi ge͡wne͡w gelirim

English	Turkish	Pronunciation
Could you call again?	*Tekrar gelebilir* ***mi siniz*** *?*	tekrur gelebilirmi-siniz ?
I expect him any minute	*Hemen her dakika avdetini bekl(i)* **yorum** (see T.G. 70ccc)	hemen her dukiku uvdetini bekli-yau͡rōōm
Have you your card?	*Kartınız var* ***mı dır*** *?*	kurti(r)ni(r)z vur-mi(r)di(r)r ?
Whose name shall I give?	*Kimin ismini vereyim? or Kim diyeyim?*	kimin ismini vere-yim ? *or* kim diyeyim ?
Mrs. Nadir is not at home	*Bayan Nâdir* ***evde değildir***	Buyun Nudir evde deghildir
She is away from home	*Misafirliğe git-* ***miştir***	misufirlighe git-mishti(r)r
How is Mrs. Nadir?	*Bayan Nâdir nasıl-* ***dır*** *?*	Buyun Nudir nu-si(r)ldi(r)r ?
Give my compliments to Miss Hayriye	*Bayan Hayriye'****ye*** *selamlarımı sununuz*	Buyun Huyriyeye selumluri(r)mi(r) sōōnōōnōōz
I must go	*Gitmeliyim*	gitmeliyim
Must you go yet?	*Hemen gitmeli* ***mi-siniz*** *?*	hemen gitmelimi-siniz ?
Good morning (greeting)	*Sabahınız hayırlı olsun, günaydın*	subuhi(r)ni(r)z huyi(r)li(r) a͡ul-sōōn, gewnuy-di(r)n
Good evening (greeting)	*Akşamınız hayırlı olsun, tünaydın*	akshumi(r)ni(r)z huyi(r)rli(r) a͡ulsōōn, tewnuydi(r)n

Notices

(İlân***lar***)

Admission free	*Duhuliye meccanen-* ***dir***	dōōhōōliye mejju-nendir
Apartment to let	*Kiralık apartman*	kiruli(r)k upurt-mun
Bedroom to let	*Kiralık yatak odası*	kiruli(r)k yutuk a͡udusi(r)

English	Turkish	Pronunciation
Dogs not admitted	*Köpeklere müsaede yoktur* or *Köpeklerin girmesi yasaktır*	ke͡upeklere me͡w-suede ya͡ukto͡or *or* ke͡upeklerin gir-mesi yusukti(*r*)r
Entrance ; exit	*Giriş yeri ; Çıkış yeri*	girish yeri ; chi(*r*)ki(*r*)sh yeri
Fire alarm	*Yangın çanı*	yungi(*r*)n chuni(*r*)
Information bureau	*İstihbarat odası*	istihburut a͡udusi(*r*)
Free library (public)	*Meccanî kütüphane (umumî)*	mejjune͡e ke͡wte͡wp-hune (o͡omo͡ome͡e)
Furnished house to let	*Kiralık mefruş ev*	kiruli(*r*)k mefro͡osh ev
Furnished rooms	*Mefruş odalar*	mefro͡osh a͡udulur
Knock ; ring	*Tokmağı çal; Zili çal*	ta͡ukmughi(*r*) chul ; zili chul
No admittance	*Girilemez*	girilemez
No smoking allowed	*Sigara içilemez*	siguru ichilemez
No thoroughfare	*Geçilemez*	gechilemez
Please do not touch	*Lûtfen dokunmayınız*	lûtfen da͡uko͡on-muyi(*r*)ni(*r*)z
Please wipe your feet	*Lûtfen ayaklarınızı siliniz*	lûtfen uyukluri(*r*)-ni(*r*)zi(*r*) sili-niz
Private	*Hususî*	ho͡oso͡ose͡e
Public notices	*Umuma mahsus ilânlar*	o͡omo͡omu muhso͡os ila͡anlur
Pull ; push	*Çekiniz ; itiniz*	chekiniz ; itiniz
Refreshments	*Büfe*	be͡wfe
To be let	*Kiralık*	kiruli(*r*)k
Unfurnished rooms	*Gayrimefruş odalar* or *döşenmemiş odalar*	guyrimefro͡osh a͡u-dulur *or* de͡ushen-memish a͡udulur
Warning ; caution	*İhtar ; dikkat*	ihtur ; dikkut

Changing Money
(Sarrafiye)

English	Turkish	Pronunciation
Where can I get my money changed?	*Param**ı** nere**de** değişti**re** bili**rim**?*	purumi(*r*) nerede deghishtire bilirim?
Where is the Iş bank?	*İş banka**sı** nere**de dir**?*	ish bunkusi(*r*) neredir?
I want change for a £5 note	*Beş lira**lık** bankonot için ufak para ist(e)**yorum*** (see T.G. 70cc)	besh liruli(*r*)k bunka͡una͡ut ichin o͡ofuk puru isteya͡uro͡om
Will you cash this cheque for me?	*Bu çek**i** ban**a** değiştiri**r mi siniz**?*	bo͡o cheki bunu deghishtirirmisiniz?
A bank-note	*Bir bankonot*	bir bunka͡una͡ut
A sovereign	*Bir altın*	bir ulti(*r*)n
This cheque needs endorsing	*Bu çek ciro **edil-meli dir***	bo͡o chek jira͡u edilmelidir
Will you give me Turkish money?	*Ban**a** Türk para**sı** veri**r mi siniz**?*	bunu Te͡wrk purusi(*r*) verirmisiniz?
What is the exchange on English money?	*İngiliz para**sının** rayici ne**dir**?*	ingiliz purusi(*r*)ni(*r*)n ruyici nedir?
Small change	*Bozukpara, ufak**lık***	ba͡uzo͡okpuru, o͡ofukli(*r*)k
How will you take it?	*Bun**u** nasıl ister**siniz**?*	bo͡ono͡o nusi(*r*)l istersiniz?
I will take it in silver	*Gümüş ol**arak** ister**im***	ge͡wme͡wsh a͡uluruk isterim
Can you change a pound for me?	*Ban**a** bir lira değiştiri**r misiniz**?*	bunu bir liru deghishtirirmisiniz?
I am sorry I cannot (change)	*Maalesef değiştir**e-mem***	muulesef deghishtiremem
Reserve capital	*İhtiyat sermaye*	ihtiyut sermuye
Current accounts	*Câri hisap**lar***	ja͡ari hisuplur

Shopping
(Öte beri satın alma)

English	Turkish	Pronunciation
I wish to buy —	*Satın al**mak** ist*(*e*)-***yorum*** (see T.G. 70cc)	suti(*r*)n ulmuk isteya͡uro͡om
I will buy this	*Bu**nu** satın al**ırım***	bo͡ono͡o suti(*r*)n uli(*r*)ri(*r*)m
I should like to see some ribbons	*Müteaddit kurdela**lar** gör**mek** ister**im***	me͡wteaddit ko͡or-delulur ge͡urmek isterim
Show me some pencils	*Ban**a** bir iki kurşun kalem göster**iniz***	bunu bir iki ko͡or-sho͡on kulem ge͡usteriniz
How much is it ?	*Kaç para**dır** ?*	kuch purudi(*r*)r ?
What is the price ?	*Fiyatı **nedir** ?*	fiyuti(*r*) nedir ?
That is too much	*O çok fazla**dır***	a͡u cha͡uk fuzlu-di(*r*)r
This colour is too dark (light)	*Bu renk çok koyu**dur** (açık**tır**)*	bo͡o renk cha͡uk ka͡uyo͡odo͡or (uchi(*r*)kti(*r*)r)
Have you any narrower (wider) ?	*Siz**de** daha **ensizi** var **mı** (geniş**i**) ?*	sizde duhu ensizi vurmi(*r*) (genishi) ?
What is this a metre ?	*Bu **nedir,** metre **mi** ?*	bo͡o nedir, met-remi ?
Its colour is faded	*Reng**i** sol**muştur***	rengi sa͡ulmo͡oshto͡or
Let it not be so fine	*O kadar ince ol**masın***	a͡u kudur inje a͡ul-musi(*r*)n
This will do (me)	*Bu iş**ime** yarar*	bo͡o ishime yurur
Show me some gloves	*Ban**a** bir iki eldiven göste**riniz***	bunu bir iki eldiven ge͡uste-riniz
What price a pair are they ?	*Bun**ların** çift**i** kaç para**dır** ?*	bo͡onluri(*r*)n chifti kuch purudi(*r*)r ?
I want . . .	*İst*(*e*)***yorum*** . . .	isteya͡uro͡om . . .
I want some envelopes	*Bir kaç zarf ist*(*e*)***yorum***	bir kuch zurf isteya͡uro͡om
I want some pins	*Toplu iğne ist*(*e*)-***yorum***	ta͡uplo͡o ighne isteya͡uro͡om

English	Turkish	Pronunciation
Half a kilo	*Yarım kilo*	yuri(*r*)m kila͡u
How much does the bill come to?	*Hisab**ın** yekün**ü** ned**ir**?*	hisubi(*r*)n yeke͡w-ne͡w nedir?
Will you serve me, please?	*Lûtfen ban**a** bak**ar** **mı sınız**?*	lûtfen bunu bukurmi(*r*)si(*r*)-ni(*r*)z?
Do you sell —?	*Sat**ar** **mı sınız**?*	sutur mi(*r*)si(*r*)-ni(*r*)z?
Have you a different pattern?	*Siz**de** başka bir ör-neğ**i** var **mı dır**?*	sizde bushku bir e͡urneghi vur mi(*r*)di(*r*)r?
I want to give an order	*Sipariş ver**mek** ist(e)**yor um*** (see T.G. 70*cc*)	sipurish vermek isteya͡uro͡om
Show me a better quality	*(Ban**a**) daha iyi cins**ini*** (or *iyisini*) *göster**iniz***	bunu duhu iyi jinsini (*or* iyisini) ge͡usteriniz
Show me a cheaper one	*(Ban**a**) daha ucuz-**unu** göster**iniz***	bunu duhu o͡ojo͡oz-o͡ono͡o ge͡usteriniz
Show me some others (will you)	*(Ban**a**) başka**ların**ı göster**iniz**,* or *(gösterir **mi siniz**)*	bunu bushkulu-ri(*r*)ni(*r*) ge͡uste-riniz, *or* (ge͡uste-rir misiniz)
Can you recommend it?	***Bunu** tavsiye ede-**bilir** **mi siniz**?*	bo͡ono͡o tuvsiye edebilir misiniz?
We can recommend this	***Bunu** tavsiye ed**e**-bili**r iz***	bo͡ono͡o tuvsiye ede-biliriz
Will it wash?	*Yikan**mağa** gel**ir** **mi**?*	yikunmughu gelir-mi?
Do you guarantee this?	***Bunu** garanti edi-**yor mu sunuz**?*	bo͡ono͡o gurunti ediya͡urmo͡oso͡o-no͡oz?
I will take them with me	*Onl**arı** beraber götür**ü r üm***	a͡unluri(*r*) beruber ge͡ute͡wre͡wre͡wm
Send them to my house	*Onl**arı** ev**im e** gön-der**iniz***	a͡unluri(*r*) evime ge͡underiniz
Can you send them to me at once?	*Onl**arı** bana hemen gönder**e** **bilir mi-siniz**?*	a͡unluri(*r*) bunu hemen ge͡undere bilirmisiniz?

English	Turkish	Pronunciation
I will pay on delivery	*Parayı eşyaların eve teslimınde tediye ederim*	puruyi(*r*) eshyuluri(*r*)n eve teslìminde tediye ederim
Will you please wrap it up?	*Lûtfen kâğıda sarar mı sınız?*	lûtfen kiaghi(*r*)du sururmi(*r*)si(*r*)ni(*r*)z?
Will you kindly make it into a parcel?	*Lûtfen bir paket yapar mı sınız?*	lûtfen bir puket yupurmi(*r*)si(*r*)ni(*r*)z?

The Dressmaker

(Modistra)

English	Turkish	Pronunciation
Can you recommend a dressmaker?	*Bana bir modistra tavsiye edebilir mi siniz?*	bunu bir mau͡distru tuvsiye edebilirmisiniz?
I cannot wait	*Bekleyemem*	bekleyemem
Show her in	*İçeriye gelsinler*	icheriye gelsinler
Have you brought my dress?	*Elbisemi getirdiniz mi?*	elbisemi getirdinizmi?
Here it is	*İşte buradadır*	ishte bo͞orududi(*r*)r
I will try it on	*Prova edeyim*	prau͡vu edeyim
The sleeves are not wide (long) enough	*Kollar kâfi derecede geniş (uzun) değildir*	kau͡llur kiafi derejede genish (o͞ozo͞on) deghildir
The skirt is too narrow (short)	*Eteklik pek dardır; Eteklik pek kısadır*	eteklik pek durdi(*r*)r; eteklik pek ki(*r*)sudi(*r*)r
It is too short-waisted	*Beli lûzumundan fazla kısadır*	beli lûzo͞omo͞ondun fuzlu ki(*r*)sudi(*r*)r
It is not a good fit	*Muvâfık bir elbise değildir*	mo͞ovaafi(*r*)k bir elbise deghildir
This is the latest style	*(Bu) en son modadır*	bo͞o en sau͡n mau͡dudi(*r*)r
The style does not suit me	*Bu biçim bana yakışm(a)yor* (see T.G. 59*l*)	bo͞o bichim bunu yuki(*r*)shmuyau͡r
It is very fashionable	*Bu çok modadır*	bo͞o chau͡k mau͡dudi(*r*)r

English	Turkish	Pronunciation
I would like a " v " neck	*Aç**ık** ve sivri bir yaka ister**im***	uchi(*r*)k ve sivri bir yuku isterim
I would like a round neck	*Yuvar**lak** bir yaka ister**im***	yo͡ovurluk bir yuku isterim
Make the necessary alterations	*Lâzım olan tâdilatı yapı**nız***	la͡azi(*r*)m a͡ulun ta͡a-diluti(*r*) yupi(*r*)-ni(*r*)z
It fits me very well	*Vucudu**ma** çok uy**gundur***	vo͡ojo͡odo͡omu cha͡uk o͡oygo͡on-do͡or
What trimming will you put on ?	*Ne gibi garnitür koya**cak sınız** ?*	ne gibi gurnite͡wr ka͡uyujuksi(*r*)-ni(*r*)z ?
When can you let me have it ?	*Ne vakıt hazır ede-bili**r siniz** ?*	ne vuki(*r*)t huzi(*r*)r edebilirsi-niz ?
Do not disappoint me	*Ümit**lerimi** boşa çıkar**mayınız**,* or *Beni inkisarı hayâle uğrat-**mayiniz***	e͡wmitlerimi ba͡ushu chi(*r*)kur-muyi(r)ni(*r*)z, *or* beni inkisuri(*r*) huya͡ale o͡oghrut-muyi(*r*)ni(*r*)z

The Shoemaker
(Kundura**cı**)

I wish to see some shoes	*Bir iki kundura görmek **isterim***	bir iki ko͡ondo͡oru ge͡urmek isterim
Ladies' shoes	*Kadın kundura**ları***	kudi(*r*)n ko͡ondo͡oru-luri(*r*)
I would like a shoe-horn	*Bir kundura (çekeceği) keratası ister**im***	bir ko͡ondo͡oru (chekejeghi) kerutusi(*r*) isterim
Have you a shoe-horn ?	*Ayakka**lı** çekeceği var **mı** ?*	uyukkubi(*r*) chekejeghi vurmi(*r*) ?
The soles are too thick	*Taban**lar** lüzumun**dan** fazla kalın**dır***	tubunlur lûzo͡o-mo͡ondun fuzlu kuli(*r*)ndi(*r*)r

English	Turkish	Pronunciation
They are too large; tight	*Fazla büyüktür; Fazla dardır*	fuzlu bewyewktewr; fuzlu durdi(*r*)r
I cannot get my foot in	*Ayağım içine gir-m(e)yor* (see T.G. 59*l*)	uyughi(*r*)m ichine girmeyaur
They hurt my heels	*Topuklarımı acıtıyor*	taupookluri(*r*)mi(*r*) uji(*r*)ti(*r*)yaur
I cannot walk in them	*Onlarla yürüye-m(e)yorum* (see T.G. 59*l*)	áunlurlu yewrew-yemeyauroom
Is it a soft leather?	*Yumuşak bir deri midir?*	yoomooshuk bir deri midir?
I want low heels	*Alçak topuklu sunu isterim*	ulchuk taupookloo soonoo isterim
I want high heels	*Yüksek topuklu olsun*	yewksek taupookloo aulsoon
I want some shoe (boot) laces	(*Potin*) *ayakabı bağı ist*(*e*)*yorum* (see T.G. 70*cc*)	(potin) uyukubi(*r*) bughi(*r*) isteyau-room
Take my size	*Ölçümü alınız*	eulchewmew uli(*r*)-ni(*r*)z
These shoes want soling and heel-ing	*Bu kunduralara yeni taban ve to-puk konmalıdır*	boo koondooruluru yeni tubun ve taupook kaunmu-li(*r*) di(*r*)r
Send my shoes to be mended	*Kunduralarımı tâmire gönderi-niz*	koondooruluri(*r*)-mi(*r*) taamire geunderiniz
When will they be finished?	*Onları ne vakıt bitirebilecek-siniz?*	aunluri(*r*) ne vuk-i(*r*)t bitirebilejeksi-niz?
must have them back quickly	*Onları bana* (*sü-ratla* or *çabuk*) *iade ediniz*	aunluri(*r*) bunu (sewrutlu *or* chu-book) iude ediniz

Laundry
(Çamaşır)

English	Turkish	Pronunciation
I want these clothes washed *or* Get these clothes washed	*Bu çamaşırları yıkatınız*	boo chumushi(*r*)rlu-ri(*r*) yi(*r*)kuti(*r*)-ni(*r*)z

English	Turkish	Pronunciation
When can I have it ?	*Onları ne vakıt alabilirim ?*	a͡unluri(*r*) ne vuki(*r*)t ulubilirim ?
Please return this laundry on Friday	*Bu çamaşırı lûtfen cuma günü iade ediniz*	bo͡o chumushi(*r*)-ri(*r*) lûtfen jo͡o-mu ge͡wne͡w iude ediniz
You must bring back this list	*Bu listeyi beraber getirmeli siniz*	bo͡o listeyi beruber getirmelisiniz
You do not put enough starch in	*Kâfi miktarda kola koymayorsunuz*	kiufi mikturdu ka͡ulu ka͡uymuya͡urso͡o-no͡oz
A collar is missing	*Bir yakalık eksiktir*	bir yukuli(*r*)k eksik-tir
See how badly this is done	*Bakınız, bu ne kadar fena yapılmış(tır)*	buki(*r*)ni(*r*)z, bo͡o ne kudur fenu yu-pi(*r*)lmi(*r*)shti(*r*)r
You must re-wash this	*Bunu tekrar yıkamalı sınız*	bo͡ono͡o tekrur yi(*r*)kumuli(*r*)-si(*r*)ni(*r*)z
That is badly ironed	*O fena halde ütülenmiş(tir)*	a͡u fenu hulde e͡w-te͡wlenmishtir
You put too much blue in it	*Fazla çivit koyuyor sunuz*	fuzlu chivit ka͡uyo͡o-ya͡urso͡ono͡oz
This is too limp	*Bu çok yumuşak(tır)*	bo͡o cha͡uk yo͡omo͡o-shukti(*r*)r
This is not my handkerchief	*Bu benim mendilim değil(dir)*	bo͡o benim mendi-lim deghildir
You have scorched my dress	*Elbisemi alazladınız*	elbisemi uluzludi(*r*)-ni(*r*)z
Have you the bill ?	*Hisabımı çıkardınız mı ?*	hisubi(*r*)mi(*r*) chi(*r*)kurdi(*r*)n-i(*r*)zmi(*r*) ?
I shall pay you your money	*Paranızı vereceğim*	puruni(*r*) zi(*r*) verejeghim

Amusements
(Eğlenti**ler**)

Shall we go to the theatre ?	*Tiyatroya gidelim mi ?*	tiyutra͡uyu gide-limmi ?
What is on ?	*Hangi piyes oynanıyor ?*	hungi piyes a͡uynu-ni(*r*)ya͡ur ?

English	Turkish	Pronunciation
Where can we book seats ?	*Nere**den** bilet al**a**bili**r iz** ?*	nereden bilet ulubiliriz ?
Is the box-office open ?	*Gişe **açık mı**(**dır**) ?*	gishe uchi(*r*)kmi(*r*)-di(*r*)r ?
I should like to see a plan of the seats	*Yer**leri** gösteri**r** bir plan gör**mek** ister**im***	yerleri ge͡usterir bir plun ge͡urmek isterim
These seats are reserved	*Bu yer**ler** tutul**muş**(**tur**)*	bo͡o yerler to͡oto͡ol-mo͡oshto͡or
Let us take —	*. . . alalım*	. . . ululi(*r*)m
We want four seats	*Dört yer tut**mak** iste**yor uz***	de͡urt yer to͡otmuk isteya͡uro͡oz
Where are our seats ?	*Yer**lerimiz** nere-**de**(**dir**) ?*	yerlerimiz nere-dedir ?
Where is the cloak-room ?	*Gardörop nere**de**-(**dir**) ?*	gurde͡ura͡up nerede-dir ?
There is no charge	*Ücret**siz dir***	e͡wjretsizdir
Will you give me a programme ?	*Ban**a** bir program ver**irmi siniz** ?*	bunu bir pra͡ugrum verirmisiniz ?
Who is the conductor ?	*Şefdorkestir kim-**dir** ?*	shefda͡urkestir kimdir ?
Shall we go to the buffet ?	*Büf**eye** gide**lim mi** ?*	be͡wfeye gidelim mi ?
Is there a good museum ?	*İyi bir müze var **mıdır** ?*	iyi bir me͡wze vurmi(*r*)di(*r*)r ?
Are tickets required ?	*Bilet al**mak** lâzım **mıdır** ?*	bilet ulmuk la͡azi(*r*)m mi(*r*)di(*r*)r ?
How much will it cost ?	*Kaç**a** mal ol**ur** ?*	kuchu mul a͡ulo͡or ?
It will take all day	*Bütün gün sür**er***	be͡wte͡wn ge͡wn se͡wrer
We must take some sandwiches with us	*Bir kaç sandviç beraber al**malı-yız***	bir kuch sundvich beruber ulmuli(*r*)-yi(*r*)z
Can we go by coach ?	*Otobüs ile gidebili**r miyiz** ?*	a͡uta͡ube͡ws ile gide-bilirmiyiz ?
The coach leaves at ten	*Otobüs saat **onda** hareket ed**er***	a͡uta͡ube͡ws suut a͡undu hureket eder

English	Turkish	Pronunciation
When does the coach leave for Taksim?	*Taksime giden otobüs nevakıt hareket eder?*	tuksime giden a͡uta͡ube͡ws nevuki(*r*)t hureket eder?
We return from Ankara at three o'clock	*Biz Ankaradan saat üçte döneriz*	biz unkurudun suut e͡wchte de͡uneriz
Every Wednesday	*Her Çarşamba günü*	her churshumbu ge͡wne͡w
We should like some refreshment	*Yiyecek bir şey isteriz*	yiyejek bir shey isteriz
Can you get some light refreshments for us?	*Bizim için yiyecek hafif bir şeyler tedarik edebilir misiniz?*	bizim ichin yiyejek hufif bir sheyler tedurik edebilirmisiniz?
Is there a good place for lunch?	*Öğle yemeğini yiyecek güzel bir yer var mıdır?*	e͡ughle yemeghini yiyejek ge͡wzel bir yer vurmi(*r*)di(*r*)r?
When does the performance commence?	*Oyun ne vakıt başlar?* (or *başlayor*) (see T.G. 70ccc)	a͡uyo͡on ne vuki(*r*)t bushlur? (*or* bushluya͡ur)
What time do the doors open?	*Kapılar kaçta açılır?*	kupi(*r*)lur kuchtu uchi(*r*)li(*r*)r?
An interval of fifteen minutes	*On beş dakikalık bir antrak*	a͡un besh dukikuli(*r*)k bir untruk

Cycling
(Bisikletile gezinti)

English	Turkish	Pronunciation
I want to hire a bicycle	*Bir bisiklet kiralamak ist(e)yorum*	bir bisiklet kirulumuk isteya͡uro͡om
Fitted with all accessories	*Bütün teferuatiyle mücehhez (olarak)* or *(olsun)*	be͡wte͡wn tefero͡outiyle me͡wjehhez (a͡uluruk) *or* (a͡ulso͡on)
What are your terms?	*Şaraitiniz nedir?*	shuruitiniz nedir?
By the day	*Gündelikle,* or *Gündeliği*	ge͡wndelikle, *or* ge͡wndelighi

English	Turkish	Pronunciation
Have you a cycle shelter?	*Bisiklet kon**acak** yer**iniz** var **mı dır**?*	bisiklet kaunujuk yeriniz vurmi(r)di(r)r ?
Tighten; loosen this nut	*Şu somunu sıkış**tırınız**; Şu somunu gevşet**iniz*** or *gevşetir **misiniz**?*	shoo saumoonoo si(r)ki(r)shti(r)ri(r)ni(r)z ; shoo saumoonoo gevshetiniz *or* gevshetir misiniz?
I have broken —	*Kır**dım***	ki(r)rdi(r)m
Are you ready?	*Hazır **mı sınız**?*	huzi(r)rmi(r)si(r)ni(r)z ?
My tyre is punctured	*Lastiğ**im** delin**miştir***	lustighim delinmishtir
The chain is off	*Zincir kurtul**muştur***	zinjir koortoolmooshtoor
I must pump up the tyres	*Lastik**leri** şişir**meliyim***	lustikleri shishirmeliyim
We will start at noon	*Öğle zaman**ında** yol**a** çık**arız***	eughle zumuni(r)ndu yaulu chi(r)kuri(r)z
Ring your bell	*Çıngırağ**ınızı** çal**ınız***	chi(r)ngi(r)rughi(r)ni(r)zi(r) chuli(r)ni(r)z
Do not go so fast	*Okadar hızlı git**meyiniz***	aukudur hi(r)zli(r) gitmeyiniz
Do I turn to the right; left?	*Sağ**a mı** dön**eyim**? Sol**a mı** dön**eyim**?*	sughumi(r) deuneyim ? ; saulumi(r) deuneyim ?
Do I keep straight on?	*Dos doğru **mu** gid**eyim**?*	daus daughroomoo gideyim ?
Have you a road-guide?	*Siz**de** yol**ları** gös**teren** harita var **mı**?*	sizde yaulluri(r) geusteren huritu vurmi(r) ?
Yes, sir, which do you require?	*Evet, bay, hangi**sini** ist(e)**yor sunuz**?* (see T.G. 70cc)	evet, buy, hungisini isteyaursoonooz ?
The one for Ankara and neighbourhood	*Ankara ve civar**ına** mahsus ol**anı** ister**im***	unkuru ve jivuri(r)nu muhsoos auluni(r) isterim

English	Turkish	Pronunciation
Where can I get my bicycle mended ?	Bisikleti**mi** nere**de** tâmir et**tir**ebili**rim** ?	bisikletimi nerede ta͡amir ettirebilirim ?
Can you repair this for me ?	Bun**u** ban**a** tâmir edebili**r misiniz** ?	bo͡ono͡o bunu ta͡amir edebilimisiniz ?
I want my cycle cleaned	Bisikleti**mi** temizlet**mek** ist(e)**yorum** (see T.G. 70cc)	bisikletimi temizletmek isteya͡uro͡om
How long will it take ?	Ne kadar süre**r** ?	ne kudur se͡wrer ?
At what time will it be ready ?	Ne vakıt hazır olu**r** ?	ne vuki(*r*)t huzi(*r*)r a͡ulo͡or ?
I am a member of the cyclists' touring club	Bisikletçi**ler** turinğ kulübü azası**ndanım**	bisikletchiler to͡oringh ko͡ole͡wbe͡w uzusi(*r*)nduni(*r*)m
Here is my membership card	İşte âza**lık** vesika**m** bura**da**dır	ishte a͡azuli(*r*)k vesikum bo͡orududi(*r*)r
How far are we from Adana ?	Adana'**dan** ne kadar uzağı**z** ?	udunudun ne kudur o͡ozughi(*r*)z ?
Are the roads good ?	Yol**lar** iyi **midir** ?	ya͡ullur iyimidir ?
The roads are in good condition	Yol**lar** iyi bir hal**dedir**	ya͡ullur iyi birhuldedir
The roads are dusty	Yol**lar** toz**ludur**	ya͡ullur ta͡uzlo͡odo͡or
This is a bad road	Bu fena bir yol**dur**	bo͡o fenu bir ya͡uldo͡or
This hill is dangerous	Bu yokuş tehlike**lidir**	bo͡o ya͡uko͡osh tehlikelidir
Ride with caution	İhtiyat**la** gid**iniz**	ihtiyutlu gidiniz
Where is the nearest cycle shop ?	Bura**ya** en yakın bisiklet**çi** dükkânı nere**dedir** ?	bo͡oruyu en yuki(*r*)n bisikletchi de͡wkkiani(*r*) nerededir ?
Is it time to light up ?	Lamba yakmak zamanı **mıdır** ?	Lumbu yukmuk zumuni(*r*)mi(*r*)di(*r*)r ?

English	Turkish	Pronunciation
Can you mend a tyre for me ?	*Bana bir lastik tâmir eder misiniz ?*	bunu bir lustik taa mir edermisiniz ?
Will you please fill my lamp ?	*Lûtfen lambamı gaz yağı ile doldurur musunuz ?*	lûtfen lumbumi(r) guz yughi(r) ile dauldooroormoo-soonooz ?
It wants a new wick	*Yeni bir fitil ister*	yeni bir fitil ister
May I borrow your pump ?	*Tulumbanızı bir az alabilir miyim ?*	tooloombuni(r)zi(r) bir uz ulubilirmi-yim ?
Lend me a spanner	*Âriyeten bana bir civata anahtarı veriniz*	aariyeten bunu bir jivutu unuhturi(r) verini(r)z
Have you accommodation for cyclists ?	*Bisikletçileri yatıracak yeriniz var mı ?*	bisikletchileri yu-ti(r)rujuk yeriniz vurmi(r) ?
Could you give me a match ?	*Bir kibrit verebilir misiniz ?*	bir kibrit verebilir-misiniz ?
Can you put us up for the night ?	*Bir gece için istirahatımızı te'min edebilir misiniz ?*	bir geje ichin istiruhuti(r)mi(r)-zi(r) te'min edebi-lirmisiniz ?

Motoring
(Otomobil**le** seyahat)

English	Turkish	Pronunciation
Will you repair — ?	*Tâmir eder mi siniz ?*	taamir edermisi-niz ?
Have you examined my speed-changing gear ?	*Vites çarkını muayene ettiniz mi ?*	vites churki(r)ni(r) moouyene ettiniz-mi ?
The clutch is out of order	*Motörün abriyaj pedalı bozuktur*	mauteurewn ubriyuj peduli(r) bauzooktoor
I want a carburettor for the motor	*Motör için bir karbüratör ist(e)yorum* (see T.G. 70cc)	mauteur ichin bir kurbewruteur isteyauroom

English	Turkish	Pronunciation
Replace my brake	*Frenlerimi değiştiriniz*	frenlerimi deghishtiriniz
The spring is broken	*Yay kırılmıştır*	yuy ki(*r*)ri(*r*)l-mi(*r*)shti(*r*)r
Change it	*Onu değiştiriniz*	a͡uno͡o deghishtiri-niz
I have lost my horn	*Kornemi kaybettim*	ka͡urnemi kuybet-tim
Have you an accumulator, four volts ?	*Dört volt kuvvetinde bir akümülatörünüz var mı ?*	de͡urt va͡ult ko͡ovve-tinde bir uke͡w-me͡wlute͡ure͡wne͡wz vur mi(*r*) ?
Can you put a new tyre on this wheel ?	*Bu tekerleğe yeni bir dış lastiği takar mısınız ?*	Bo͡o tekerleghe yeni bir di(*r*)sh lustighi tukurmi(*r*)si(*r*)-ni(*r*)z ?
Give me a litre of petrol	*Bana bir litre benzin veriniz*	bunu bir litre ben-zin veriniz
Give me some motor oil	*Bana makine yağı veriniz*	bunu mukine yug-hi(*r*) veriniz
Give me a motoring map	*Bana bir otomobil yolu haritası veriniz*	bunu bir a͡uta͡uma͡u-bil ya͡ulo͡o huritu-si(*r*) veriniz
To motorists : Drive slowly through this town ; (village)	*Otomobilcilere : Bu şehirden, bu (köyden) geçerken yavaş gidiniz*	a͡uta͡uma͡ubiljilere : bo͡o shehirden, bo͡o (ke͡uyden) ge-cherken yuvush gidiniz
Speed not to exceed 10 Km. per hour	*Sürat saatte on kilometroyu geçmemelidir*	se͡wrut suutte a͡un kila͡umetra͡uyo͡o gechmemelidir
Danger, cross-roads	*Tehlike var, dört yol ağzıdır*	tehlike vur, de͡urt ya͡ul ughzi(*r*)-di(*r*)r
Is there a motor garage in this town ?	*Bu şehirde bir otomobil garajı var mı ?*	bo͡o shehirde bir a͡uta͡uma͡ubil guru-ji(*r*) vur mi(*r*) ?
What is the power of this motor ?	*Bu motörün kuvveti nedir ?*	bo͡o ma͡ute͡ure͡wn ko͡ovveti nedir ?
It is forty horse-power	*Kırk beygir kuvvetindedir*	ki(*r*)rk beygir kuv-vetindedir

English	Turkish	Pronunciation
I want my accumulator charged	*Akümülatörümün imlasını isteyorum*, or *isterim*	ukewmewluteurewmewn imlusi(*r*)ni(*r*) isteyauroom, *or* isterim
Are you an experienced driver ?	*Siz tecrübeli bir şoför müsünüz ?*	siz tejrewbeli bir shaufeurmewsewnewz ?

The Steamboat
(İstimpot)

English	Turkish	Pronunciation
Is this the boat for Bandirma ?	*Bandırma'ya gidecek vapur bu mudur ?*	bundi(*r*)rmuyu gidejek vupoor boomoodoor ?
When do we start ?	*Ne vakıt hareket ediyoruz ?*	ne vuki(*r*)t hureket ediyaurooz ?
What time are we due at Bandirma ?	*Bandırma'ya muvasalat saatı kaçtır ?* or *Bandırma'ya kaçta varıyoruz ?*	bundi(*r*)rmuyu moovusulut suuti(*r*) kuchti(*r*)r ? *or* bundi(*r*)muyu kuchtu vuri(*r*)yaurooz
Wait for me	*Beni bekleyiniz*	beni bekleyiniz
Time is up	*Vakıt geldi*	vuki(*r*)t geldi
Where is your luggage ?	*Eşyanız neredеdir ?*	eshyuni(*r*)z nerededir ?
When shall we arrive ?	*Ne vakıt varacağız ?*	ne vuki(*r*)t vurujughi(*r*)z ?
Let us go into the cabin	*Kamaraya inelim*	kumuruyu inelim
Where is my cabin ?	*Kamaram nerededir ?*	kumurum nerededir ?
I want a cabin to myself	*Yalnız bana mahsus bir kamara ist(e)yorum* (see T.G. 70*cc*)	yulni(*r*)z bunu muhsoos bir kumuru isteyauroom
Is the sea smooth ?	*Deniz sâkin midir ?*	deniz saakinmidir ?
The sea is rough	*Deniz serttir*	deniz serttir

English	Turkish	Pronunciation
It is blowing a gale	*Bora çıktı* or *Bora kopuyor*	bauru chi(r)kti(r) *or* bauru kaupooyaur
I feel ill (sick)	*Mîdem bulanıyor*	meedem booluni(r)-yaur
Can you get me some tea?	*Benim için çay yaptırabilir misiniz?*	benim ichin chuy yupti(r)rubilir-misiniz?
Call the stewardess	*Bayan kamarotu çağırınız*	buyun kumurautoo chughi(r)ri(r)ni(r)z
Look for my things	*Eşyalarımı arayınız*	eshyuluri(r)mi(r) uruyi(r)ni(r)z
Look after my things	*Eşyalarıma bakınız*	eshyuluri(r)mu baki(r)ni(r)z
There is another trunk	*Bir bavul daha olacak*	bir buvool duhu aulujuk
Passengers are requested to keep clear of the gang-way	*Yolculardan yol üzerinde durmamaları rica olunur*	yauljoolurdun yaul ewzerinde door-mumuluri(r) riju-auloonoor
How far are we from the sea?	*Denizden ne kadar uzağız?*	denizden nekudur oozughi(r)z?
Are there any sea-side places near here	*Buraya yakın plaj var mıdır?*	booruyu yuki(r)n pluj vurmi(r)-di(r)?
I should like to go for a short sea trip	*Kısa bir deniz seyahatına gitmek isterim*	ki(r)su bir deniz seyuhuti(r)nu git-mek isterim

Photography
(Fotografçılık)

Have you brought your camera?	*Fotograf makinenizi getirdiniz mi?*	fautaugruf mukine-nizi getirdi-nizmi?
This is my camera	*Bu benim fotograf makinemdir*	boo benim fautau-gruf mukinem-dir
Must permission be obtained to photograph?	*Fotograf çekmek için izin alınmalı mıdır?*	fautaugruf chekmek ichin izin uli(r)nmuli(r)-mi(r)di(r)r?

English	Turkish	Pronunciation
I wish to photograph the interior	*İçer**sinin** fotografını almak ist(e)**yorum*** (see T.G. 70cc)	ichersinin fa͡uta͡ugrufi(r)ni(r) ulmuk isteya͡uro͡om
What exposure must I give it ?	*Ne kadar pozla al**malıyım*** or *al**ayım** ?*	ne kudur pa͡uzlu ulmuli(r)yi(r)m *or* uluyi(r)m ?
This light is too strong	*Bu ziya fazla kuvvet**lidir***	bo͡o ziyu fuzlu ko͡ovvetlidir
This light is bad	*Bu ziya fena**dır***	bo͡o ziyu fenudi(r)r
It is out of focus	*Görüş saha**sından** hariç**tir***	ge͡ure͡wsh suhusi(r)ndun hurichtir
What size of plate do you use ?	*Ne büyük**lükte** cam kullanı**yorsunuz** ?*	ne be͡wye͡wkle͡wkte jum ko͡olluni(r)ya͡urso͡ono͡oz ?
This plate is spoiled	*Bu cam bozu**lmuştur***	bo͡o jum ba͡uzo͡olmo͡oshto͡or
Have you a dark-room ?	*Karan**lık** oda**nız** var **mıdır** ?*	kurunli(r)k a͡uduni(r)z vur mi(r)di(r)r ?
I want to develop some plates	*Bir kaç cam develope et**mek** ist(e)**yorum***	bir kuch jum devela͡upe etmek isteya͡uro͡om
I am going to print some copies	*Bâzı**larını** kâğı**da** çeke**ceğim***	ba͡azi(r)luri(r)ni(r) kiaghi(r)du chekejeghim
This was spoilt in the printing	*Bu kâğı**da** çekilir**ken** bozul**muştur***	bo͡o kiaghi(r)du chekilirken ba͡uzo͡olmo͡oshto͡or
That is due to over-exposure	*Bu fazla poz netice**sidir***	bo͡o fuzlu pa͡uz netijesidir
What a beautiful photograph !	*Ne kadar güzel bir fotograf**tır** !*	ne kudur ge͡wzel bir fa͡uta͡ugrufti(r)r !
The grouping is very good	*Grup tarzı çok iyi**dir***	gro͡op turzi(r) cha͡uk iyidir
I have secured some very fine views	*Gayet güzel bir takım manzara**lar** elde **ettim***	guyet ge͡wzel bir tuki(r)m munzurulur elde ettim

English	Turkish	Pronunciation
Do you sell photographic materials; photographic chemicals?	*Fotograf levazımatı; Fotograf mevadı kimyeviye**si** satı**yor musunuz**?*	fa͡uta͡ugruf levuzi(*r*)muti(*r*); fa͡uta͡ugruf mevudi(*r*) kimyeviyesi suti(*r*)ya͡urmo͡oso͡ono͡oz
What do you require?	*Ne ist(e)**yor sunuz**?* (see T.G. 70cc)	ne isteya͡urso͡ono͡oz?
I want some more films	*Bir kaç pelikül daha ist(e)**yorum***	bir kuch pelike͡wl duhu isteya͡uro͡om
I want some pretty mounts	*Güzel bir iki karton iste**rim***	ge͡wzel bir iki kurta͡un isterim
Were your photographs successful?	*Resim**leriniz** iyi çık**tı mı**?*	resimleriniz iyi chi(*r*)kti(*r*) mi?
I want to buy a camera	*Bir fotograf makine**si** satın al**mak** ist(e)**yorum***	bir fa͡uta͡ugruf mukinesi suti(*r*)n ulmuk isteya͡uro͡om
I am afraid they are failures	*Korkarım ki bun**lar** bozuk**tur***	ka͡urkuri(*r*)m ki bo͡onlur ba͡uzo͡okto͡or
An amateur photographer	*Amatör bir fotografçı*	umute͡ur bir fa͡uta͡ugrufchi(*r*)
Sensitive to light	*Ziya**dan** çok mütehassis*	ziyudun cha͡uk me͡wtehussis
I was very disappointed	*İnkisarı hayale uğra**dım***	inkisuri(*r*) huyule o͡oghrudi(*r*)m

Post, Telegraph, and Telephone

(Posta, telegraf ve telefon)

Where is the post-office?	*Postane nerede**dir**?*	pa͡ustune neredеdir?
Post this letter	*Bu mektubu posta**ya** veri**niz***	bo͡o mekto͡obo͡o pa͡ustuyu veriniz
Pay the postage on it	*Posta ücreti**ni** veri**niz***	pa͡ustu e͡wjretini veriniz

English	Turkish	Pronunciation
What is the postage on this letter?	*Bu mektubun posta ücreti nedir?*	bo͡o mekto͡obo͡on paûstu ewjreti nedir?
Were you in time for the post?	*Postaya yetişdiniz mi?*	paûstuyu yetishdinizmi?
Office hours (civil service)	*Daire saatları*	duire suutluri(r)
Is this letter overweight?	*Bu mektubun ağırlığı fazla mıdır?*	bo͡o mekto͡obo͡on ughi(r)rli(r)ghi(r) fuzlu mi(r)di(r)r?
Yes, it wants another stamp	*Evet, bir pul daha ister*	evet, bir po͡ol duhu ister
Maximum weight	*Âzamî ağırlık*	aazumee ughi(r)rli(r)k
Write your name and address here	*İsim ve adresinizi buraya yazınız*	isim ve. udresinizi bo͡oruyu yuzi(r)ni(r)z
I wish to register this letter	*Bu mektubu taahütlü olarak göndermek isterim*	bo͡o mekto͡obo͡o tuuhewtlew aûluruk gewndermek isterim
A registered letter	*Taahütlü mektup*	tuuhewtlew mekto͡op
Printed matter	*Matbua*	mutbo͡ou
Have you any letters for the post?	*Postaya verilecek mektuplarınız var mı?*	paûstuyu verilejek mekto͡opluri(r)ni(r)z vurmi(r)?
You are too late for this post	*Bu posta için çok geç kaldınız*	bo͡o paûstu ichin chaûk gech kuldi(r)ni(r)z
Am I in time for the mail?	*Postaya yetişebildim mi?*	paûstuyu yetishebildimmi?
The mail has gone	*Posta gitmişdir*	paûstu gitmishdir
The next mail goes at 3 o'clock	*Gelecek posta saat üçte gider*	gelejek paûstu suut ewchte gider
Is it time for the post?	*Posta zamanı mıdır?*	paûstu zumuni(r)mi(r)di(r)r?

English	Turkish	Pronunciation
When is the next collection ?	*Gelecek toplama saat kaçtadır ?*	gelejek tau͡uplumu suut kuchtudi(*r*)r ?
Is there another delivery to-night ?	*Bu gece başka bir tevzi daha var mıdır ?*	bo͞o geje bushku bir tevzi duhu vur-mi(*r*)di(*r*)r ?
Please forward	*Lûtfen sevk ediniz*	lûtfen sevk ediniz
Is your letter ready for posting ?	*Mektubunuz postaya verilmeğe hazır mıdır ?*	mekto͞obo͞ono͞oz pau͡ustuyu veril-meghe huzi(*r*)r-mi(*r*)di(*r*)r ?
Will you post this letter for me ?	*Bu mektubu postaya verir misiniz ?*	bo͞o mekto͞obo͞o pau͡ustuyu verirmi-siniz ?
When does the post office close ?	*Postahane ne vakıt kapanır ?*	pau͡ustuhune ne vuki(*r*)t kupu-ni(*r*)r ?
At what time does the office close ?	*Daire saat kaçta kapanır ?*	duire suut kuchtu kupuni(*r*)r ?
Customs declaration	*Gümrük beyannamesi*	ge͡wmre͡wk beyun-numesi
Name and address of sender	*Gönderenin isim ve adresi*	ge͡underenin isim ve udresi
Value of contents	*Muhteviyatının kıymeti*	mo͞ohteviyuti(*r*)n-i(*r*)n ki(*r*)ymeti
Place of destination	*Gideceği yer*	gidejeghi yer
Have you any letters for Mr. — ?	*Bay — için mektup var mı ?*	buy — ichin mek-to͞op vurmi(*r*) ?
Will this letter go to-night ?	*Bu mektup bu gece gider mi ?*	bo͞o mekto͞op bo͞o geje gider mi ?
When does the mail leave for London ?	*Londra'ya posta ne vakıt hareket eder ?*	lau͡undru'yu pau͡ustu ne vuki(*r*)t hure-ket eder ?
Is the London mail in yet ?	*Londra postası geldi mi ?*	lau͡undru pau͡ustusi(*r*) geldimi ?
I want to send a telegram	*Bir telgraf göndermek ist(e)yorum* (see T.G. 70cc)	bir telgruf ge͡un-dermek isteyau͡u-ro͞om

English	Turkish	Pronunciation
What is the charge ?	*Ücreti* ***nedir*** *?*	e͡wjreti nedir ?
The first twelve words	*İlk on iki kelime*	ilk a͡un iki kelime
Every extra word	*Her fazla kelime*	her fuzlu kelime
I want a money-order	*Bir havalename ist(e)****yorum***	bir huvulenume isteya͡uro͡om
Are you on the telephone ?	*Telefon****unuz*** *var* ***mı ?***	telefa͡uno͡ono͡oz vurmi(*r*) ?
What is your number ?	*Numara****nız*** *kaç****tır*** *?; Numara****nız*** *ne****dir***	no͡omuruni(*r*)z kuchti(*r*)r ? ; no͡omuruni(*r*)z nedir ?
Ring up Mr. Orhan	*Bay Orhan'****a*** *telefon edi****niz***	buy a͡urhunu telefa͡un ediniz
Are you there ?	*Siz* ***misiniz*** *?*	sizmisiniz ?
Who are you ?	*Kim****siniz*** *?*	kimsiniz ?
I want number —	*. . . numara****yı*** *ist(e)****yorum***	. . . no͡omuruyi(*r*) isteya͡uro͡om ?
You are through	*Görüş****ünüz***	ge͡ure͡wshe͡wne͡wz
Time is up	*Vakıt gel****di****, (vaktınız bitmiştir)*	vuki(*r*)t geldi, (vukti(*r*)ni(*r*)z bitmishtir)
I cannot hear you	*Sizi işide(****me****)****yorum*** (see T.G. 59*l*)	sizi ishidemeya͡uro͡om
I cannot get number —	*. . . . numara****yı*** *bula(****ma****)****yorum*** (see T.G. 59*l*)	. . . no͡omuruyi(*r*) bo͡olumuya͡uro͡om
No reply from Ankara	*Ankara'****dan*** *cevap yok*	unkurudun jevup ya͡uk
Your call is cancelled	*Mükâleme****niz*** *iptal edil****miştir***	me͡wkialemeniz iptul edilmishtir

Correspondence
(Muhaberat)

English	Turkish	Pronunciation
I must write a letter	*Bir mektup yaz****malıyım***	bir mekto͡op yuzmuli(*r*)yi(*r*)m
I want some paper	*Bir az kâğıt ist(e)****yorum***	bir uz kiaghi(*r*)t isteya͡uro͡om

English	Turkish	Pronunciation
Have you any ink ?	*Mürekkebiniz var mı ?*	mewrekkebiniz vurmi(*r*) ?
Will you please give me some ?	*Lûtfen bana bir az mürekkep verir misiniz ?*	lûtfen bunu bir uz mewrekkep verirmisiniz ?
I have some letters to write	*Yazılacak bâzı mektublarım var*	yuzi(*r*)lujuk baazi(*r*) mektooblu-ri(*r*)m vur
Can you lend me a pen (pencil) ?	*Bana âriyeten bir kalem (kurşun kalem) verir misiniz ?*	bunu aariyeten bir kulem (koorshoon kulem) verirmisiniz ?
Will you please give me some note-paper ?	*Lûtfen bana not-kâğıdı verir misiniz ?*	lûtfen bunu not-kiaghi(*r*)di(*r*) verirmisiniz ?
One sheet will be enough	*Bir tabaka kâfidir*	bir tubuku kiafidir
I shall want an envelope	*Bir zarfa ihtiyacım olacaktır*	bir zurfu ihtiyuci(*r*)m aulujukti(*r*)r
How much a packet ?	*Paketi kaç paradır ?*	puketi kuch purudi(*r*)r ?
I will take a quire	*Bir deste alırım*	bir deste uli(*r*)ri(*r*)m
I want a postcard	*Bir kartpostal ist(e)yorum*	bir kurtpaustul isteyauroom
I want a postcard with a view	*Manzaralı bir kartpostal ist(e)yorum* (see T.G. 70cc)	munzuruli(*r*) bir kurtpaustul isteyauroom
I want some picture postcards	*Resimli kartpostal isterim*	resimli kurtpaustul isterim
I use a fountain-pen	*Mürekkepli kalem kullanıyorum*	mewrekkepli kulem koolluni(*r*)yauroom
Will you please refill my pen ?	*Kalemimi lûtfen mürekkeple doldurur musunuz ?*	kulemimi lûtfen mewrekkeple dauldooroor moosoonooz ?
I have a note to enclose	*İçine konacak bir notum vardır*	ichine kaunujuk bir nautoom vurdi(*r*)r

English	Turkish	Pronunciation
Lend me a sheet of paper, please	*Lûtfen bana âriyeten bir tabaka kâğıt veriniz*	lûtfen bunu aari-yeten bir tubuku kiaghi(*r*)t veriniz
Do you like a hard nib?	*Sert bir uç mu seversiniz?*	sert bir oochmoo seversiniz?
What is the day of the month?	*Ayın (ne günüdür)?* (or *kaçıdır*)?	uyi(*r*)n ne gew-newdewr? (*or* kuchi(*r*)di(*r*)r)
To-day is the first	*Bu gün biridir*	boo gewn biridir
Seal your letter	*Mektubunuzu mühürleyiniz*	mektoobooonoozoo mewhewrleyiniz
There is no sealing wax	*Mühür mumu yoktur*	mewhewr moomoo yauktoor
I have a letter to answer	*Yazılacak bir mektubum var*	yuzi(*r*)lucuk bir mektooboom vur
Wait for an answer	*Cevap için bekleyiniz*	jevup ichin bek-leyiniz
Shall I wait for an answer?	*Cevap için bekleyeyim mi?*	jevup ichin bek-leyeyimmi?

Beginning and Ending Letters
(Mektup başı ve nihayeti)

Dear Sir	*Sayın Bay*	suyi(*r*)n buy
Dear Mr.	*Sayın Bay*	suyi(*r*)n buy
Dear Miss	*Sayın Bayan*	suyi(*r*)n buyun
Dear Madam	*Sayın Bayan*	suyi(*r*)n buyun
By beloved Sister	*Sevgili Hemşireciğim*	sevgili hemshire-jighim [ghi(*r*)m
My dear Father	*Sevgili Babacığım*	sevgili bubuji(*r*)-
Dearest Mother	*Çok Sevgili Anneciğim*	chauk sevgili unne-jighim
Dear Cousin	*Aziz yeğenim*	uziz yeghenim
The Proprietor (House)	*Ev* (or *mal*) *Sahibi*	ev (*or* mul) suhibi
The Manager	*Şef*	shef
The Secretary	*Kâtip*	kiatip
The Postmaster	*Posta Müdürü*	paustu mewdewrew
The Stationmaster	*İstasyon Şefi*	istusyaun shefi
With many good wishes	*Temenniyatı hâlisane ile*	temenniyuti(*r*) haalisune ile

English	Turkish	Pronunciation
Yours obediently	*Arzı mutâvaat**la***	urzi(*r*) mo͡otaa͡vuut-lu
Yours faithfully	*Arzı sadâkat ile*	urzi(*r*) suda͡akut ile
Your obedient servant	*Muti kulu**nuz***	mo͡oti ko͡olo͡ono͡oz
Yours truly	*Arzı muhalesetl**e***	urzi(*r*) mo͡ohule-setle
Yours sincerely	*Arzı samimiyet**le***	urzi(*r*) sumimiyetle
Yours most sincerely	*Çok fazla samimi-yet**le***	cha͡uk fuzlu sumi-miyetle
Yours affectionately	*Arzı muhabbet**le***	urzi(*r*) mo͡ohubbetle
Your affectionate friend	*Samimî dost**unuz***	sumime͡e da͡usto͡o-no͡oz
Ever your devoted daughter	*Ebediyen siz**e** sadık ve merbut kız**ınız***	ebediyen size su-di(*r*)k ve merbo͡ot ki(*r*)zi(*r*)ni(*r*)z

The Time

(Vakıt)

English	Turkish	Pronunciation
What time is it ?	*Saat kaç**tır** ?*	suut kuchti(*r*)r ?
Tell me the time	*Lûtfen ban**a** saatı söyle**yiniz***	lûtfen bunu suu-ti(*r*) se͡uyleyiniz
Is it late ?	*Geç **midir** ?*	gechmidir ?
It is early	*Erken**dir***	erkendir
It is two o'clock	*Saat iki**dir***	suut ikidir
It will soon strike six	*Yakın**da** altı**yı** çal**acak**tır*	yuki(*r*)ndu ulti(*r*)-yi(*r*) chulujukti(*r*)r
It has just struck five	*Şimdi**cik** beş**i** çal**dı***	shimdijik beshi chuldi(*r*)
It is time to get up	*Kalk**mak** zamanı-**dır***	kulkmuk zumuni(*r*)-di(*r*)r
It is day *or* it is morning	*Gün doğ**muş**,* or *sabah olmuş*	ge͡wn da͡ughmo͡osh, *or* subuh a͡ulmo͡osh
It is not late	*Geç değil**dir***	gech deghildi(*r*)r
It is five minutes past seven	*Yediy**i** beş geç**iyor***	yediyi besh gechi-ya͡ur
It is a quarter past one	*Bir**i** çeyrek geç**iyor***	biri cheyrek gechi-ya͡ur

English	Turkish	Pronunciation
Exactly five o'clock	*Saat tam beş*—	suut tum besh
Between four and five o'clock	*Saat dört ile beş arasında*	suut deûrt ile besh urusi(*r*)ndu
It is twenty minutes past two	*Saat ikiyi yiğirmi dakika geçiyor*	suut ikiyi yighirmi dukiku gechiyaûr
It is half past six	*Saat altı buçuktur*	suut ulti(*r*) bōō-chōōktōōr
It is later than I thought	*Zan ettiğimden fazla geçtir*	zun ettighimden fuzlu gechtir
At a quarter to eight	*Sekize çeyrek kala*	sekize cheyrek kulu
It is time for breakfast	*Kahve altı zamanıdır*	kuhve ulti(*r*) zumuni(*r*)di(*r*)r
It will soon be nine o'clock	*Nerede ise saat dokuza gelecek*	nerede ise suut daûkōōzu gelejek
Has it struck eleven yet ?	*Aceba on biri çaldı mı ?*	ujebu aûn biri chuldi(*r*)mi(*r*) ?
I shall be late	*Geç kalacağım*	gech kulujughi(*r*)m
Tell her to hurry	*Acele etmesini ona söyleyiniz*	ujele etmesini aûnu seûyleyiniz
Come quickly	*Çabucak geliniz*	chubōōjuk geliniz
It is only four o'clock	*Saat ancak dörttür*	suut unjuk deûrttewr
Twenty minutes to six	*Altıya yiğirmi dakika var*	ulti(*r*)yu yighirmi dukiku vur
It is nearly midnight	*Nerede ise gece yarısıdır*	nerede ise geje yuri(*r*)si(*r*)di(*r*)r
At what time ?	*Ne vakıt ?*	ne vuki(*r*)t ?
At seven-fifteen p.m.	*Akşam saat yediyi çeyrek geçe*	ukshum suut yediyi cheyrek geche
By your watch	*Sizin saatınızla*	sizin suuti(*r*)ni(*r*)zlu
My watch has stopped	*Saatım durmuştur*	suuti(*r*)m dōōrmōōshtōōr
I had forgotten to wind it up	*Saatı kurmağı unuttum*	suuti(*r*) kōōrmughi(*r*) ōōnōōttōōm
My watch gains	*Saatım ileri gidiyor*	suuti(*r*)m ileri gidiyaûr
Does your watch lose ?	*Sizin saatınız geri kalıyor mu ?*	sizin suuti(*r*)ni(*r*)z geri kuli(*r*)yaûrmōō ?

English	Turkish	Pronunciation
Yesterday (it) gained 10 minutes	*Dün (saatı**m**) on dakika ileri **idi***	de͡wn (suuti(*r*)m) a͡un dukiku ileri idi
To-day it has lost half an hour	*Bu gün (saatı**m**) yarım saat kaybet**ti***	bo͡o ge͡wn (suuti(*r*)m) yuri(*r*)m suut kuybetti
It is not going	*(Saatı**m**) işle(**me**)-**yor*** (see T.G. 59*l*)	(suuti(*r*)m) ishlemeya͡ur
My watch does not keep good time	*Saatı**m** doğru git(**me**)**yor*** (see T.G. 59*l*)	suuti(*r*)m da͡ughro͡o gitmeya͡ur
It keeps very correct time	*Çok doğru gidi**yor*** or *Çok güzel işl(e)**yor*** (see T.G. 70*cc*)	cha͡uk da͡ughro͡o gidiya͡ur *or* cha͡uk ge͡wzel ishleya͡ur
You are an hour late	*Siz bir saat geç**siniz***	siz bir suut gechsiniz
We have plenty of time	*Çok vaktı**mız** var**dır*** (see T.G. 23*f*)	cha͡uk vukti(*r*)mi(*r*)z vurdi(*r*)r
Let us be early	*Erken davrana**lım***	erken duvrunuli(*r*)m
He came in good time	*O tam vaktı**nda** gel**di*** (see T.G. 23*f*)	a͡u tum vukti(*r*)ndu geldi
At ten a.m.	*Sabah**leyin** saat on**da***	subuhleyin suut a͡undu
Three-thirty	*Üç buçuk*	e͡wch bo͡ocho͡ok
Seven forty-five	*Yedi**yi** kırk beş geçe**rek***	yediyi ki(*r*)rk besh gecherek

Time, Seasons, and Weather
(Vakıt, Mevsim***ler*** ve hava)

English	Turkish	Pronunciation
A short time ago	*Az bir zaman evvel*	uz bir zumun evvel
It was only two days ago	*Ancak iki gün mukaddem **idi***	unjuk iki ge͡wn mo͡okuddem idi
It is at least a month ago	*Hiç ol**mazsa** bir ay evvel **idi***	hich a͡ulmuzsu bir uy evvel idi

English	Turkish	Pronunciation
A few days ago	*Bir kaç gün evvel* ***idi***	bir kuch ge͡wn evvel idi
This day week; From to-day a week ago	*Bund**an** bir hafta sonra ; Bun**dan** bir hafta evvel*	bo͡ondun bir huftu sa͡unru ; bo͡ondun bir huftu evvel
That was two or three days ago	*O iki veya üç gün evvel* ***idi***	a͡u iki veyu e͡wch ge͡wn evvel idi
At about this time	*Takriben bu saatta* (see T.G. 23*f*)	tukriben bo͡o suuttu
Next year	*Gele**cek** sene*	gelejek sene
Next week	*Gele**cek** hafta*	gelejek huftu
next month	*Gele**cek** ay*	gelejek uy
In a month's time	*Bir ay zarfı**n da***	bir uy zurfi(*r*)ndu
On the first of next month	*Gele**cek** ayın birin-de*	gelejek uyi(*r*)n birinde
At the end of this month	*Bu ayın nihayetin-de*	bo͡o uyi(*r*)n nihuye-tinde
The end of the year	*Sene**nin** nihayeti*	senenin nihuyeti
Since December 19th	*Bir**inci** kânunun on dokuz**undan**-**beri***	birinji kiano͡ono͡on a͡un da͡uko͡ozo͡on-dunberi
Until March 25th	*Mar**tın** yiğir**mi** beş**ine** kadar*	murti(*r*)n yighirmi beshine kudur
The middle of April	*Nisa**nın** orta**sı***	nisuni(*r*)n a͡urtusi(*r*)
From time to time	*Zaman zaman*	zumun zumun
Before long	*Çoğa kal**maz***	cha͡ughu kulmuz
Every day	*Her gün*	her ge͡wn
It was only last week (as recently as)	*Daha geç**en** hafta* ***idi***	duhu gechen huftu idi
The twentieth century	*Yiğirm**inci** asır*	yighirminji usi(*r*)r
Before the season	*Turfan**da***	to͡orfundu
In season	*Mevsim**inde***	mevsiminde
During the season	*Mevsim esnası**nda***	mevsim esnusi(*r*)n-du
How long does the season last?	*Mevsim nekadar devam ed**er**?*	mevsim nekudur devum eder?
Out of season	*Vakıt**sız***	vuki(*r*)tsi(*r*)z

English	Turkish	Pronunciation
About three months	*Takri**ben** üç ay*	tukriben ewch uy
How the time flies	*Zaman ne kadar çabuk geç**iyor***	zumun ne kudur chubook gechiyaur
It is like a spring day	*Bir bahar gün**üne** benz(e)**yor***	bir buhur gewnewne benzeyaur
What a lovely spring	*Ne kadar latif bir ilk bahar*	ne kudur lutif bir ilk buhur
It is just like summer	*Ayni**yle** yaz gibi-**dir***	uyniyle yuz gibi-dir
The days are long	*Gün**ler** uzun**dur***	gewnler oozoon-door
Winter will soon be here	*Nere**de** ise kış**a** gireceğiz*, or *giriyor**uz***	nerede ise ki(*r*)shu girejeghiz, *or* giriyauroo z
It is as cold as winter	*Kışın oldu**ğu** kadar soğuk**tur**, kış gibi soğuk**tur***	ki(*r*)shi(*r*)n aul-dooghoo kudur saughooktoor, ki(*r*)sh gibi sau-ghooktoor
What kind of weather is it ?	*Ne biç**im** hava**dır** ?*	ne bichim huvu-di(*r*)r ?
It is beautiful weather	*Güzel bir hava*	gewzel bir huvu
The weather is beautiful	*Hava güzel**dir***	huvu gewzeldir
It is very windy	*Çok rüzgâr**lı dır***	chauk rewzgiarli(*r*)-di(*r*)r
It is very warm	*Çok sıcak**tır***	chauk si(*r*)jukti(*r*)
Is it windy ?	*Rüzgâr var **mı** ?*	rewzgiar vurmi(*r*) ?
No, it is quite calm	*Hayır, gayet sakin-**dir***	huyi(*r*)r, guyet sukindir
I think it will rain	*Yağmur yağ**acağı**-**nı** zanned**erim***	yughmoor yughu-jughi(*r*)ni(*r*) zun-nederim
The sky is overcast	*hava bulut**ludur***	huvu boolootloo-door
It will not last long	*Bu çok sür**mez***	boo chauk sewrmez
The sun is coming out	*Güneş meydan**a** çık(**ı**)**yor*** (see T.G. 70ccc)	gewnesh meydunu chi(*r*)ki(*r*)yaur

English	Turkish	Pronunciation
I do hope it will be fine	*Havanın iyi olduğunu çok ist(e)yorum*	huvuni(*r*)n iyi a͡uldo͡ogho͡ono͡o cha͡uk isteya͡uro͡om
If it does not rain I shall go out	*Yağmur yağmaz sa dışarıya çıkarım*	yughmo͡or yughmuzsu di(*r*)shuri(*r*)yu chi(*r*)kuri(*r*)m
It is frosty	*Ayaz var*	uyuz vur
I am so cold	*O kadar soğuğum ki*	a͡u kudur sa͡ugho͡oghо͡om ki
I am shivering with cold	*Soğuktan titr(i)yorum* (see T.G. 70*cc*)	sa͡ugho͡oktun titriya͡uro͡om
Has it been raining ?	*Yağmur mu yağdı ?*	yughmo͡ormo͡o yughdi(*r*) ?
It is snowing fast	*Kar çok hızla yağ(ı)yor*	kur cha͡uk hi(*r*)zlu yughi(*r*)ya͡ur
It rains	*Yağmur yağ(ı)yor*	yughmo͡or yughi(*r*)ya͡ur
It hails	*Dolu yağ(ı)yor*	da͡ulo͡o yughi(*r*)ya͡ur
It is going to rain	*Yağmur yağacak*	yughmo͡or yughujuk
The weather is very changeable	*Hava çok kararsızdır*	huvu cha͡uk kururst(*r*)zdi(*r*)r
How strong the wind is !	*Ruzgâr ne kadar kuvvetli dir !*	ro͡ozgiar ne kudur ko͡ovvetlidir !
We shall have a storm	*Fırtına kopacaktır*	fi(*r*)rti(*r*)nu ka͡upujukti(*r*)r
The wind is in the east	*Ruzgâr şarktan es(i)yor; Gün doğrusu esiyor* (see T.G. 70*ccc*)	ro͡ozgiar shurktun esiya͡ur ; ge͡wn da͡ughro͡oso͡o esiya͡ur
The dust is very thick	*Toz çok kesiftir*	ta͡uz cha͡uk kesiftir
We were covered with dust	*Toza boğulduk*	ta͡uzu ba͡ugho͡oldo͡ok
Oh dear ! What dreadful weather	*Aman! Ne kadar fena hava*	umun ! ne kudur fenu huvu

English	Turkish	Pronunciation
How it pours	*Nasıl da yağıyor*	nusi(*r*)l du yughi(*r*)-ya͡ur
I am wet through	*Kemiklerime kadar ıslandım*	kemiklerime kudur i(*r*)slun-di(*r*)m
I would like an umbrella	*Bir şemşiye isterim*	bir shemshiye isterim
Look at the rainbow	*Alâimisemaya bakınız*	ala͡aimisemuyu buki(*r*)ni(*r*)z
Oh, how hot it is	*Aman, ne kadar sıcaktır*	umun, ne kudur si(*r*)jukti(*r*)r
I heard the thunder	*Gök gürlemesini duydum*	ge͡uk ge͡wrlemesini do͡oydo͡om
It is lightning	*Şimşek çak(ı)yor* (see T.G. 70*ccc*)	shimshek chuki(*r*)-ya͡ur
There is a full moon	*Ayın on beşidir*	uyi(*r*)n a͡un beshi-dir
There is a new moon	*Yeni ay çıktı*	yeni uy chi(*r*)kti(*r*)

Health

(Sıhhat)

English	Turkish	Pronunciation
How are you ?	*Nasılsınız ?*	nusi(*r*)lsi(*r*)ni(*r*)z ?
Are you quite well ?	*Pek iyi misiniz ?*	pek iyimisiniz ?
Very well, thanks	*Çok iyiyim, teşekkür ederim*	cha͡uk iyiyim, teshekke͡wr ede-rim
Not very well	*Pek iyi değilim*	pek iyi deghilim
I am quite well	*Pek iyiyim*	pek iyiyim
I feel faint	*Baygınlık hissediyorum*	buygi(*r*)nli(*r*)k hiss-ediya͡uro͡om
I am constipated	*İnkıbazım var, pekliğim var*	inki(*r*)buzi(*r*)m vur, peklighim vur
I am ill	*Hastayım*	hustuyi(*r*)m
I don't feel well	*İyi değilim*	iyi deghilim
I have caught a chill	*Soğuk kaptım*	sa͡ugho͡ok kupti(*r*)m

English	Turkish	Pronunciation
I have a headache	*Baş**ım** ağr**ıyor***	bushi(*r*)m ughri(*r*)ya͡ur
I have a cold	*Nezl**em** var*	nezlem vur
I want to see the doctor	*Doktor**u** gör**mek** ist(e)**yorum*** (see T.G. 70cc)	da͡ukta͡uro͡o ge͡urmek isteya͡uro͡om
Send for the doctor	*Doktor**a** haber gönder**iniz***	da͡ukta͡uru huber ge͡underiniz
She has a bad cough	(*O**nun***) *fena bir öksürü**ğü** var*	a͡uno͡on fenu bir e͡ukse͡wre͡wghe͡w vur
How much is the doctor's fee for a visit ?	*Doktor**un** vizit**ası*** (*kaç para**dır***) or (ne***dir***)	da͡ukta͡uro͡on vizitusi(*r*) (kuch purudi(*r*)r) *or* (nedir)
Where is there a chemist's shop ?	*Eczane nerede**dir** ?*	ejzune nerededir ?
I feel better	*Kendim**i** daha iyi bulu**yorum***	kendimi duhu iyi bo͡olo͡oya͡uro͡om
I hope you will soon be better	*Yakın**da** daha iyi ola**cağınızı** ümit **ederim***	yuki(*r*)ndu duhu iyi a͡ulujughi(*r*)ni(*r*)zi(*r*) e͡wmit ederim
Do you sleep well ?	*İyi uyu**yor musunuz** ?*	iyi o͡oyo͡oya͡urmo͡oso͡ono͡oz ?
When shall I call again ?	*Tekrar nevakıt gel**eyim** ?*	tekrur nevuki(*r*)t geleyim ?
Will you give me a prescription ?	*Ban**a** bir reçete ver**ir misiniz** ?*	bunu bir rechete verirmisiniz ?
Have this prescription made up	*Bu reçete**yi** yap**tırınız***	bo͡o recheteyi yupti(*r*)ri(*r*)· i(*r*)z
See me again on Wednesday	*Ben**i** çarşamba gün**ü** tekrar gör**ünüz***	beni churshumbu ge͡wne͡w tekrur ge͡ure͡wne͡wz
A soupspoonful three times a day	*Gün**de** üç çorba kaşı**ğı***	ge͡wnde e͡wch cha͡urbu kushi(*r*)ghir
To be taken after each meal	*Her yemek**ten** sonra alın**acaktır***	her yemekten sa͡unru uli(*r*)nujukti(*r*)r

English	Turkish	Pronunciation
Where shall I find a dentist	*Nerede bir dişçi bulabilirim*	nerede bir dishchi bo͡olubilirim
I want a tooth extracted	*Bir diş çektirmek isteyorum*	bir dish chektir-mek isteya͡uro͡om
Please use chloroform	*Lûtfen kloroform kullanınız*	lûtfen kla͡ura͡ufa͡urm ko͡olluni(*r*)ni(*r*)z
Please give an injection	*Lûtfen enceksiyon yapınız*	lûtfen enjeksiya͡un yupi(*r*)ni(*r*)z
I want this tooth filled	*Bu dişi doldurtmak ist(e)yorum* (see T.G. 70cc)	bo͡o dishi da͡ul-do͡ortmuk iste-ya͡uro͡om
How much do you charge ?	*Kaç para ist(e)-yorsunuz ?*	kuch puru iste-ya͡urso͡ono͡oz ?
Shake the bottle	*Şişeyi çalkayınız*	shisheyi chulkuyi(*r*)-ni(*r*)z
Poison, not to be taken	*Zehirlidir, içilemez*	zehirlidir, ichile-mez
For outward application only	*Yalnız hariçten istîmal içindir*	yulni(*r*)z hurichten isteemul ichindir

Religion

(Din)

English	Turkish	Pronunciation
Is there an English church here ?	*Burada (bir) protestan kilisesi var mıdır ?*	bo͡orudu (bir) pra͡u-testun kilisesi vurmi(*r*)di(*r*)r ?
What time is the service ?	*İbâdet saat kaçta yapılıyor ?*	iba͡adet suut kuchtu yupi(*r*)li(*r*)ya͡ur ?
Is it far from here ?	*Buradan uzak mıdır ?*	bo͡orudun o͡ozuk-mi(*r*)di(*r*)r ?
Who is the preacher ?	*Vâiz kimdir ?*	va͡aiz kimdir ?
The seats are free	*Yerler parasızdır*	yerler purusi(*r*)z-di(*r*)r
The seats must be paid for	*Yerler için para vermek zarurîdir*	yerler ichin puru vermek zuro͡ore͡e-dir
Where is the verger ?	*Kilisenin (zamgoçu) neredeđir ?*	kilisenin (zumga͡u-cho͡o) nerededir ?

English	Turkish	Pronunciation
Can you find me a seat, please?	*Lûtfen* ***bana*** *(bir) yer* ***bulabilir misiniz?*** ***[lim***	lûtfen bunu (bir) yer bo͡olubilirmisiniz?
Let us wait, (go)	*Bekl(e)****yelim,*** *gide-*	bekleyelim, gidelim
Please lend me a hymn book	*Lûtfen* ***bana*** *(âriyeten) bir dua kitabı ver****iniz***	lûtfen bunu (a͡ariyeten) bir do͡ou kitubi(*r*) veriniz
What other services are there?	*Başka ne gibi âyin****ler*** *var?*	bushku ne gibi a͡ayinler vur?
There is a strong choir	*Ora****da*** *pek çok muganni****ler*** *var*	a͡urudu pek cha͡uk mo͡ogunniler vur
Have you a Bible?	*Sende (bir) kitabı mukaddes var* ***mı?***	sende (bir) kitubi(*r*) mo͡okuddes vur mi(*r*)?
Is there a collection?	*Para toplan(ı)****yor mu?*** (see T.G. 70ccc)	puru ta͡upluni(*r*)-ya͡urmo͡o?
An offertory is taken	*Teberru suretiyle verilen para alın(ı)****yor*** (see T.G. 70ccc)	teberro͡o so͡oretiyle verilen puru uli(*r*)ni(*r*)ya͡ur

Legal and Judicial Phrases

(Adlî ve kanûnî cümle***ler***)

English	Turkish	Pronunciation
Call the police	*Polisi çağırı****nız***	pa͡ulisi chughi(*r*)ri(*r*)ni(*r*)z
Take this man in charge	*Bu adamı tevkif ed****iniz***	bo͡o udumi(*r*) tevkif ediniz
He has stolen my purse	*Ben****im*** *çanta****mı*** *çal****dı***	benim chuntumi(*r*) chuldi(*r*)
Where is the court?	*Mahkeme nere****dedir?***	muhkeme neredédir?
Can we make an arrangement?	*Aranızı* ***bulabilir miyiz?***	uruni(*r*)zi(*r*) bo͡olubilirmiyiz?
Can you recommend me a solicitor?	***Bana*** *bir avukat tavsiye* ***edebilir misiniz?***	bunu bir uvo͡okut tuvsiye edebilirmisiniz?
Where is the legation?	*Sefaret****hane*** *nere****dedir?***	sefurethune neredédir?

English	Turkish	Pronunciation
What case is on ?	*Hangi dâva rü'yet* ***edil(i)yor*** *?* (see T.G. 70*ccc*)	hungi da͡avu re͡w'yet ediliya͡ur ?
Who is the plaintiff ?	*Müddei **kimdir** ?*	me͡wddei kimdir ?
Will you take charge of this case ?	*Bu dâvayı siz üzeri**nize** alır **mısınız** ?*	bo͡o da͡avuyi(*r*) siz e͡wzerinize uli(*r*)r-mi(*r*)si(*r*) ni(*r*)z ?
What do you advise ?	*Ne tavsiye ede**r**-**siniz** ?*	ne tuvsiye edersi-niz ?
Can we have an interpreter ?	*Bir tercüman el**de** ede**bilir miyiz** ?*	bir terje͡wmun elde edebilirmiyiz ?
Does the judge speak English ?	*Hâkim İngiliz**ce** bili**yor mu** ?* or *bilir **mi** ?*	ha͡akim ingilizje biliya͡urmo͡o *or* bilir mi ?
I want bail	*Kefalet ist(**e**)-**yorum***	kefulet isteya͡uro͡om
Send to my friends	*Dost**larımı** çağır-**tınız***	da͡ustluri(*r*)mi(*r*) chughi(*r*)rti(*r*)-ni(*r*)z
This is quite wrong	*Bu tamami**yle** yan-lış**tır***	bo͡o tumumiyle yunli(*r*)shti(*r*)r
It is not just	*Doğru değil**dir***	da͡ughro͡o deghildir
I apologize	*Af diler**im***	uf dilerim
I accept your apology	*Tarziye**nizi** kabul ede**rim***	turziyenizi kubo͡ol ederim
I will pay	*Para**yı** ben veri-**rim** ; Ben öde**rim***	puruyi(*r*) ben veri-rim ; ben e͡uderim
It was all a mistake	*He**psi** bir hatâ **idi***	hepsi bir huta͡a idi
I claim damages	*Zarar ziyan talep ed(**i**)**yorum***	zurur ziyun tulep ediya͡uro͡om
The case is long	*Bu dâva uzun**dur***	bo͡o da͡avu o͡ozo͡on-do͡or
It is adjourned until to-morrow	*Yarın**a** kadar te'hir edi**ldi***	yuri(*r*)nu kudur te-hir edildi
Shall I have to come ?	*Gel**mekliğim**,* or *Gel**mem** lâzım **mı** ?*	gelmeklighim, *or* gelmem la͡azi(*r*)mmi(*r*) ?
I will be there	*Ben ora**da** buluna-**cağım***	ben a͡urudu bo͡olo͡o-nujughi(*r*)m

English	Turkish	Pronunciation
I appeal to the court of appeal	*Ben temyiz mahkemesine müracaat ed(i)yorum*	ben temyiz muhkemesine mewrujuut ediyauroom
Must I come	*Gelmem zarurî mi ?*	gelmem zurooi cee mi?

Commercial and Trading Terms
(Tüccar ve esnafa mahsus istilahlar)

English	Turkish	Pronunciation
I represent the firm of —	*. . . firmasını temsil ed(i)yorum*	. . . firmusi(*r*)ni(*r*) temsil ediyauroom
May I show you my samples ?	*Nümunelerimi göstereyim mi ?*	newmoonelerimi geustereyim mi ?
Send our account monthly	*Hisabımızı ayda bir gönderiniz*	hisubi(*r*)mi(*r*)zi(*r*) uydu bir geunderiniz
Give me a receipt	*Bana bir makbuz veriniz*	bunu bir mukbooz veriniz
What assets (*or* liabilities) are there ?	*Ne kadar matlubat* (or *düyunat*) *gösteriliyor ?*	ne kudur mutloobut (or dewyoonut) geusteriliyaur ?
Show me a balance sheet	*Bana bir bilanço gösteriniz*	bunu bir bilunchau geusteriniz
There is an error in your account	*Hisabınızda bir yanlışlık vardır*	hisubi(*r*)ni(*r*)zda bir yunli(*r*)shli(*r*)k vurdi(*r*)r
I shall send in a claim	*Matlubatımı bildireceğim*	mutloobuti(*r*)mi(*r*) bildirejeghim
Will you accept a bill (at three months) ?	*Otuz bir gün vâdeli bir bono kabul eder misiniz ?*	autooz bir gewn vaadeli bir baunau kubool edermisiniz ?
What dividend is declared ?	*İlân edilen* (or *gösterilen*) *temettü nedir ?*	ilaan edilen (*or* geusterilen) temettew nedir ?
This cheque needs endorsing	*Bu çek ciro edilmelidir*	boo chek jirau edilmelidir
Quote me a price for —	*. . . için bir fiyat veriniz*	. . . ichin bir fiyut veriniz
How soon can you deliver ?	*Ne vakıt teslim edebilirsiniz ?*	ne vuki(*r*)t teslim edebilirsiniz ?

English	Turkish	Pronunciation
Do you add the delivery charge? (do you deliver-free?)	*Nakliye ücretini ilâve ediyor musunuz?*	nukliye ew͡jretini ilaave ediyaur moosoonooz

Arrival

(Muvasalat)

Call a taxi (open); (closed)	*Bir otomobil çağırınız (açık); (kapalı)*	bir autaumaubil chughi(*r*)ri(*r*)-ni(*r*)z uchi(*r*)k; (kupuli(*r*))
What is the fare?	*Ücretiniz nedir?*	ewjretiniz nedir?
Do you charge by the hour?	*Ücretinizi saatla mı hisap edersiniz?*	ewjretinizi saatlu-mi(*r*) hisup edersiniz?
Put my luggage in the taxi	*Eşyamı otomobile koyunuz*	eshyumi(*r*) autau-maubile kauyoo-nooz
Drive me to Bebek	*Beni Bebeğ'e götürünüz*	beni bebeghe geu-tewrewnewz
Drive quickly	*Süratlı gidiniz*	sewrutli(*r*) gidiniz
Drive slowly	*Yavaş gidiniz*	yuvush gidiniz
stop; go on!	*durunuz; devam ediniz!*	doorooonooz; devum ediniz!
wait	*bekleyiniz*	bekleyiniz
I wish to get out	*İnmek ist(e)yorum*	inmek isteyauroom